STRATEGIC MANAGEMENT
FOR PUBLIC LIBRARIES

Strategic Management for Public Libraries

A HANDBOOK

Robert M. Hayes
and Virginia A. Walter

THE GREENWOOD LIBRARY MANAGEMENT COLLECTION
Gerard B. McCabe, Series Adviser

GREENWOOD PRESS
Westport, Connecticut • London

Library of Congress Cataloging-in-Publication Data

Hayes, Robert Mayo, 1926–
    Strategic management for public libraries : a handbook / Robert M.
Hayes and Virginia A. Walter.
      p. cm.—(The Greenwood library management collection, ISSN
0894–2986)
    Includes bibliographical references and index.
    ISBN 0–313–28954–9 (alk. paper)
    1. Public libraries—United States—Planning. 2. Strategic
planning—United States. I. Walter, Virginia A. II. Title.
III. Series.
Z678.H39   1996
027.4—dc20   96–2548

British Library Cataloguing in Publication Data is available.

Library of Congress Catalog Card Number: 95–2548
ISBN: 0–313–28954–9
ISSN: 0894–2986

First published in 1996

Greenwood Press, 88 Post Road West, Westport, CT 06881
An imprint of Greenwood Publishing Group, Inc.

Printed in the United States of America

The paper used in this book complies with the
Permanent Paper Standard issued by the National
Information Standards Organization (Z39.48–1984).

10 9 8 7 6 5 4 3 2 1

Contents

Preface

INTRODUCTION

In 1993, the reference text *Strategic Management for Academic Libraries* was published. In the three years since then, dramatic changes have occurred in the strategic environment, and an update seems well called for. Rather than just producing a second edition, though, it was felt that something more could be accomplished by shifting the focus from academic to public libraries. While there are many aspects of the two types of libraries that are similar, there are significant differences, especially in the natures of the communities served and the types of users. We felt that by shifting the coverage to include another context and by identifying such essentially different strategic considerations, the book could be more than simply an update in discussions of the environment. Furthermore, it gave us the opportunity to bring about a collaboration that we had long wanted.

Of course, the structure of this book is essentially identical to that of the first one, and some chapters (such as the one reviewing industrial models for strategic management) are, at most, minimally different. However, most of the chapters are substantively new and completely focused on issues important to public libraries.

THE ORIGINS OF THIS BOOK

As described above, this book is intended to be a companion and, to some extent, an update to the prior reference text on the same topic for academic libraries.[1] The prior book was an outgrowth of a project, conducted under sponsorship of the Council on Library Resources, on Strategic Planning for Libraries and Information Resources in the Research University.[2] The project was undertaken at UCLA, during the four years from the beginning of 1987 through the end of 1990, to explore means by which a major university could carry forward such planning, with emphasis on involvement of faculty. It was the outgrowth of a conference held at Lake Arrowhead Conference Center in December 1981.[3] Both the project and the conference were conducted under the management of Robert M. Hayes.

This new book, focused on public libraries, was similarly derived from another conference held in March 1984, also at the UCLA Lake Arrowhead Conference Center, under the management of Robert M. Hayes, with sponsorship by the California State Library.[4] It brought leaders in government, communities, libraries, information industries, and universities together to identify the role of libraries within the information economy of the state of California. That conference was useful not only in setting out an agenda for the state of California but as a model for similar efforts elsewhere in the country.[5] It also served as a stimulus for initiating a series of discussions among the United States, the United Kingdom, and Canada about similarities among those three countries with respect to their information economies and related governmental policies; that series led to what was called The Glenerin Resolution (named after the site of the third meeting in 1987, in Canada just outside Toronto), a statement of general principles.[6]

Virginia A. Walter has had the opportunity to reflect on changes in the environment and organization of public libraries throughout a long career in both practice and academia, beginning in the mid-1960s at the San Francisco Public Library, as urban libraries were discovering the need to reach out to nontraditional users. Later, she worked to redefine public library services in Latino neighborhoods of Los Angeles. The wrenching changes in public finance wrought by California's Proposition 13 in 1978 sent her back to school to seek new organizational responses to turbulent environmental changes. A Ph.D. in Public Administration brought a new understanding of the political context of the public library and the urgency of its strategic mission in a democratic society. After managing LAPL's Central Library Business and Economics Department and its Office of Children's Services, Walter joined the faculty at UCLA to teach management and children's services to students in the Department of Library and Information Science and to conduct research that would help shed light on the institution of the public library, in particular the services it provides to children and young people.

Walter played a major role in two national efforts to strengthen the public library and to develop its capability to provide excellent service. As the principal investigator and author of both *Output Measures for Public Library Service to Children* and *Output Measures and More: Planning and Evaluating Public Library Services for Young Adults*, she developed techniques for measuring service products intended for children, young adults, and their caregivers.[7] Testing these techniques in sites throughout the United States, she gained a national perspective on the challenges facing public libraries and the resilience and resourcefulness with which librarians are meeting those challenges. Her contributions to this book reflect her conviction that public library managers want and need tools to help them direct their resources toward the goal of creating a flexible "learning" organization that is able to respond effectively to a whirlwind of change while retaining its traditional value of providing community-based access to information to all.

OBJECTIVES

This reference text is intended to serve practicing public library managers and members of governing boards at all levels, from metropolitan to rural, from city/county library systems to single, stand-alone community libraries in small towns. In every context, there is need to prepare for the strategic changes that are occurring in developments such as the National Information Infrastructure and the onrush of electronic information. While many issues discussed may seem relevant primarily to the larger, metropolitan libraries and systems, they are in fact of vital importance even to small libraries that are the means by which their communities can participate in these national developments.

For the library manager, the book will provide tools to aid in strategic management. For the members of governing boards, it will provide a perspective on the role of their library in meeting the needs of their community and a framework for policy making. For students in schools of library and information science, it will serve as a textbook for their course work in library management and in the operations and services of the public, community-based library.

The book is generally written at a level that requires intellectual commitment, but without need for specific technical skills. However, chapters 9 and 10 involve accounting and mathematics to an extent that make it valuable to have some knowledge of their use.

The contents of chapters 3 through 6 are based on assessments of the strategic situation for public libraries during the years leading up to completion of the manuscript in 1995. While it is likely that the issues identified in them as important will continue to be so for some time to come, it must be recognized that strategic situations change. In the same vein, the contents of chapters 7 through 10 are based on current theories and techniques for strategic management. While they are likely to continue to be valuable, presumably they also will develop over time, both within business management contexts and in application to libraries. As a result, while it is hoped that the basic structure and philosophy presented in this text will have continuing validity, its content is rather specific to the current situation faced by public libraries.

STRATEGIC MANAGEMENT RATHER THAN
STRATEGIC PLANNING

One point must be established at the outset. Planning in this area cannot keep pace with developments as they actually occur. Public libraries generally are highly dynamic organizations, constantly at the forefront of developments of every kind. Any planning effort repeatedly is faced with the reality of implementation of services and facilities within the library, not at some planned future time, but today. Something more than "planning" is needed if this kind of dynamic environment is to be dealt with. The answer is evident and is represented by a simple though vital change in one word. We need to be concerned with strategic *management*, within which planning may play a role but at most a supportive one.

This is well reflected in the fact of changes during the past decades, changes so dramatic and in so many ways that the need for strategic management in public libraries is today greater than it ever has been. It must deal not only with the role of public libraries in general but with their role in the national information economy and with the future of public information needs.

ORGANIZATION OF THIS VOLUME

The book is organized into three major groups of chapters: (1) concepts, (2) contexts, (3) techniques for assessment. The first provides definitions, emphasizes the importance of *vision* on the part of the managers of the library, provides a structure for strategic management, and discusses specific issues of current importance to strategic management of public libraries. The second discusses the context, both from within the public library and from the external environment; the former, of course, reflects the immediate situation in which communities throughout the country are facing immense pressures of all kinds and, as a result, are experiencing unprecedented change; the latter represents both immediate and long-term effects with which library management must deal. The third section provides a set of technical tools, procedures, and theories by which the process of strategic management can be supported, in assessment of the internal and external situations.

ACKNOWLEDGMENTS

There are persons to whom we wish to convey our deep gratitude. Whatever value this book may have is in large part due to them; deficiencies are due solely to us. Robert Hayes acknowledges the central role played by persons at OCLC with whom he has had the opportunity to work for the past five years—C. Wayne Smith, Rich Van Orden, Clarence Walters, and Kate Nevins, especially. The opportunity they provided for him to see the public library scene from a truly national perspective was invaluable. Virginia Walter acknowledges the influence of three professors of public administration at the University of Southern California: Wesley Bjur, Robert Biller, and Eli Glogow. She also wishes to thank the many librarians across the country who worked with her on the children's and young adult output measures projects, in particular Clara Bohrer, Kathleen Reif, Elaine Meyers, Patrick Jones, and Penny Markey. These dedicated, creative library managers know how to "do the right thing."

NOTES

1. Robert M. Hayes, *Strategic Management for Academic Libraries* (Westport, Conn.: Greenwood Press, 1993).

2. Robert M. Hayes, "Long-range strategic planning for information resources in the research university," in *Advances in Library Administration and Organization*, ed. Gerard B. McCabe and Bernard Kreissman (New York: JAI Press, 1992). This reprinted the final report to the Council on Library Resources on this project.

3. Robert M. Hayes, *Universities, Information Technology, and Academic Libraries: The Next Twenty Years. The Report of the CLR Sponsored Frontiers Conference, Lake Arrowhead, December 1981* (Norwood, N.J.: Ablex Press, 1986).

4. Robert M. Hayes, ed., *Libraries and the Information Economy of California* (Los Angeles: GSLIS/UCLA, 1985). A Conference sponsored by the California State Library.

5. Alphonse F. Trezza, ed., *Effective Access to Information: Today's Challenge, Tomorrow's Opportunity* (Boston: G.K. Hall, 1989). The report on a conference in 1988 sponsored by the Florida State University School of Library and Information Studies and the Center for Professional Development and Public Service.

6. Barry Lesser, *The Glenerin Report: Access: Information Distribution, Efficiency, and Protection* (Halifax, N.S.: Institute for Research on Public Policy, 1988?). A report on a conference held at the Glenerin Inn, Mississauga, Ontario, May 13–15, 1987.

7. Virginia A. Walter, *Output Measures for Public Library Service to Children: A Manual of Standardized Procedures* (Chicago: American Library Association, 1995); Virginia A. Walter, *Output Measures and More: Planning and Evaluating Public Library Services for Young Adults* (Chicago: American Library Association, 1995).

PART I

Concepts

1

Definitions, Objectives, Alternatives

This chapter defines "Strategic Management," provides a conceptual framework for it, and identifies its major concerns and relationships to tactical and operational management of community libraries. The concepts of strategic management derive largely from its application in the commercial and industrial environment. To apply it to community libraries requires changes in the definitions of "product," "market," and performance criteria.

LEVELS OF MANAGEMENT

Definitions

Strategic management is a concept of increasing importance in modern industrial management.[1] The purpose of this text is to demonstrate the values in applying it to community libraries and to provide tools to assist in such application.[2] The following is a definition of the term as it will be used in this text:

Strategic management is that part of general management of organizations that emphasizes the relationships to external environments, evaluates the current status of them and the effects of future changes in them, and determines the most appropriate response of the organization to them.

Strategic management is oriented toward long-range institutional goals and objectives. It is concerned with identifying those goals and objectives, with creating a political consensus concerning their validity, with establishing priorities among them, with determining the resources that will be needed to meet them, with creating the environment within which those resources can be marshalled. The time frame of concern may be quite short—even months—especially if goals and objectives are in a state of change, uncertainty, or controversy; it can be quite long—from five to twenty years—if there is institutional stability and if the environment is reasonably predictable.

A distinction is made between such long-range, externally focused management and that which is internally focused, which will be characterized as either "tactical management" (concerned with the most effective deployment of resources within the organization) or "operational management" (concerned with assuring maximum effectiveness in use of the available resources).[3]

Tactical management is oriented toward implementation of the means for meeting goals and objectives, either as defined on strategic bases or as may be needed to meet immediate needs. It must assure that the necessary resources are allocated consistent both with the goals and with what in fact are at hand or can be obtained. The time frame of concern is likely to be quite immediate—on the order of months to at most a year.

Operational management is oriented toward the most immediate needs in maintaining an effective operation. It is concerned with using the resources at hand in the most effective and efficient manner to meet those immediate needs. The time frame of concern is usually days to weeks.

Relationships among Levels

The crucial point, given these definitions, is that if they are to be effective, the three levels of management must be in close interaction. While one might, in the abstract, conceptualize about long-range goals, especially in the context of speculations and enthusiasms about such resources as information technology, the fact is that such abstract speculations become remote from reality. The future must be built upon what is happening today, and the needs that will be of paramount importance are those that will be evidenced in current development. Strategic planning must deal with that fact.

The evident disadvantage of this approach is that it ties planning to what is currently known and thus may fail to adequately recognize potentials that depart radically from present trends. It tends, therefore, to be conservative and constrained by traditional means for dealing with information resources. Despite that disadvantage, though, this text will argue that strategic management should identify goals, objectives, external developments, and internal pressures by examining current community programs and proposed changes in them, rather than speculating on future developments that are divorced from actual community concerns. This means that current community perspectives and projects serve as the starting point for determining needs.

The result, however, is that perceived needs become inevitably reflected in demands for immediate capabilities. It would otherwise be a disappointment if citizens were encouraged to consider means for meeting their needs only to find that the information facilities—the libraries, computers, referral centers, and others—were incapable of implementing those means.

As a result, at the same time that strategic objectives are identified from community needs, those concerned with tactical implementation must be completely aware of their implications. And, in most cases, there will be operational requirements that must be met as well.

A specific example in this respect is the role of the on-line public access catalog of the library. Developed as a full service support to technical processing and to public access to catalog data, it is a capability with exceptional importance, both strategically and tactically. In itself, the database can serve the needs of individuals and organizations requiring catalog data to be downloaded for their own special bibliographic purposes. It can serve as the technical means for creating single point access to community-wide information resources; by establishing MARC formats as the standard for inclusion of data records for holdings of databases, films, and other media, the public access catalog contributes directly to that strategic goal.

The tactical implications are also exceptionally important, since use of on-line public access catalog (OPAC) software requires a high level of expertise, placing a burden on the library for training users and making the technical additions necessitated by user demands. And the operational implications are also important, since the ability to meet user needs depends upon having adequate hardware, storage capabilities, and access terminals. The library must assure that computing facilities can meet these needs.

THE POLITICAL CONTEXT OF STRATEGIC PUBLIC LIBRARY MANAGEMENT

Strategic management of public libraries takes place in the arena of government. While managing a public library has much in common with managing any other enterprise, at least at tactical and operational levels, the public library's relationship to political authority sets constraints on strategic management and complicates the process. The legitimacy of the public library is based in almost all instances on political authority, usually represented by mandates in local charters. In many communities, elected or appointed trustees represent the will of the public in deciding policy issues for the library. Virtually all public libraries rely on public money for the biggest share of their budgets.

A primary constraint is inherent in the uncertain tenure of elected officials. Another is the traditional lock-step of the annual budget in local government. These combine to make long-term planning very difficult. Except for some capital projects, it is very difficult to predict revenues or policy positions of elected decision makers from year to year.

Another constraint is the nature of public personnel systems under which many public libraries operate. Civil service rules and regulations often make it difficult to respond to changing organizational needs in a timely manner. It may be impossible to add a needed position or to change a job description outside of the annual budget process. Layoffs are usually subject to union negotiation and/or elaborate regulations for "reductions in force." Cumbersome civil service systems are implemented in creaky bureaucratic structures, making innovation and flexible response the exception rather than the norm.

Additionally, the criteria for evaluating organizational performance are often elusive or ambiguous. In the past, public managers often felt they had done a good job if they were successful in increasing their budgets; in the current period of retrenchment, this criterion is no longer applicable. One of the watchwords of newer reform movements in public managements, however, is accountability, and considerable effort has gone into developing useful indicators of organizational performance. As David Osborne and Ted Gaebler put it in *Reinventing Government*, it is necessary for government organizations to become more results-oriented, to focus more on outcomes than inputs.[4]

The Public Library Association started looking for ways to measure and quantify public library performance some time ago. The publication of *Output Measures for Public Libraries*, second edition, in 1987, gave public library managers some tools for quantifying service outcomes other than the traditional circulation and reference counts of the past. These output measures are linked to the planning process described in *Planning and Role Setting for Public Libraries: A Manual of Options and Procedures*, enabling library decision makers to assess their progress toward measurable objectives. The portfolio of output measures has been further expanded by the publication of *Output Measures for Public Library Service to Children* and *Output Measures and More: Planning and Evaluating Public Library Service to Young Adults*, which provide ways to look at library service to important specialized segments of the public library's population.[5]

However, output measures still represent fairly unsophisticated efforts to measure a library's performance. They represent internally generated measures of a public library's service output. They do not measure productivity or the impact of a library's services on the user. Perhaps most significantly, they are not necessarily the performance measures that political figures, ultimately controlling the library's destiny, wish to see.

The elected officials who are the custodians of political authority are unlikely to agree on the performance measures that truly determine a public library's effectiveness. This is largely due to a final constraint on strategic management in the public sector: the competing and often conflicting claims on the public interest. One year, the city council may be championing services for youth at risk. The next year, service to business may get priority, followed by an interest in literacy programs. It is a highly volatile environment in which the public interest is determined by a frequently irrational political process, not by the rational, analytical techniques of management professionals.

Barry Bozeman and Jeffrey D. Straussman outline a number of strategic management activities which all public managers can practice.[6] These include defining the appropriate sphere for action in their organizations; this keeps managers focused not on the political aspect of framing broad policy outlines but rather on the professional activities of assessing policy consequences and implementing policy initiatives.

Bozeman and Straussman also advocate that public managers "go forward by going backward." This apparently contradictory advice rests on conventional wisdom that the career bureaucrat has access to the policy memory. The public library director typically stays in his or her position and watches elected officials come and go. By tracking issues over time, the strategic library manager can be ready with preinvented wheels for newly invented policy wagons. The strategic library manager can sometimes see trends emerging before the newly elected official can formulate them.

Public managers also can work harder at framing the strategic issues, avoiding the perennial problem of goal ambiguity. For example, a public library director could meet the fuzzy city council mandate to "promote economic development" by framing the library's strategic response as an enhanced electronic information retrieval service for local business or as a package of services for job retraining. It may be politically necessary to present the organizational responses as alternatives; it is still the manager's prerogative to define the alternatives for implementation and to suggest possible outcomes for each. The key is that the strategically minded library director frames the operational responses to the policy initiative rather than waiting for public officials to define them.

STRATEGIC MANAGEMENT IN COMMUNITY LIBRARIES

Considering the overall character and quality of the management of public libraries, both now and as it has been for decades, it is clear that strategic management has been of paramount importance. In a very real sense, in fact, the community library embodies the very objective of the concept, since to fulfill its most fundamental imperative, providing access to information both past and present, it must continually assess the value of information in meeting future needs. As a result, the perspective of the community library is essentially long term and strategic, so it is not surprising that community library directors have been highly effective in strategic management, dealing with problems by long-term solutions rather than immediate quick fixes.

However, to apply an industrial management approach to libraries requires some necessary changes in definition of such concepts as "product," "market," "competition," and performance criteria. The concerns in strategic management—goals and objectives, administration, constituency and market, sources and resources, competition and cooperation, politics, technology, economics, social policy, sources for staff—all need to be reinterpreted and applied with clear knowledge of the nature of the community being served and of the library within it.

Overall Community Library Strategy

The overriding strategic concern must be with the community library as a whole—its mission, its relationship to the community and the people in it, its means for dealing with other libraries in cooperative arrangements. Most of this text will be at this scope of concern, and Chapter 3 will explicitly identify the issues, tactical and operational as well as strategic, involved in overall community library strategy.

The mission of the community library to date has been embodied in two imperatives: collecting materials of value to its community and providing access to those records and their contents. The primary issue of overall importance for the community library is whether the two imperatives are still the focus of its mission, still the basis of its role in the community, still of value to the people it serves. The strategic answer of the community library to that issue has been a resounding YES.

Strategies for Individual Products and Services

In implementing that strategic answer, though, the community library has faced some critical decisions with respect to individual products and services. One arises in balancing the relative importance of the two imperatives, in the choice between "acquisition" and "access."

Another set of critical decisions lies in balancing the relative importance of the traditional printed forms of information with the newer electronic ones. The array of potential records, of course, has been greatly expanded, and the traditional tools of reference have been augmented by a variety of electronic tools. Which of them should take priority in the future?

Specific assessment of individual products and services of the community library, aside from their roles in meeting overall objectives, is also necessary in strategic management. Chapter 3 will consider in detail the array of products and services that today characterize the community library. The strategic issue with respect to specific products and services is whether each will continue in the coming decades to be the essential ones. Does the need in the community for any of them justify continuing it? Will the electronic forms of records and means for access require instituting new services? Should the community library provide services other than simply preserving and providing access to its own materials?

Community Library Markets

Chapter 5 will consider in detail the needs of the various groups that today are the market for the products and services of the community library. They are primarily the needs that are self-evident in the nature of the community within which the library operates—individuals, local government and community-based organizations, local commerce and industry, local educational needs, specialized cultural and ethnic groups, specific age groups. It seems unlikely that there will be substantial change in this array of markets, but the strategic issue is whether there will be changes in their needs. It is primarily this question that is addressed in Chapter 5.

Community Library Competition

It is perhaps strange to think of competition for community libraries, since their position in the community is so accepted, so well entrenched and with such momentum of investment. But competition there is, if not for the library as an institution, at least for many of its products and services. There is a variety of alternative means for access to information. The public library, as a "discretionary" public service, is always in competition with all other demands on its users' time. In fact, almost any survey of users of community libraries will show that the library is somewhere between number four and seven in the order of priority of sources for information. Today, a number of commercial services are being added to the traditional sources—database access services and document delivery services, especially; the potential for significant competition from them, as they aim for larger markets by selling directly to the users rather than simply through libraries, is a very real threat to community library services for information access.

A preschool library story hour is not only in competition with children's television programming, the Mommy and Me program at the local recreation center, and the appearance of Ruffles the Clown at the local shopping mall. It is also in competition with all of the other non-child-related activities in a caregiver's day. A mother or father may choose to go shopping or bowling or decide to just stay home rather than take the kids to the library. Beyond the functional competition, though, is that for resources. The community library competes with the most fundamental community services—police and fire protection, health, maintenance of roads, trash collection and sewers, education—for resources within the community.

The strategic challenge, of course, is to deal with the competition in ways that will best maintain the continued viability of the community library. That may mean the necessity of strategic decisions about specific products and services in ways that will maintain the overall viability of the community library as a whole.

OBJECTIVES IN STRATEGIC MANAGEMENT

There is a range of objectives that, individually and combined, can serve as the motivation for strategic management.

Management for Change

The most dramatic surely is the need to deal with an accelerating rate of change and to increase the ability of management to anticipate crises. In this respect, strategic management, as a continuing process, provides the basis for response of the organization to the environment.

Historically, the picture of management in any organization was one of careful, considered assessment in specific decision-making contexts. In that picture, the role of the manager was to identify problems, determine what information was needed to deal with them, initiate whatever action was needed to assemble that information, and then make a reasoned decision based on analysis of it. The good manager was seen as someone who was virtually a technician in the application and use of information resources and methods for scientific management, such as operations research.

Today, though, there is a different picture of management, one that both is consistent with reality and highlights the role of strategic planning. In this newer picture, the manager is seen as someone who responds to situations with rapidity and decisiveness. The reality underlying this picture is the fact that problems requiring management decisions are likely to have immediate importance and must be dealt with in a context of uncertainty, without the time to acquire information so necessary to the more technical picture.

Support to Decision Making

If this newer picture has any substantial validity, it requires that the manager continually be monitoring the environment, whether consciously or subconsciously. The good manager is likely to be someone who is constantly talking with people at every level of operation, internally and externally, thus assuring an understanding of what is happening and what the effects of change in that environment will be. The result is that decisions will be made that prevent problems, rather than having to solve them, because there is an intuitive grasp of what is happening. When a problem cannot be prevented, the same intuitive understanding provides the basis for immediate, effective decision making because necessary information already is embedded in that understanding. This truly is what strategic management is all about.

In that respect, then, strategic planning has the supporting role to such management by providing the formal basis for continually acquiring, analyzing, and integrating information into systematic decision making.

Provide a Basis for Accountability

It also serves as the means to integrate planning with operations and to provide a basis for accountability. In strategic management, expectations must be communicated and individuals must be motivated to meet them. In this way, management can assure that accomplishments are directed to objectives.

Encourage Creativity

A somewhat different set of objectives for strategic management is to encourage innovation and creativity. By its nature, it must identify new opportunities and it calls for the generation of new ideas.

Assess Individual Products and Services

An objective may be simply to assess one or more community library products or services for the purpose of determining costs, markets, competition, needed resources, and relative priorities. Such an objective might arise from a proposal to implement a new product or service, or from concern about the value in an existing one, or from a need to reallocate resources.

Improve System Operations

The ultimate objective perhaps is to improve library operations, and many of the issues discussed in subsequent chapters will focus on aspects of this objective.

ALTERNATIVE STRATEGIES FOR MEETING OBJECTIVES

The literature for strategic management has generally been focused on business, commerce, and industry. Can the alternatives meaningful in those contexts be applied in community libraries? To explore that question, three major categories of alternatives will be identified: those that build on the core business (i.e., the library as it now is), though perhaps with changes in the way in which it is conducted; those that involve substantial change in the core business; and those that involve change in the environmental contexts. For each, examples will be provided to illustrate their application to strategic alternatives for community libraries.

Build on the Core Business

If the core business is essentially successful, and that generally is the case for the community library, alternatives that maintain it, though possibly with modification to meet new opportunities, would seem to be the ones most important to consider.

Maintain the Status Quo. The most conservative option, as represented by the traditional adage, "If it ain't broke, don't try to fix it," is to preserve the status quo. In the case of the community library, this may well be the option of choice, given the long history of successful integration of libraries into their communities, the overall quality of strategic management exhibited to date, the stability and existing momentum (or perhaps the equivalent, inertia).

Innovate and Diversify. The strategies of greatest excitement, of course, are those that innovate by expanding the core business, implementing new kinds of services, new ways of doing things, new relationships with the constituencies served. Certainly these options underlie the efforts to automate library services and internal operations. This option, in fact, will be the one most evident in this text as it considers issues faced by the community library in serving its community and its users, and in dealing with the external environment. During the past couple of decades it is the strategy that has been followed in community libraries, with great success in doing so.

Concentrate. A reverse option would be concentration, a narrowing of focus and of objectives to specific library roles. A community library might consider focusing its collection on identified groups in the community, rather than continuing an effort to cover the entire range of community interests. It might consider focusing its attention on specific community needs, such as support to education. It might concentrate on specific media. It might eliminate some existing services.

Retrench, Divest, Liquidate. The extreme options in this respect must also be considered, negative though they may seem—retrenchment, divestment, and liquidation. To an extent these may be necessary results of concentration as the means for dealing with the residual activities not included in the focus. They may be more deliberate options, though, reflecting conscious decisions to close down operations. There is nothing really new or threatening about this option, negative though it is. Community libraries have eliminated branches, have sold collections, have reduced staff, and have contracted out for replacement services.

Reconceive the Core Business and Innovate

Another set of options involves substantial change in the core business, moving into new and different kinds of activities.

Horizontal Integration. One strategy would be horizontal integration—an active effort to encompass a wide range of community information activities within a single organizational structure. For many, this option is a natural consequence of the perception that referral centers, community information centers, and the library are essentially similar. By bringing them administratively together, there could be economies of scale, efficiencies in performance of common functions, sharing of resources and facilities. This option is by no means new or revolutionary. Community libraries indeed have incorporated referral centers within their services; they are providing community information. The current options for horizontal integration, though, appear to be substantially larger and more complex. The most dramatic example of horizontal integration is found in the various consortia and cooperative arrangements among community libraries. These have been especially effective in the coordination of collections, in the provision of reciprocal borrowing privileges, and in the sharing of resources.

Vertical Integration and Joint Ventures. A related strategy is vertical integration, in which additional functions are added to those traditionally seen as the responsibility of the library. This option is one with which community libraries have less experience, but there are those who have suggested that they should expand services into areas of commercial information brokerage. In that respect, the development of joint ventures, whether with other libraries, with other information agencies, or with commercial partners such as information entrepreneurs, represents a component strategy and an approach to vertical integration. A second example would be entry of the community library into publishing ventures—CD-ROM publication of local history materials perhaps, or on-demand publication as a replacement for circulation.

Modify the Environment

A final set of strategies turns to the larger frame of reference, the environment, considering alternatives that change that environment or the relationship that the community library bears to it. It must be said that by their nature these alternatives appear to be meaningful for the entire set of community libraries of the country, rather than for individual libraries.

Expand the Societal Role of Information. It is now well recognized that the United States, along with other highly industrialized nations, has moved from an economy focused on production of physical goods and services to one in which information is dominant. It has been estimated that well over 50 percent of the nation's work force is engaged in information work, and that percentage is growing. The problem, though, is that national policies and accounting for economic activity have not kept pace with the times. Those policies and accounts need to be changed to reflect today's reality.

If that kind of change can be made, the role of libraries as contributors to economic success will be made more evident, providing an added basis for commitment of resources to their services. The growing emphasis on access to information resources, stimulated by policies of the Clinton administration aimed at development of the ''information superhighway,'' clearly provides a context in which such expanded roles for the community library are almost essential to successful implementation.

Modify the Political, Legislative, and Legal Environment. The library community generally has been reasonably effective in lobbying, and the specific interests of community libraries have been well represented. But, political decisions are being made about intellectual property rights, about availability of information from the federal government, about privatization of government activities, about the development of the information superhighway that vitally affect the operations, services, and even mission of community libraries. The need is to develop means for the community library community to influence those decisions.

Change the Nature of Sources. Community libraries have for decades had a stable set of sources for the materials and technologies they acquire—the publishers, distributors, and booksellers; the computer manufacturers, database services, and local systems vendors. Now, though, those sources are themselves in a turmoil of change, and the opportunity is in principle here for community libraries to influence the changes that are occurring. And indeed, community libraries have been doing just that. The creation of the bibliographic utilities as a partnership among libraries is one evident example.

The major force arguing for this kind of impact is the important role that libraries have, given the magnitude of investment and the history of success in meeting community objectives. The major differences from the past in that respect are effects of the information technologies in stimulating change, but with the community library as the crucial component in delivery of electronic services.

The implications are clear. There is an opportunity for community libraries to be dominant players in shaping the future of the delivery of information in all forms.

Change Relationships with the Environment

To an extent, this alternative is represented by approaches to vertical integration. By combining with other agencies in the broadening of scope of joint responsibilities, the community library changes its relationship to the environment from that of recipient to that of participant. The National Information Infrastructure is likely to provide opportunities for such collaboration, in partnership with community telecommunications companies and in statewide networks, opportunities that will be explored in a later chapter.

EVALUATION OF ALTERNATIVE STRATEGIES

Each of these strategic options must be evaluated for its effectiveness, likelihood of success, level of resulting performance, and cost. In the context of systems analysis and evaluation, the relevant encompassing measure would be efficiency (i.e., cost-effectiveness). Clearly, however, in the political environment of the public library, efficiency and cost-effectiveness are not the only or even most important criteria for determining alternative strategies. The public library must demonstrate its responsible use of public funds, but cost-effectiveness may be more relevant to tactical and operational activities than to strategic management responses.

Criteria for Evaluation

To assess these several alternatives and choose among them, the strategic manager should consider a range of criteria.

Internal. Is the alternative congruent with the mission of the library and of the community it serves? Does it draw on existing skills? Is there the potential for sharing resources within the scope of management? Will the results be measurable? Is the alternative aimed at prevention of problems or as a cure for them?

External. Will the alternative appeal to groups who will be affected by it and will it gain their support? Is it fundable and will there be funding stability? What is the size and concentration of client base implied by the alternative, and will it grow? Is there resistance on the part of existing or future clients? Are there barriers to change in the alternative, once chosen? Is the alternative one in which the library can be self-sufficient, or will it be dependent on other agencies?

Competitive Position. Is the library well located and logistically capable of handling the alternative? Is there loyalty to the library's interests by those with a stake in the outcome? Is there history of prior funding, a track record of fund-raising ability and performance to justify confidence? What is and would be the market share? Is there momentum derived from prior performance? Is there a basis for assessing likely quality? Are there advocates for the option, and who are they?

Program Position. Are there adequate policies—programmatic, client, costing, funding? Are there adequate internal procedures for control of funds and management of staff? Is there demonstrable leadership capability? Are the requisite skills—technical, organizational, research and development—at hand? Will the option be cost-effective?

Strategic Positions and Associated Options

Chapter 7 will present the range of issues involved in assessment of strategic positions, together with several models that can assist in evaluation of alternative strategies. One among them seems especially valuable and applicable to evaluation in community libraries.[7] It is based on an overall assessment of three variables: (1) relative value of services provided by the community library, (2) relative strength of the community library's position, and (3) relative strength of the competition faced by the community library. The cells of the resulting three-dimensional matrix then provide contexts in which to identify the strategic options of choice. The ones identified here are derived from conventional wisdom for the not-for-profit context, and they appear to apply with great force to community libraries. It is important to note, as we have several times to this point, that the assessments of position and options apply both to the community library as a whole and to individual products and services.

High Value: Strong Position, Strong Competition. This appears to be the case in most strong communities. Their libraries are in strong positions within the communities; the library's services are valued; there is strong competition from other means for information access—especially alternative referral and community information centers. The primary strategy for not-for-profit agencies is *cooperation with the competition,* leading to efficient division of responsibilities. That indeed is the strategy that has been generally followed by community libraries. The potential secondary strategy is to dominate and shut out competition; that does not appear to have been generally followed.

High Value: Strong Position, Low Competition. In cases in which the competition is weak, the primary strategy is to consolidate and to expand aggressively the library's position. Such might occur in a community for which alternative information facilities are poorly managed.

High Value: Weak Position, Strong Competition. This applies if the community library is in a poor position—underfunded, badly managed, with bad relations to the community and its government—but with other strong information structures in the community. The recommended primary strategy is to transfer programs to the strong competing services. For example, responsibility for computer support of library operations might go to the community's computing facility.

High Value: Weak Position, Low Competition. Under these conditions, the community itself clearly faces a severe problem. The recommended primary strategy must be for the community to commit resources and to build strength as rapidly as possible.

Low Value. Fortunately for most community libraries, overall they have high value. These conditions are therefore not likely to apply to the community library as a whole. However, individual products or services may not be valued, of course, so they should be individually assessed. The strategy generally would be to get out of any undervalued products or services, whatever the position of the library or the competition may be.

NOTES

1. There are literally dozens of standard texts for courses in strategic management for business, all roughly equivalent in organization and substantive content. The following is a brief sample of half a dozen of them that will serve to illustrate the generic approach and, in later chapters, the coverage of specific models.

David A. Aaker, *Developing Business Strategies,* 2d ed. (New York: John Wiley, 1988); William R. Boulton, *Business Policy: The Art of Strategic Management* (New York: Macmillan, 1984); Samuel C. Certo and J. Paul Peter, *Strategic Management* (New York: Random House, 1988); William F. Glueck and Lawrence R. Jauch, *Business Policy and Strategic Management* (New York: McGraw-Hill, 1984); Arnoldo C. Hax and Nicolas S. Majluf, *Strategic Management: An Integrative Perspective* (Englewood Cliffs,

N.J.: Prentice-Hall, 1984); Robert T. Justis et al., *Strategic Management and Policy* (Englewood Cliffs, N.J.: Prentice-Hall, 1985).

2. In addition to the business-oriented references, the following focus on not-for-profit organizations, and therefore are especially relevant to community libraries: Jack Koteen, *Strategic Management in Public and Nonprofit Organizations* (New York: Praeger, 1989); Ian C. Macmillan, "Competitive strategies for not-for-profit agencies," in *Advances in Strategic Management*, vol. 1, ed. Robert Lamb (Greenwich, Conn.: JAI Press, 1983), pp. 61–82.

3. The identification of these three levels of management and the definitions for them are specific to this text and do not seem to be part of the general vocabulary of strategic management.

4. David Osborne and Ted Gaebler, *Reinventing Government: How the Entrepreneurial Spirit Is Transforming the Public Sector from Schoolhouse to Statehouse, City Hall to the Pentagon* (Reading, Mass.: Addison-Wesley, 1992).

5. Charles R. McClure et al., *Planning and Role Setting for Public Libraries: A Manual of Options and Procedures* (Chicago: American Library Association, 1987); Nancy A. Van House et al., *Output Measures for Public Libraries*, 2d ed. (Chicago: American Library Association, 1987); Virginia A. Walter, *Output Measures and More: Planning and Evaluating Public Library Services for Young Adults* (Chicago: American Library Association, 1995); Virginia A. Walter, *Output Measures for Public Library Service to Children: A Manual of Standard Procedures* (Chicago: American Library Association, 1995).

6. Barry Bozeman and Jeffrey D. Straussman, *Public Management Strategies: Guidelines for Managerial Effectiveness* (San Francisco: Jossey-Bass, 1990), pp. 36–46.

7. Macmillan, "Competitive strategies for not-for-profit agencies."

2

Top Management Responsibility

This chapter discusses the strategic responsibilities of managers—the board of trustees, the director of the public library, and the key members of the professional staff. It identifies the need for a vision of the role and importance of the library to its community, its state and region, and the nation. It discusses the professional responsibility for assuring access to information resources by the entire community. In that context, it discusses the mission of the public library, its relationship to community objectives, and the resulting commitments, goals, and objectives. It then discusses alternative scopes for strategic management: internal to the library, broadened to the community, external to the community including national in scope. It discusses requirements and generic issues related to the needs of users.

The chapter will cover concerns of library managers in such areas as the organizational structure of the library, its personnel policies and numbers of staff, space, finances, expenditures and revenues, internal operations and quality of service, the contributions of individual products and services. In doing so, however, it is not the objective of this chapter, or of the book in general, to replace the excellent texts on public library administration, such as Wheeler and Goldhor's classic, *Practical Administration of Public Libraries*,[1] but to assure that the entire array of administrative issues has been considered for their relationships to strategic issues. There is much more to be considered than can possibly be presented here, so in this chapter and elsewhere in this book as appropriate, Wheeler and Goldhor will be cited for their advice so the reader can expand the discussion here with the much more comprehensive presentation there.

VISION, MISSION, AND PROFESSIONAL COMMITMENTS

Vision for the Individual Library

The primary responsibility of management must be to have a vision of the role of the library.[2] Is that role seen as minor and at best supportive? Or is it seen as central and critical, as essential and of vital importance? Is the intent to emphasize excellence and breadth of collection, or is it to be a focal point for access to information? Is it to be a major source within the national library system, or primarily a user of other sources? Is it to focus on the traditional media, or is it to be a leader in the use of new ones?

Of course, each community and the library within it doubtless has high levels of aspiration, but vision is not merely aspiration. Is top management able to obtain resources—money, facilities, staff—and willing to commit them to the vision, bringing aspirations to reality? The point, of course, is that strategic management of information resources is determined both by the vision held by the community and by the degree to which resources can be and are committed to fulfillment of that vision. It is commitment of resources that constitutes leadership.

State and National Vision

Strategic management of libraries, however, involves a wider perspective than the individual community. There has been a history of vision for the profession as a whole, a perception of the entire set of public libraries as a resource for the state and even the nation. That vision has established a basis for grand strategies. One is exemplified by the national bibliographic utilities—OCLC (the Online Computer Library Center, which serves all kinds of libraries, from public to academic to major research), RLIN (the Research Libraries Information Network, which focuses on major research libraries), and WLN (the Washington Library Network, which focuses on the northwestern section of the country). Another is reflected in state and national efforts to create networks (well exemplified by the states of California, Washington, New York, and Illinois, each of which includes vast public library networks) for collaboration in sharing of resources.

The result is a hierarchy of objectives, from the individual library, to the community, to the state and the nation. Underlying them all is the vision of the public library as the means for information resource management to meet the needs of society at every level. It is wonderful to see the extent to which public library management has embodied that vision in the full range of contexts.

Community Mission

Historically, the broad mission of the library has been twofold: To preserve the record of knowledge and to provide access to that record and its contents. In the past, the two aspects of the mission have been mutually supportive, since the primary concern was with access to the individual library's own collection by its primary constituency. Today, while they are still largely mutually supportive, there are growing tensions between them. Increasingly, libraries are facing a crisis in determining their missions, and are being forced to make a choice in commitment of resources between collection development on the one hand, and information access services on the other.

It is that which today makes the context for strategic management so crucial. Does the individual library focus its mission on the needs of the community, perhaps emphasizing collections designed to meet the specific current needs, or does it see its mission in the context of the "nation's library," perhaps emphasizing information access and sharing of the wide range of national resources?

Of course, the choice is by no means so dichotomous, and every community will surely balance collection development with means for information access. But, when choices must be made, where are resources committed? Do they go to capital investment in maintenance of the collection to serve needs directly, or do they go to operating costs in obtaining information only when needed, from wherever it may be available?

Even the small community library must deal with this issue, since it must focus resources on maintaining collections and services for its primary users— children through adults of all ages—and so must depend on cooperation with other libraries in order to assure access to the wider range of materials needed for more specialized purposes.

Public libraries may be unique among types of libraries in their emphasis on services. Even the basic function of collection development is typically seen as an element in the provision of services rather than as an end in itself. Public libraries provide access to information through a wide variety of delivery systems and methods which become part of their product mix. The classic example, of course, is public library service to children which traditionally includes a wide variety of programming in addition to the provision of an age-appropriate collection of library materials.

Public libraries often provide a wide array of services for adults as well, however. For example, a public library may provide information about AIDS through a variety of means: a collection of books, pamphlets, periodicals, and audiovisual materials; informational bulletin boards, information and referral services, on-line databases, film and lecture programs, group discussions, and cooperative efforts with other community agencies for various outreach activities. The intensity of this effort would of course be determined by community needs, the library's mission and stated role in the community, and the availability of resources.[3]

Many public libraries have used some form of the planning and role-setting process developed by the Public Library Association (PLA) to identify the particular niche they should occupy in their communities. The planning and role-setting process involves an assessment of community needs followed by an effort to identify the particular roles that would be most appropriate for the library to play in that community, based on both external community factors and internal factors such as library resources. PLA offers a menu of eight roles which, taken together, offer a good array of options:

1. Community Activities Center

2. Community Information Center

3. Formal Education Support Center

4. Independent Learning Center

5. Popular Materials Library

6. Preschoolers' Door to Learning

7. Reference Library

8. Research Center

Libraries are encouraged to select one primary and perhaps two or three secondary roles on which to concentrate their efforts. This enables the library to focus its energies and resources on the particular activities which most closely match its community's needs. A suburban community with many well-educated young families may thus select Popular Materials Library as its primary role, with Reference Library and Preschoolers' Door to Learning as its secondary roles, while an inner-city library whose community residents are struggling for economic survival may select Independent Learning Center as its primary role, with Community Information Center and Preschoolers' Door to Learning as secondary roles. Each role suggests a different cluster of strategies for collection development and service delivery. This approach to public library service is much like the niche marketing practiced by many successful corporations and represents a considerable conceptual change from the more traditional, standardized model of public library service.[4]

Professional Commitments

There have been evident corollary commitments by the library: to open availability of collections, without essential barriers, to free service (at least as far as the individual user is concerned), and to cooperation (since it has long been recognized that no library, however large, can encompass the full range of recorded knowledge). Increasingly, though, those commitments are becoming burdens. Libraries are faced with conflicts between meeting needs of their primary constituency and meeting those of others, with increasing costs in access to commercial information services, and with complications as well as costs in participating in national cooperative programs. As a result, they frequently must consider imposing restrictions on use, payment by users for special services, and fees for interlibrary lending.

In some cases, the professional commitments which public library managers bring to their jobs become more than burdensome; they may actually become value conflicts. For example, the traditional library commitment to intellectual freedom is sometimes in conflict with the need to respond to community norms and standards. A balanced collection representing all points of view on a topic may actually be inappropriate in some communities, a fact that contradicts the professional training of most librarians.

ALTERNATIVE CONTEXTS

The point, in any event, is that the board and the director must set the context for strategic management. What are the priorities among the several scopes to be considered? Should emphasis be given to external factors that are related to politics, social policy, legislation, and legal aspects? To cooperation with other communities? To internal community issues? To information sources and resources? To economics? To the needs of the constituencies for services and to the mix of services provided to them? To technology? To improving management of operations, production, personnel, and finances?

The first step in dealing with those questions should be identification of the opportunity or need for change. Since change is a fact of life, this may seem to be superfluous, but it is important that they continually emphasize its importance, that it identify the relevant policy problems, and that it establish the means for effecting and managing change.

Second is setting the objectives for planning and management. Are the objectives, aside from dealing with change per se, to be growth? Improved efficiency? Better resource utilization? Greater levels of contribution to the public and the community?

Third is assignment of responsibility. Strategic management itself clearly should be at the highest levels of administration in both the community and the library. But who is to do the associated planning? Where will they be in the administrative hierarchy?

Identification of Scope

Strategic management in general must consider a range of contexts, both internal and external, and at various levels of detail. With respect to libraries and information resources, in particular, one must simultaneously deal with at least three levels:

• The "library," taken narrowly as the traditional collection of books, journals, and a wide range of other media, with its inherent set of facilities, operations, and services;

• The "library of the future," taken broadly as the entire set of information resources and facilities, including libraries taken narrowly but adding to them computing centers, media centers, film and data archives, museums, and telecommunications networks;

• The "national library network," consisting of the entire set of libraries and other kinds of information resources acting as a cooperative and integrated whole.

It is not easy to keep these separate, and the temptation to slip from one to the other is great, sometimes without realizing that one has done so.

If boundaries are not set, the entire process of analysis will be based on shifting sand. Requirements will reflect mixed and varying perceptions of context; functional components and their relationships to one another will be unclear; the criteria for evaluation will be amorphous. Of course, having set boundaries for the scope does not prevent subsequent change of them. But the important point is that, at any given time, the focus should be clearly defined and known to all participants and that, if changes are made, it is made evident that such has happened.

THE HIERARCHY OF STRATEGIC CONTEXTS

These can be viewed as a sequential hierarchy of strategic contexts. For purposes of description here, that structure will be restricted simply to three levels (although it should be evident that the hierarchy will extend both outward and inward to many levels)—(1) the strategic focus, (2) the set of contexts, and (3) the set of sub-systems.

As Figure 2.1 shows, the Strategic Focus will fall within a number of contexts. Principal among them is (or are) the administrative context(s), reflecting the hierarchy of reporting. Others include the sources of funding, the various groups of users (i.e., the market or constituencies served), the sources of information and services, the suppliers of technologies, the political environment (including aspects of social policy, legislation, and legal decisions), and the potentials for cooperation and perhaps competition with other libraries.

Within the Strategic Focus there are now and in any future alternative will be components of various kinds. Some represent issues of tactical significance, such as administrative structures within the Strategic Focus that provide the means for management. Others are of operational significance, such as the matching of expectations with performance. Some of the components are individual products or services of the public library. Strategic management will frequently need to assess them. That may be necessary in assessing their contribution to the overall effectiveness of the public library in meeting its objectives. It may also be necessary in assessing their individual effectiveness.

Figure 2.1
Hierarchy of Systems

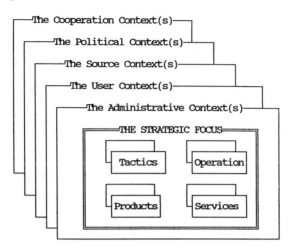

THE OBJECTIVES OF THE STRATEGIC FOCUS

As Figure 2.1 should make evident, the objectives of the Strategic Focus are derived from the complex interaction of a variety of interests—those of the focus itself, those of the several contexts, and those of the constituent components. The objectives can be categorized into three groups—Strategic Objectives, Tactical Objectives, and Operational Objectives—reflecting perhaps the three major categories in the hierarchy of systems: "context," "strategic focus," and "components." Later in this chapter, we will examine these in more detail as we look at "Requirements."

Political Factors

The objectives are rarely in complete congruence but must be balanced among one another by a political process of reconciling divergent views, priorities, and needs. Good strategic managers recognize that these political factors may be covert elements in any decision-making process and will remember to take them into consideration. They will recognize that they themselves are not indifferent to these dynamics. Self-knowledge is an important attribute for successful managers. The following factors can each be operative:

• *Personal Politics*: reflecting personal ambition, personal animosities, personal characteristics

• *Administrative Responsibilities*: reflecting the defined functions of the position of each individual in the hierarchy of systems and administrative structures

- *Professional Perspective*: reflecting the focus of commitment, of societal responsibility, of community orientation
- *Capital Commitments*: reflecting the existing status of resources and the effects of alternatives upon them
- *Personal Perspectives*: reflecting the differences in perception of risks, of the effects of problems, of the relationships among priorities.

The first, personal politics, is the most difficult to deal with, though perhaps ultimately the most significant. The other four are also significant and must be carefully considered. They each have profound impact on the assessment of alternatives.

TACTICAL ISSUES IN STRATEGIC MANAGEMENT

At the risk of stating the obvious, library management must be concerned with tactical issues related to the library's organizational structure, with personnel management, and with financial management.

Administrative Structure

Paramount among the tactical concerns is the nature of the library's administration. In part, administration is reflected in the administrative structure: divisions between and within public and technical services, between central and branch library operations, and between operations and central management services (finance, personnel, procurement, research and development, and management information systems). Wheeler and Goldhor devote their entire Chapter 6 to these aspects of the organization of the library.

In this respect, virtually all public libraries are bureaucracies, with the classic hierarchical structure of interlocking administrative authority. Reporting relationships and spheres of activity tend to be clearly defined. It is usually obvious who is on the administrative team and who should be involved in strategic management decisions. Strategic managers should also be aware, however, of other informal leaders and stakeholders who may not be as visible on the organization chart. It may be advisable to include a representative of the employees' bargaining unit, for example, or the children's librarian who is not on the management team but is responsible for service to 40 percent of the community's population.

It should also be noted that most public libraries are actually very small, with very simple organizational structures. In these small libraries, with fewer than five staff members, the assignment of responsibility for strategic management decisions is almost a nonissue. Everybody will be involved. There is sometimes a temptation in small organizations to do everything informally, on the fly. The level of planning and decision making described in this book may seem overly burdensome and even irrelevant. However, there are advantages for even the smallest libraries to thinking strategically about their external environment and about potential changes in their circumstances.

But in a larger, strategic sense, administration reflects the management style. Is it responsive to the environment? Is it flexible? Is it effective for internal communication and control? Does it aid in attracting and retaining creative people? Is it able to handle changing technology, to deal with inflation and other financial crises?

In many public libraries, trustees or board members serve in an advisory capacity to the library management. As representatives of the public, their advice on strategic decisions should be sought and carefully considered, but library managers will have the responsibility for actually determining policy. In other situations, the elected or appointed library board has administrative oversight, and library managers will craft strategy in partnership with these citizens. In either case, library managers must be very clear about their sphere of responsibility.[5]

The administrative structure is represented in part by the library's administrative hierarchy and in part by a matrix of functional relationships.[6] Should the existing structure be changed to provide a better response to the strategic environment? To an extent, this question represents the *tactical* response to strategic objectives, since it provides the primary basis for allocation of internal resources. But it may also be a strategic response, especially as it results in improved relations with community government and administration and with the population served.

Technology provides the potential for new approaches to administrative structures. Electronic systems for information support to management have led to a current debate in management theory, as important to community libraries as it is to commercial and industrial companies, about the appropriate size of middle management. Should the structure be based on the traditional concepts of span of control, which result in the typical pyramid? Or do modern management information systems permit a much flatter structure, eliminating the middle manager and coming to a cusp at the highest levels of management?[7]

With all due respect to the current "wisdom" about the presumed effects of automated management information systems, is the elimination of middle management a realistic approach? There is a need for awareness of reality that absolutely requires day-to-day knowledge of what is happening, as represented not by data accumulating in a file but by personal observation; that requires middle-level managers who can function close to operations.[8] There is also the need for a process of testing and evaluation of persons. Where are the future managers to come from if the positions through which they currently advance are eliminated? What will be the means for participatory management if the mechanisms for communication are reduced simply to processing of data?

A second effect of the technology is provided by the electronic linking of locations. How does the resulting structure relate to the constituency being served? How does it affect centralization versus decentralization of functions?

Personnel Management

Another strategic concern with tactical implications relates to policies for both professional and nonprofessional personnel. Wheeler and Goldhor devote their Chapter 5 to Personnel Policies and Procedures, covering all levels of staff, from the library director through administrative support, unit heads, professionals, and nonprofessionals.[9]

A strategic issue of special importance in medium to large public libraries is the source for staff and especially of professionals. They depend largely upon educational programs in "library and information science" for their professional staff; but those programs serve a much broader set of constituencies than the community library. The quality of those programs, the numbers and quality of graduates, the skills and attitudes they bring to their work—these must be of concern to strategic management.

Strategies for human resources are implemented tactically through policies of personnel management. Within the constraints of existing civil service regulations, these policies should deal with needs for cultural and ethnic diversity; they should forecast employment needs; they should determine the means for recruitment and retention; they should identify the measures for staff effectiveness; they should determine the basis for distribution of staff among professional and support; they should determine the structure of compensation.

A crucial element of strategy for human resources is the appropriate commitment of resources to training of staff and educational development of library administration. In particular, what percentage of library resources should be allocated to staff development—for staff to train trainers, for staff doing training, for supervision, for staff being trained? What is the appropriate level of commitment in management planning? Data from the industrial context suggest that it should be at least 2 percent of the total staff budget and preferably as much as 4 percent.[10] Wheeler and Goldhor place special emphasis on this element of personnel policies and procedures, and rightly so, given its importance. For the small library, these needs may be met through the workshops provided by the state library, but even so there must be funds to cover the costs in attendance.

Volunteers play an increasingly large role in public library work forces. Where they once worked primarily as fund-raisers or as sources of supplementary labor, they are now often integral to the library's service delivery system. Where libraries are dependent on volunteers for essential services, library managers must plan for their recruitment, retention, and training as well as that of regular paid staff. Jeffrey L. Brudney, who has studied public sector voluntarism extensively, has noted that public agencies are in stiff competition for a declining pool of qualified volunteers. Library managers will need to develop strategies for attracting and retaining excellent citizen volunteers as well as the professional and clerical staff required for the library's operations.[11]

Financial Management

Wheeler and Goldhor devote Chapter 7 to issues in Budgeting and Finance.[12] Beyond those administrative issues, though, public libraries have in the past faced and increasingly in the future will face some major financial strategic issues: the effects of technology, of inflation, of reduced resources and the potential need to charge fees, of the costs of interlibrary borrowing and lending, and of the costs of consortial arrangements. Beyond those issues that essentially are internal to the library, a dominating concern today is the economics of community libraries resulting from financial pressures on the communities they serve. This strategic concern will be discussed in Chapter 4 when we examine the factors currently affecting the community and, as a result, the library. The point here is that it affects the tactical management of finances—the sources and distribution of funds, control and accountability, cash flow.

Effects of Technology. In part the financial concern is related to technological change. Libraries have been forced to make major investments in automation of operations and services, in programming, in installation of equipment, in conversion of catalogs and other files, in training of staff and of the population being served. Those costs have been of great magnitude, both as capital investments and for operating expenses; they will continue in the future as obsolescent and even obsolete equipment and related software must be replaced to deal with the dizzying pace of development of the information technologies.

Libraries have been forced to deal with costs incurred in new means of data access—the on-line computer databases. They must respond to the demand for new media, such as optical disk stores, that are acquired to serve the needs of the population. Indeed, the pressures on the acquisition budget are almost certainly the most pernicious economic problem faced by community libraries. They are creating conflicts within the library in fighting the diversion of funds from books to journals to databases to external services. They may create conflicts between the library and the community, as different choices adversely affect different community groups.

Effects of Inflation. For more than a decade the rates of inflation have threatened acquisition budgets. The rising costs of books and other media combined with the need to consider new formats, all within the context of declining financial support, complicate making choices.

Effects of Charges for Use. In large communities, an emerging issue is whether to charge fees. It requires that the library determine which costs the users will bear and which users will bear them. In many communities special surcharges have served as means for funding of libraries, especially for the development of automated services. Implementation of a full-cost charge-back program is becoming an option with high priority, especially for charging users from business and industry for special services, for use of electronic resources, for reference and user intermediation services, for document delivery services.

Effects of ILL. The costs of resource sharing and remote access are becoming critical, as interlibrary loan (ILL) is being buried under an avalanche of requests. Libraries throughout the country are therefore being forced to reconsider the issue of charging for ILL services. For the small library, even a modest increase in demand is almost beyond their ability to handle.

Effects of Demographic Changes. During the past five decades, there has been a succession of "baby booms" and the nation is now entering another of them. Within a short time, as the number of births begins to soar again, the pressures on the library's limited financial resources, like those on the schools, will increase from the need to commit them to more and more children's services.

Effects of Declining or Unpredictable Government Revenues. The complexities of local government finance, combined with economic downturns over the past decade, have made tax revenues uncertain. While some public libraries may be guaranteed a certain level of revenue by local charter, many are dependent on annual negotiations with a city council or county board for operating funds. As local tax revenues decrease, often the library budget decreases as well. Strategic managers must become skilled not only in fighting for their share of local revenues but also in developing alternative funding sources. In California, public library directors who have grappled with the financial chaos and uncertainty caused by Proposition 13 and the Gann Initiative are suggesting statewide reforms that would affect the governance and the funding base of public libraries.[13]

Outsourcing of Operations

The decision to have operations performed outside an organization rather than within it is called "outsourcing."[14] It is a tactical decision, since it determines how resources will be allocated, but it is one with vital strategic implications. In businesses today, overall about 25 percent of their information activities—in data processing, accounting, software development, computer hardware facilities, even training, libraries, and research and development—are being outsourced.[15] It is likely that the proportion of outsourced information work will gradually increase over time. The reasons are multiple: access to specialized capabilities, sharing of costs with other businesses, focusing resources on core business needs, expectation of efficiencies in operation.

The concept of outsourcing can be fearful for librarians, and members of governing boards may be reluctant to spend money on things they cannot see. But it is well exhibited in libraries already. The most central example is the choice between acquisition and access; if access is chosen, clearly the library has decided to outsource some portion of its services, to that extent depending on other libraries or commercial document delivery services to meet patron needs.

A similar example is in reference, where an outsourcing decision could be to replace local printed collections of indexes and abstract by on-line database services. Another example is in cataloging, in which the decision has been made by virtually every library to outsource to central bibliographic services for the majority of its catalog data—to the book distributors, to the bibliographic utilities, perhaps even to other libraries. For many years, this has extended to having vendors provide books "shelf ready," that is, fully processed, with book cards and pockets, bar codes and security system targets already in place.

Through their participation in state library networks, such as those mentioned earlier, small libraries may outsource access to needed materials, thus obtaining the advantages of large collections without depleting financial resources. Indeed, participation in such centrally sponsored networks is among the most successful means for outsourcing. Some public libraries have outsourced to their community computing facilities for management of the hardware and software to support their local systems. In some cases, even the function of systems work in the library has been outsourced in that way.

A good rule of thumb is to outsource tasks and procedures that are not directly related to primary services to users. These may include computer processing, payroll management, maintenance of facilities and grounds, in addition to the internal library processes in ordering and cataloging. The kind of costing analysis presented in Chapter 9 can provide the means for assessing whether outsourcing will be more cost-effective than keeping certain functions in-house.

TECHNOLOGICAL ISSUES IN TACTICAL MANAGEMENT

Automation of Internal Operations

For the past twenty to twenty-five years, automation of internal library operations has been a significant strategic issue in community libraries.[16] Today, though, it is a part of every major library's operations, used for control of book circulation in its central downtown library and in neighborhood branches, for management of the technical processes in acquisition and cataloging of materials, for exchange of information with other libraries, for administrative functions such as finance and personnel, for management of staff and costs; and for assessment of the popularity of library services, the frequency of use of library materials, and the types of books and information in greatest demand. Of special importance is an ongoing process to maintain the quality of the catalog, assuring that it accurately reflects the actual holdings. Even small public libraries can gain the advantages of automation of internal operations through use of the on-line bibliographic utilities, such as OCLC.

The use of automated systems in support of internal operations in cataloging and technical processing is changing the ground rules for production planning and for measurement of production effectiveness. It is changing the mix of professional and nonprofessional staff. What changes are required, therefore, in management of the production and delivery of these internal operations? This question represents the *operational* response to the strategic environment.

Automation of Public Services

Today, most major public libraries provide an on-line public access catalog (OPAC) that enables patrons in central downtown libraries and in any of the neighborhood libraries to inspect references to their combined book holdings by author, title, and subject from remote computer terminals. Beyond just the holdings of the public library itself, the OPAC may include access to other data files concerning Community Resources, Contacts (organizations and services), Events, and Facts; direct connection with the agencies outside the library can permit them to update the relevant data for their own operations. The OPAC may also include access to catalogs of other libraries, such as those of the state university and of regional library systems. Of special importance has been the potential of access to the Internet. As will be discussed, it is a basis for development of the "information superhighway" that promises to revolutionize access to library catalogs, national data files, and an almost overwhelming array of information resources.

Even the small public library can gain virtually all of the advantages of automation in services through participation in its statewide library networks. In most cases, the state's union catalog provides the means for access to the broad range of statewide resources, as well exemplified in New York, Illinois, and Nevada. The library need only provide the means for access from the local community to that union catalog.

The OPAC provides an operational base not only for adding new data files (such as those related to public and private service agencies and the catalogs of other libraries), but for augmenting the data within all of those files. Specific examples would be: addition of tables of contents, analytics, and deeper indexing of cataloged materials. The bibliographic utilities and other database services already have begun to provide such augmentations of the basic bibliographic data.

Currently, terminals within the library provide the on-site means for such public access to the OPAC. But in addition, dial-in ports can allow library patrons to have the same capability from their homes and offices through their own personal computers. The importance of both capabilities is highlighted by the results of a recent survey showing that one home in three now has a computer, and the number is growing rapidly, so dial-in access is meaningful;[17] but, as is so often the case, there are differences among economic levels in that distribution, so access at the library is essential if all needs are to be served. In that respect, it is important to note the efforts at the public library to serve patrons who have special needs—workstations with large print screens, voice output, braillewriters, special keyboards, and speech synthesizers.

Of course, beyond the OPAC and its other data files, access to on-line databases through various national services and utilities continues to be provided at the reference departments of the central downtown library and the branches. In addition, most large public libraries have acquired large amounts of reference material in the form of CD-ROMs; they cover almost every conceivable subject. CD-ROMs are of special importance because they save space, are relatively inexpensive, have extensive capabilities for computer searching, and their content can be communicated over telephone lines and processed easily by computers. In addition to reference materials, a steadily increasing number of sound recordings, electronic databases, government documents, and printed materials are now being published in this format. Currently, access frequently is through independent, stand-alone terminals, one for each CD-ROM, but the tactical need is early on to create a CD-ROM network which will facilitate access to the entire set from any terminal.

At most central downtown libraries and at many branches, microcomputers are available for the public to use for word processing and for spreadsheet and database processing. The result is a dramatic enhancement of the ability for library users to gain information literacy and to combine data from the array of resources to serve their own specific needs. A necessary element of collection development policy is to assure that there is appropriate computer software so that these microcomputers can be really useful to library users.

THE MANAGEMENT OF STRATEGIC PLANNING

Strategic management is clearly the responsibility of the director of the public library, but it is essential that the board encourage the director and assist with ideas, especially as they reflect the needs of the community. Within it, though, planning is an essential element, serving as the means for acquiring, analyzing, and presenting the data needed to make effective decisions.

Management Style

The style of library management is determined in part by the community environment, in part by the relationships between the library director and the governing board of trustees, in part by personal views and philosophy, in part by the demands of the management task. The style may be externally determined if the board of trustees plays a dominating role in establishing policies. It may be directive or controlling, in which the library manager unilaterally determines policy; such management has been characteristic of entrepreneurial enterprises, but it also has been the style in many public libraries with strong directors. It may be analytic or objective, in which management draws on means for measurement and formal assessment; such management would use tools of scientific management, such as operations research. The style may be participatory or political, in which the library manager involves others in the decision processes; such management was fostered during the past two decades. The style may be conceptual or behavioral, in which decision making derives from perceptions of the purposes of the library; the library director who is a renowned "lover of books" may well adopt this style. Each of these styles has its advantages and disadvantages and the likelihood is that any given library is managed with some mixture, but strategic management is consistent with any of them.

In particular, critical to success whatever the management style may be is the ability to foresee and even to avert or prevent problems. In itself, this adds importance to the strategic approach to management, since it requires a continuous monitoring of the environment, maintaining an awareness about potential problems that will trigger decisions when subsequent events occur.

Also critical is the proper perception and use of time. The focus should be on both present and future. The style should allow sufficient time to generate alternatives, without the need to hurry the processes in evaluation and selection. Yet one must be able to deal with problems decisively and rapidly. This too adds importance to the strategic approach to management, since it requires that the information and other bases for decision have been developed before, not after, problems occur.

The management style must provide means for translation of problems into challenges and opportunities, means for handling complexity. There must be a tolerance for ambiguity and uncertainty, a willingness to accept dissonance and inconsistency in available information, an ability to separate facts from opinions and judgments, an ability to handle conflict.

The Locus for the Planning Effort

Strategic planning requires a substantial dedication of effort on the part of a responsible person. It requires an ability to establish working relations with persons at many levels—technical, administrative, professional, and political—in a wide range of community contexts. It requires continual discussion with everyone who has a stake in the outcome. It requires both technical skills and political awareness. It requires some degree of vision about the planning issues and their relationships, both existing and potential, to strategic management of the library.

What is the suitable locus for such planning? The most likely locus would be within the community library itself, and there are good reasons for eventually moving responsibility to that locus, however the effort may have been initiated. Another might be outside the library—using a contractor, perhaps—and such might be the choice if the board of trustees wishes to play a dominant role. A third might be within the community administration, and again there are good reasons for such a choice, given the increasing importance of broadly defined information resources to community programs.

The Process of Strategic Planning

Information Gathering. Strategic management depends upon a continuing environmental scan to acquire information, not so much to provide a basis for response to specific problems as to provide awareness of the strategic situation.

Strategic planning, therefore, must implement that process and make the resulting information files usable for strategic management. Chapter 7 will consider the means for providing this kind of support to management.

Assessment of Current Strategy. Strategic management requires an objective assessment, at periodic intervals, of the status of the current situation. Chapter 7 will provide a set of techniques and models for assessment of the current strategy focusing on the collection, the operational performance, and the value to the community. Chapter 9 will present details of a costing model to support that part of such assessment for both the current situation and potential future ones. Chapter 10 will present an economic model intended to assist in assessment of one of the most crucial strategic contexts for public libraries.

Forecasting Future Needs. Strategic management must be long term in its perspective and therefore requires means for assessing likely futures. Chapter 8 will provide a set of techniques for assessing the future—the needs of the markets served by public libraries, both quantitative and qualitative, and the several external environments. It will also discuss some means for determining political positions and the effects of them. Chapter 10 will provide means for assessing the specific effects of changes in the structure of the local economy especially as represented by the increasing importance of information and the growing national information infrastructure.

Analysis and Evaluation of Alternatives. The set of descriptive models and associated techniques for assessing alternative options presented in Chapters 7, 9, and 10 can then be applied as well to decisions about moving from the current strategic positions into the future.

Planning Studies

Beyond the formalized tools presented in Chapters 7 through 10, planning studies can serve as means for identification of specific public needs and operational effects. The result is that strategic planning gains substantial leverage in furthering its data-gathering objectives through participation of many more individuals.

DETERMINATION OF REQUIREMENTS

We turn now to the more specific and concrete issue of "requirements." They fall into the following categories:

- Performance Expectations: high performance, frugal, or subsistence
- Boundary Conditions: funding, staffing, equipment, acceptable (and prescribed) alternatives
- Functional Requirements: identified functions to be provided by the system

• Parametric Requirements: amounts of activity, response times, measures of quality and quantity.

Performance Expectations

Strategic management should identify the performance expectations. At one extreme is "high performance"—the expectations of the engineer, the economic "developer," the military-industrial complex, the highly industrialized world in general. At the other extreme are "subsistence" expectations, represented by peasant societies. In the middle are "frugal" expectations. Libraries in the past would seem to have been characterized as frugal systems, reflected in their operation and their role in society as the preservers of the records of the past. The strategic management question, of course, is whether they should continue to be so.

Boundary Conditions

Strategic management should also identify boundary conditions, especially as represented by available resources. Of course, parallel with the picture of "expectations" there is a comparable spectrum of resource requirements, so the resources must be congruent with the expectations:

Subsistence	Resource Balance
Frugal	Resource Creation and Conservation
High Performance	Resource Exploitation

Subsistence economies live essentially in balance with the available resources, consuming only at the rate at which the resources are renewed. Frugal economies also limit the use of resources, but they attempt to create and to conserve capital as the organization of excess resources, beyond those strictly necessary for simple subsistence; thus there is an element of saving not characteristic of the subsistence economies. High performance expectations lead to the intensive use, exploitation, and consumption of resources in order to meet performance objectives, frequently without regard to cost.

Problems in Determining Requirements

With each and every method for determining requirements, one faces the problem of reliability. In questionnaires and interviews, one cannot guarantee that the respondent is honest, that the memory of events is correct, that there has not been confusion between different events or different sources, that the description of outcomes isn't just wishful thinking. Even with usage logs, there may be inaccuracies. Even if the data are reliable, one still faces the question of whether they represent valid user needs.

Another problem is the extent to which the results can be generalized beyond simply the specific respondents, time periods of monitoring, specific events observed or described. So one has identified, with reliability and validity, that a particular group of respondents had an identified set of needs, that the activity on the system demonstrated particular characteristics during a specific time. So what? Does that mean that other users at other times will have the same needs and experience the same results? Many of these problems reflect the underlying statistical problems of sample size and representativeness.

FACTORS AFFECTING USER NEEDS

Chapter 5 will provide a detailed discussion of various specific needs. Here, we will summarize the aspects of those needs that are of generic importance to strategic management responsibilities.

Nature of Users

The demographics of user groups need to be considered in strategic management. They affect the needs of users, the extent to which individuals will use an information resource, and the ways in which they will do so. Age, sex, education, social or economic class, ethnicity, geographic location—these have all been considered as potentially relevant demographic variables. They affect such management decisions as branch library location, local collection policies, staffing needs, hours of opening, services provided. Decisions about them can all be made with at least a statistical basis in the demographics of the population served.

Aside from the demographic characteristics, individuals will differ in the nature of needs, the kinds of usage, the services that will be needed. Goal-oriented users—exemplified by science, technology, management—will differ from education-oriented users—students and teachers—and from personal interest users. In Chapter 5, we will examine in detail the range of kinds of use: reading and circulation use, reference use, browsing; support to decision making, intensive research, and data processing. Strategic management needs to recognize the extent to which each type of user depends upon the library for each kind of use, especially with respect to eliminating barriers to their use.

The different kinds of usage differ significantly in several respects, both quantitative and qualitative. First is the amount of activity that each type of usage represents. This parameter is important to strategic management because it affects the decisions concerning ''access allocation''—that is, the level of access to be provided to information materials. This decision problem requires that there be a model for distribution of use among materials on which to base the economic assessment.

There is differential use of any information resource. There are individual differences; those who know the value of an information resource will use it heavily, while those with little or no experience will not even think of it. There are differences due to distance, response time, and cost—as any of them increase, the use will be reduced. Each of these therefore must be considered in making strategic decisions about such matters as branch library location, acquiring versus borrowing, and fees for services.

NOTES

1. Carlton Rochell, *Wheeler and Goldhor's Practical Administration of Public Libraries* (New York: Harper & Row, 1981); Darlene E. Weingand, *Administration of the Small Public Library*, 3d ed. (Chicago: American Library Association, 1992); Alice Gertzog and Edwin Beckerman, *Administration of the Public Library* (Metuchen, N.J.: Scarecrow Press, 1994).

2. Each of the standard texts for strategic management in business, as listed in note 1 of Chapter 1 of this book, emphasizes this point, evident though it is in principle. In addition, the following references may be of interest: G. D'Elia, *The Role of the Public Library in Society* (Evanston, Ill.: Urban Libraries Council, 1993); Abraham Zaleznik, *The Managerial Mystique* (New York: Harper & Row, 1989).

3. W. Bernard Lukenbill, *AIDS and HIV Programs and Services for Libraries* (Englewood, Colo.: Libraries Unlimited, 1994).

4. Charles R. McClure et al., *Planning and Role Setting for Public Libraries: A Manual of Options and Procedures* (Chicago: American Library Association, 1987), p. 28.

5. Mary Biggs and Glenna Kramer, "We have been there too: Library board essentials for effectiveness," *Wilson Library Bulletin* 68(9) (May 1994): 32–35; Alexander Cameron, Betsy Cornwell, and Joanne Tate, "Public library boards: A creative balance," *CLJ* 49(2) (April 1992): 135–139; Alice B. Ihrig, *Decision Making for Public Libraries* (Hamden, Conn.: Library Professional Publications, 1989).

6. The use of a matrix for description of the structure of an organization is a relatively new concept. It is beyond the scope of this text to go into details, but the following references will provide a start: Carlton Rochell, *Wheeler and Goldhor's Practical Administration of Public Libraries*, p. 113; Kenneth Knight, ed., *Matrix Management* (New York: PBI, 1977); Anthony G. White, *Matrix Management/Public Administration: A Selected Bibliography* (Monticello, Ill.: Vance Bibliographies, 1982); David I. Cleland, *Matrix Management Systems Handbook* (New York: Van Nostrand Reinhold Co., 1984).

7. *Automation and the Middle Manager: What Has Happened and What the Future Holds* (New York: American Foundation on Automation and Employment, 1966); L. Fulop, "Middle managers—victims or vanguards of the entrepreneurial movement," *Journal of Management Studies* 28(1): 25–54; D. W. Lewis, "8 truths for middle managers in lean times," *Library Journal* 116(14) (1 September 1991): 315–316; C. L. Harris, "Columbia University Library's staff development seminar," *Journal of Academic Librarianship* 17(2) (3 May 1991): 71–73; Alvin Toffler, *Power Shift* (New York: Bantam Books, 1990) (see especially pp. 172–177 and pp. 221–222); Alvin Toffler, "Toffler's next shock," *World Monitor* (November 1990): 34–44.

8. J. L. Connors and T. A. Romberg, "Middle management and quality control," *Human Organization* 50(1) (Spring 1991): 61–65.

9. Carlton Rochell, *Wheeler and Goldhor's Practical Administration of Public Libraries*, pp. 59–100.

10. *Fortune* 127(6) (22 March 1993): 62–64ff. This article reports that Motorola spent 3.6% of payroll on education; Federal Express, 4.5%; Anderson Consulting, 6.8%; Solectron, 3.0%; and Corning, 3.0%. President Clinton proposed that at least 1.5% should be so devoted.

11. Jeffrey L. Brudney, *Fostering Volunteer Programs in the Public Sector: Planning, Initiating, and Managing Voluntary Activities* (San Francisco: Jossey-Bass, 1990), pp. 145ff.; Virginia A. Walter, "Volunteers and bureaucrats: Clarifying roles and creating meaning," *Journal of Voluntary Action Research* 16(3) (July-September 1987): 22–32.

12. Carlton Rochell, *Wheeler and Goldhor's Practical Administration of Public Libraries*, pp. 115–137.

13. "Restructuring of Calif. public libraries urged," *American Libraries* 26(7) (July/August 1995): 627–629.

14. Kelly R. Conatser, "In or out?—a simple 1-2-3 model reveals whether outsourcing is for you," *Lotus* 8(8) (August 1992): 36–40; Suzanne Platenic, "Should I or shouldn't I?" *Beyond Computing* (Premier Issue 1992): 26–33.

15. Donald Siegel and Zvi Griliches, *Purchased Services, Outsourcing, Computers, and Productivity in Manufacturing* (Cambridge, Mass.: National Bureau of Economic Research, April 1991), especially table 1.

16. Bruce Flanders, "Spectacular systems!" *American Libraries* (October 1989): 915–922.

17. *Los Angeles Times*, 24 May 1994.

3

Strategic Issues for the Community Library

This text places its strategic focus on the community library itself, with the larger contexts to be considered for their effects upon it.

GOALS

Goals are concrete and specific as the means for realizing the vision and implementing the mission. Early on in a strategic management program, an effort should be made to identify specific goals that would relate information resources to the community's goals as explicitly as possible. They should set the stage, guide the process, and serve as the basis for evaluation of results.

Goals and objectives are by no means easy to establish and indeed, one of the purposes of strategic planning is to determine what they should be. They are likely to reflect a mix of concerns that need to be resolved in a political process, not a technical one.[1]

Community Goals

While each community must establish its own goals and objectives for libraries and information resources as the means by which they respond to the external forces, we can identify the following kinds of goals for the role of information resources in support of the community's perceived objectives:

1. Increase the reputation and national visibility of the community, especially as that may depend upon or be affected by information resources;

2. Expand the role of information resources in support of community business and industry;

3. Expand the role of information resources in support of community educational programs;

4. Increase the effectiveness in use of expenditures, throughout the community, in acquiring, producing, and using information resources;

5. Increase the degree of cooperation among community units in the use of information resources.

Library Goals

More specific are the goals for the library and other information agencies:

1. Improve the quality of reader services and enrich the reading experience, at every level;

2. Increase the support to education and enrich the learning experience from the first steps for early preschoolers to continuing education programs for adults;

3. Increase the productivity of business and industry as it may depend upon or be affected by information resources;

4. Increase the information literacy (i.e., ability to use information resources) of the community;

5. Increase the amount of information available to the community;

6. Develop the means to assure that the community has access to the technical information support needed to use information resources effectively;

7. Develop single point access to the full range of information resources in the community;

8. Deliver information directly to homes and offices.

FUTURE TECHNOLOGICAL DEVELOPMENT

The national initiatives, as enunciated by President Clinton and Vice President Gore in their 1992 book *Putting People First*, are now called "the information superhighway"—a door-to-door information network to link every home, business, laboratory, classroom, and library by the year 2015.[2] It will provide the means for electronic access to public records, databases, libraries, and educational materials. Access will be available through terminals in libraries, schools, homes, and offices. Materials provided will include the riches of learning, practical information for daily life, information resources from throughout the world. The technologies encompassed include computer-controlled interactive systems—multimedia, TV, and cable—computer database retrieval, computer-based library networks for sharing of resources.

Within the context of the "information superhighway," the public library will face many developmental challenges:

- Play a major role in creating a "wired" community, making information access a crucial element of support to community interests;
- Make full and effective use of the developing national information network for the benefit of the community;
- Educate library users in new information literacy skills, as may be required to take full advantage of these developments;
- Establish a collection development policy in which print, media, and electronic forms of information are properly reflected in the public library collections, with a balance that will assure all segments of the population have access to the materials they need;
- Assure compatibility of the public library's internal automated systems with the new developments;
- Maintain an effective role in the statewide library network, as new models are established for cooperation among libraries within the new national electronic infrastructure.

The greatest challenge is to respond to all these changes at a time when public funding is under severe strain and the demand for traditional library services has never been higher. The challenges are formidable, but the rewards and new possibilities are exciting.

The objective of strategic management is to deal with the information technologies in ways that will be of value not only to the public library itself, but to create the long-term capacity to deliver information to citizens. This is clearly consistent with the mission of the public library to serve the information interests of the general public, and especially those who would otherwise not have access to information. More than that, though, it places the library at the forefront of what promises to be one of the most important initiatives in the nation's history. Chapter 6 will review the major technological developments with which strategic management will need to deal.

COLLECTION DEVELOPMENT: POLICIES

The collection is the central tool of the community library. There are at least three major strategic concerns: (1) assuring that collection development policies are well established and consistent with both community interests and professional responsibilities, (2) assuring that collection acquisitions and management are consistent with changing methods of publication and distribution as they relate to community needs and programs, (3) assuring that the balance between acquisition and access is both economic and consistent with community needs.

Overarching even these concerns is the need to be sure that the collection is tailored to the community needs, as defined by the particular public library's mission or stated role. A public library which has determined that it serves as a research center for its community will tend to have a very different approach to collection development than one which serves primarily as a circulation point for popular materials.

Turning to the most fundamental—collection development policies—the basis for them surely must be the perceived needs of the users, of all kinds.[3] In fact, Wheeler and Goldhor deal with such policies in Chapters 8 (on adult services), 11 (on young adult services), and 12 (on children's services).[4] Chapter 5 of this book will consider those needs from the perspective of users themselves and attempt to characterize them with respect to both materials and services. The problem, though, is translating those needs into the policies that will guide collection development decisions within the context of available funds.

Censorship and Other Limitations on Acquisition and Access

Unfortunately, collection development must deal with something more than just formally identified needs and available resources. Materials acquired can and frequently have become issues of political, even legal controversy when advocates of particular interests object to them and wish to eliminate or, at the least, to restrict access to them. As Wheeler and Goldhor identify in their Chapter 8, the spectre of censorship sits just outside the door of every public library, and only a well-formulated, comprehensive collection development policy provides means for assuring that such advocates can be dealt with fairly, consistently, and responsibly.[5]

Indeed, President John F. Kennedy has been quoted to the effect, ''. . . open to all—except the censor . . . ,'' but that represents exactly the opposite of what it purports to say.[6] If we truly believe in freedom of expression, it should say, ''. . . open to all *including* the censor.'' The point is that even the censor should have freedom of expression, and the library should make even those views which are abhorrent to its commitments as readily available as it does any other.

But the quote does serve as an object lesson. Each person, each group has its reasons for wishing to restrict the expression of views and to set limits on freedom of access to information. It is therefore worthwhile to consider the range of rationales that may be used to support such positions, to assess the extent to which each may or may not be valid, to determine the contexts in which they may or may not properly be applicable, and to explore the responses that the library profession and the librarian as a person might have to them.

Library Selection Criteria. Just to start with the limitations that, on the surface at least, would appear to be most consistent with principles of librarianship: Every library should have selection criteria that determine what materials it should acquire. Indeed, as stated above, this is the most effective answer to all of the efforts to place limits on acquisitions.

In formulating such policies, isn't it appropriate that they include recognition of the interests of the community being served? This isn't a matter of censorship or even of limiting access to information; it is merely incorporating good judgment in the process of selection. Obviously, we can't acquire everything, so we should use the funds available in the way that best meets the needs of the community and that recognizes their interests as a group.

Preservation versus Access. In fact, another rationale reflects a conflict between the two imperatives of the library—preservation and access. *Preservation may well require limitations on access.*[7] Brittle books, rare and intrinsically valuable books, unique materials (such as original manuscripts), books intended for specific groups of scholars—each of these and similar kinds of materials need to be protected if they are to be preserved. Indeed, some librarians, emphasizing the responsibility for preservation, will regard the user with suspicion and require clear, unequivocal justification for access to such materials. Some university libraries still maintain policies of "closed stacks," with access permitted only by the staff or by selected users. Is this "censorship?" Well, probably not in the strictest sense of that word, but it certainly is a real limitation on access to and availability of the materials in the library. The effects are no different, even though the rationale appears to be different, and it is the effects that must be recognized.

Some libraries may adopt collection strategies which emphasize providing access to current materials. Their concern with preservation issues may be minimal. However, even libraries that are not involved with building permanent research collections may have some interest in preservation. Many public libraries, for example, have local history collections which include fragile ephemera, such as old city directories printed on pulp paper and early plat maps. The strategic issue for most public libraries may be to determine which areas of the collection are targets for preservation, which are areas requiring constant replacement, and which may be allowed to simply wear out.

National Security. Congress has explicitly recognized the necessity for protection of military secrets; it has established categories of security classification, with procedures for assigning them to specific materials and for review of the assignments over time.[8] The rationale seems evident and generally has been accepted as appropriate, even by those most committed to the position of "open access to information." The point here, of course, is that national security concerns have directly affected public libraries in a number of ways, acquisition of such materials being one of them.

The problems appear to arise as the scope of "national security," to be encompassed by the statutory provisions for security classification, is broadened. And the stages in doing so are easy ones to take, as we move in succession from military security to diplomatic security to strategic security to economic security. During the decade of the 1980s, the executive branch of national government by policy wished to interpret the term "national security" in the broadest possible way. Scientific research in the field of optics was regarded as identical with military interests in development of weapons; research in the mathematics of coding was regarded as identical with interests of the national intelligence community;[9] economic data, even in the field of agricultural production, were regarded as part of national strategic security.[10] Even today, the efforts by the intelligence community to control the means for coding data reflect their concern with a broad definition of national security.[11]

The effects of these national policy directives on libraries were not hypothetical. Specific attempts were made to involve libraries in controlling access to material, even if not explicitly classified, that was deemed by the federal executive offices to affect national security broadly defined.[12]

Personal Privacy. Even libraries, despite their commitment to "open access to information," have placed restrictions in the interests of protecting the privacy of the individual. Circulation records of libraries are protected, in some states by statute but in all states by the professional position of librarians, from access except by court order.[13] More generally, it seems evident that protection of personal privacy is a proper limitation. We see it even in operations of public agencies which, in California at least, are required to do their business in public, except when they deal with "personnel actions."[14]

Again, though, while not "censorship," this kind of limitation on open access to information has the same effect. And as with the rationale on the grounds of "national security," it is easy, inch-by-inch, to expand the scope of application. From the individual person to the family group, to larger groups, to corporations. Indeed, in a corporate environment, it is essential that the special library preserve the confidentiality of materials.

An emerging issue for some public libraries is the extent to which children's privacy can and should be protected, even to the extent of limiting parent's access to information about their children's circulation records.[15]

Materials Demeaning of Individuals or Groups. The laws regarding libel and slander clearly impose limits not only on what can be said but on the responsibility of librarians to limit access to materials that are libelous or slanderous. Recent court rulings, however, have complicated the interpretation of those laws with respect to one of the defenses (i.e., that relating to "opinion").[16]

But aside from those laws, there have been increasing pressures to censor materials that are demeaning of groups. Ethnic, cultural, religious, gender, sexual preference, national origin—each of these and more has provided a context in which persons have argued that libraries should not acquire and should not make available materials that diminish the image of the group. *The Merchant of Venice* and *The Protocols of the Wise Men of Zion, Little Black Sambo* and the *Uncle Remus Stories*—shouldn't libraries just eliminate such materials?[17] Most recently, even universities which presumably are bastions of freedom of expression have debated about the acceptability of language that reflects adversely on group identity. The term "political correctness" as the identifier for these kinds of limitations on speech has itself been used for political purposes.[18]

Of course, the objectives in suggesting such restrictions are laudatory. Anything that demeans a person or a group is abhorrent. Shouldn't it be prevented?

The American Library Association itself faced serious internal debate about a film ("The Speaker") it produced in which this very issue was the theme; it presented the view that even unpopular positions should be given an audience, and it was attacked by some of its membership for presenting that view.[19]

Intellectual Property Rights. By its very intent, the copyright law places severe restrictions on open access to information. Fortunately for libraries today, the law now explicitly recognizes the principle of "fair use" and of the appropriateness (with suitable restrictions) of "library photocopying."[20] But still, there are those restrictions.

Most recently, some court rulings have dramatically extended the scope of copyright with respect to "unpublished materials."[21] That will certainly affect libraries in their treatment of access to collections of manuscripts, letters, personal archives, and so on. In fact, though, some restrictions have already been part of the management of such collections, with the donors limiting access for specified time periods or for specified kinds of uses.

Pornography. Historically, the wish to eliminate access to pornographic materials—especially as represented by "child pornography," by depictions of sexual perversions, by debasement of women—has been a primary motivation for censorship.[22] And who would deny that the young, at their most impressionable and vulnerable age, should be protected from viewing such materials?

The problem, of course, is that pornography may well be "in the eye of the beholder." As one U.S. Supreme Court justice stated, "I know it when I see it."[23] But one person's pornography may be another's art and another's political statement. Where and how is the line to be drawn? The problems arise when efforts are made to impose one person's definition of that line upon all.

Right to Control Use of Public Funds. Frequently, it is argued by public bodies, such as city councils, that they have responsibility for the proper use of public funds and therefore have the concomitant responsibility to determine that library acquisitions are consistent with that use. Again, the problem arises when one view of what is "proper use of public funds" is used to prevent those with other views from access to library materials they want.

Parental Responsibility. Parents will argue that they have the responsibility to determine what their children see and hear, and surely that sense of responsibility is important and valuable. Many libraries have, in that context, provided means by which parental oversight is made possible.[24]

Of course, the definition of "childhood" may well mean that teenagers will need to get parental approval to obtain from the library books that they can easily buy at any drugstore, tapes that they can easily obtain at any video store, films that they can see at any theater. And, as with the other rationales for restricting access, the real problem arises when parents argue that, in order to protect *their* children, access to materials must be restricted for *all* children.

Each new format which appears in library collections seems to raise the issue of parental responsibility all over again. Many public libraries have found it to be a workable policy to allow children open access to all print materials, leaving any censorship to the individual parent. The appearance of videos in library collections, with their elaborate rating systems and sometimes graphic sexual and violent content, seems to have been more problematical. The Internet is raising yet another public controversy over children's access, in Congress as well as in libraries.[25]

Religious Prerogatives. Many religious groups have argued that they have the prerogative to determine what may appropriately be read and heard by their membership.[26] That implies that they have the right to limit access to materials that contradict the canonical views of their group. Historically, the Roman Catholic Church used the Inquisition, trials for heresy (such as that of Galileo), the Index of Prohibited Books, and similar efforts to accomplish this objective.[27]

Again, the problem is that, all too frequently, religious communities will want to impose their views upon others, preventing access for everyone, not just their own membership, to information they consider inappropriate. In the United States, this rationale was perhaps most spectacularly represented by the Scopes trial, in which the concern was with access to materials espousing Darwin's "principle of natural selection," with the view that they attacked the authority of the Bible and the views of some churches on the religious basis of humanity.[28] In recent years, that debate has been renewed, with a rather intriguing twist. The religious position has been expressed in the form of "creationism," with the view that it is an alternative explanation, even scientific in its nature.[29] The twist, of course, is that scientists argue that creationism should not be taught, at least not in a scientific context, since it is not a scientific explanation; but whatever the rationale may be, the facts are that the presentation of views would thus be restricted.[30]

Strategic Responses to Efforts to Restrict Acquisition or Access

The strategic point, of course, is that every context for limitation on acquisition of materials has a rationale and the espousers cannot be dealt with as zealots, fanatical and destructive of the principles of librarianship, but must be dealt with as persons with legitimate concerns that must be recognized as such. There would seem to be four effective strategies for doing so.

First, the community librarian must be continually aware of the issues within the population served that represent focal points of concern about the nature of library materials. Meeting with those who have strong views, both for restriction and against it, is essential, and preferably in an atmosphere that encourages discussion of the pros and cons. Each person must feel that his or her views have been heard.

Second, in such discussions, the need is to recognize ranges of validity of the wishes to restrict access and then, having done so, make sure that the range is identified as distinctly and narrowly as possible. The point is that, as the array of examples given above has illustrated, the problems arise when means to deal with legitimate concerns are extended beyond their appropriate limits. When the censors attempt to impose upon others their views of what is "irreligious," "demeaning," "immoral," "poor quality," or whatever else may be the rationale for restriction, the bounds of validity are exceeded. But to make that clear, those bounds must be known.

Third, the community librarian needs to assure that there is a level of community recognition and support of those boundary conditions. Fourth, they need to be embodied, as clearly as possible, in the library's collection development policies. Only by doing so does the community library have the established basis for responding to the continuing and repeated efforts to restrict acquisition and access.

COLLECTION DEVELOPMENT: THE RANGE OF MEDIA

Both strategic and operational management must be concerned with the full range of media that may be of value to community programs: printed books and journals, manuscripts and archives, microforms, films, video and audio tapes, computer hardware and software, computer databases, optical disks and cards, means for communication.

The traditional functions of the library—selection and acquisition, intellectual and physical organization, storage and preservation, access and retrieval—all are changing. The classical imperatives of collection development and access to the information records are beginning to conflict instead of being mutually supportive; the tools for intellectual access are changing as on-line public access catalogs become universal tools and there is pressure to change the very nature of the catalog records to accommodate new needs and new methods; the problem of preservation is rapidly becoming one of monumental magnitude; the relationship of the library to other means for information access is increasingly complex. In other words, across the board of community library management responsibilities, change is the order of the day. Strategic management needs to assess each of these, both for its contribution to the mission of the community library as a whole and for individual viability.

Print

An issue of current debate is whether print form publication will continue to be viable and an important means for information distribution. Some have claimed that we will become a "paperless society," with electronic means for communication replacing print.[31] Most of that speculation, though, has been generated by the enthusiasts for "computer-based publication," with little attention paid to the paramount importance of the decisions made by publishers about what will be published and about its format. Others have pointed to the fact that the effect of the computer, of FAX, and of other new media has been to *increase* the role of paper, not diminish it.

The position of this text is unequivocal: *Print is still the essential medium for public library collections.* It will continue to be so for at least the next two decades. But it is also evident that the information technologies and the new media must be considered, not only in their own right but as essential adjuncts and supplements to the printed formats and as means for production of them.

It is important to provide some basis for projecting the likely rate of print publications and of library acquisitions of them. For the moment, the available estimates, largely based on industrialized countries, are that print publication internationally will grow at a rate between 3 and 4 percent per annum (in constant dollars).[32] The great unknown lies in the "third world"; there could be an explosive growth in publication in those developing countries or there could be stagnation.

CD-ROM Databases

CD-ROM databases have now become an evident resource in community libraries. They are standard tools for reference support, and acquisition of them will continue to increase. Interconnection among microcomputer servers, in local networks both within the library and throughout the community, is now standard in community library operations.[33] There are increasing amounts of material being distributed in these forms, some as counterparts of print and some as independent publications. Even government information is now available on CD-ROM (an example being the 1990 census). As a result, libraries of all kinds will face complex decisions about whether to acquire the print versions, the CD-ROM versions, other electronic versions, or mixes of them all. Strategic management calls for a process of evaluation of electronic media and, as part of collection development policies, establishment of criteria for determination of what budget allocation should be committed to acquire them.

The levels of use, though, do not suggest they will replace print as means for access to even the kind of information they store. CD-ROMs may sit on the shelf beside one's home computer at home, and it still is easier to turn to the print sources—the encyclopedia, the almanac, the dictionary, the thesaurus— than to find the appropriate CD, mount it, load the software for it, and then make one's way laboriously through menus to find what is wanted. Of course, if such access is needed on a day-by-day basis, CD-ROMs will be used far more, but for their specific values, not as replacements for print publications.

The use of computer-controlled access to a range of instructional materials in systems called "multimedia" and "hypermedia" has dramatically increased the potential range of uses.[34] Among the most exciting promises are those related to the potentials for use of computers and multimedia in interactive learning, exemplified by projects such as *The First Emperor*, developed by Professor Ching-chih Chen at Simmons College, and *Columbus*, developed by IBM. Strategic management should explore the potential of these systems, especially as they will support services to students in elementary and secondary schools.

The appearance of more and more useful interactive multimedia products intended for home and school use, as well as for sophisticated information retrieval, makes it imperative that public libraries decide how to integrate this format into their collection. Some public libraries are already circulating CD-ROMs; others make them available in multipurpose workstations or in specialized Homework Centers. Children's librarians may be in the vanguard on this issue, perhaps taking the cue from their colleagues in school library media centers. The Association for Library Services for Children now names notable software each year, as well as notable books and films or videos. In 1994, all of the notable software products were CD-ROMs, and all were appropriate for public library use.

Electronic Media

But clearly, as a result of the impact of technology on publishing, there are changes occurring in patterns of publication. The new media—computer databases, on-line access to them, electronic mail and facsimile, distribution of data and images in optical disk formats, desktop publishing—all provide new means for communication of information. Especially difficult for strategic management is predicting the pace at which the suppliers will shift from one mode of distribution to another. Libraries generally need to make plans for acquisition of equipment and facilities largely on the basis of speculation, and the publishers provide little data on which to base those decisions. The well-established relationships for monograph writing, editing, publishing, and distribution have as yet no counterparts in the electronic arena.[35]

Librarians have seen themselves as the professionals whose position, whose skills, whose commitments make them the natural focal point for management of these new electronic resources. Library schools have virtually preempted the title "information science" to encompass those responsibilities. The new electronic media have very naturally been added to the array of potential acquisitions. CD-ROMs, tape databases, electronic journals—these and other forms as they may appear become grist for the library acquisition mill. All of this increases the position and status of the librarians, bringing them out of the picture of mere custodians into that of dynamic participants in a wonderful new world.

Pricing policies of electronic services are in such a state of flux today that the library manager really has no basis on which even to estimate what costs will be for various kinds of products and services. "Block pricing," "differential pricing," "usage-based pricing"—each of these and others is being used by one or more publishers. When the range of alternatives to be considered—print, CD-ROM, on-line services, magnetic tape acquisition—is added to the mix, the result is chaotic.

Still, though, the mainstream publishers of books and journals are moving into this form of publication very slowly, very cautiously. That means that there is much uncertainty about when, or even whether, library materials will be available in this form.

Full-Text Digital Storage. In this respect the great leap forward would be in full-text digital storage, in which the texts of books, journals, and other forms of publication are stored in disk files or CD-ROMs for immediate access on-line. The JANUS project of Columbia University is intended to create such a large, in-depth digital text library.[36] Initiated in 1990 and currently planned for completion in 1998, this project provides means to experiment with the operation and use of digitized files. Many of them will be digitized texts and would provide the basis for full-text indexing, searching, and retrieval; others will be digitized images and other forms of digitized data. The Seattle Public Library is one of the participants in this project, serving as the representative for public libraries in general.

Among the potential services from such an electronic library is on-demand publication. While still largely experimental, it represents an important new dimension of public library services. The OCLC publication of an electronic journal is an example of this kind of development.[37] Another is an existing service that scans journal articles and provides them in electronic document delivery.[38]

Digitized Imaging. Inclusion within the JANUS project of digitized images is an exceptionally important element, with significance beyond the JANUS project itself. Digitized imaging is feasible because the supporting technologies are all now here. The scanners are available and are inexpensive; the transmission capacity is operational; the processing power is now widespread, with microcomputers capable of meeting most needs; the software development is well in hand; the capacity for image storage is available.

There is an increasing use of digitized images in every professional field. Pictures of the human body, generated by digitized imaging, are now crucial in medical practice as well as in research. Pictures of the earth, generated from satellites, are used in oil exploration, in community planning, in agriculture, and in geographical research. Pictures of buildings and of manufactured parts, generated by computer-aided design, are now part of the tool kit of every kind of creative designer.[39]

Digitized image data can derive from conversion of source data to digitized image form, as exemplified in FAX transmission, in the preservation of brittle books by conversion to optical disk images, in the conversion of motion picture film to optical disks. They also derive from algorithmic production of images, as in computer-aided design, architectural design, or cartooning. They can come from the monitoring or observation of physical processes, illustrated by data from satellites scanning the earth and other planets and data from scanning of persons, as in radiology and neurology. They can also arise from digitized image storage of administrative data files.

The use of digitized image storage for administrative data files is worth consideration here as part of library strategic management; scanned administrative documents can be stored in electronic form, with automated work assignment and scheduling, automated work-flow control, and automated indexing and file searching.[40] The benefits arise from increased staff productivity, reduced costs for paper handling, improved control, better response to needs.

COLLECTION DEVELOPMENT: ACCESS
VERSUS ACQUISITION

Throughout most of the long history of librarianship, its two imperatives— *preservation* of the records of the past and *access* to those records and their contents—have been mutually supportive. Libraries acquired materials, and access in the main was to the resulting holdings of each particular library by the constituency it served; interlibrary loan was a valuable support, but its role was relatively limited and of minor significance in the overall. In this context, the concept of "free" access was both meaningful and justifiable; the library, having made the capital investment in its collection, could easily make it freely available at essentially no additional cost, aside from wear and tear on the collection and the effects of use on availability. As a result, the library could serve its constituency within its budget and without the need to be concerned about the costs involved in meeting the needs for access. Even the real costs involved in interlibrary loan could be tolerated, given the relatively low level of use, the fiction of reciprocity, and the ability of the established staff to handle the workload.

The Alternatives for Access

Resource Sharing. Since the late 1930s, however, increasingly the argument has been made that no library can stand alone and that interinstitutional cooperation, as a basis for "sharing of resources," should be made a professional priority. For at least the last thirty years, these kinds of efforts have steadily accelerated. The result has been an increased emphasis on sharing, aiming to replace "acquisition" by "access" (meaning not just access to the individual collection, which was the historic emphasis, but access to materials wherever stored, especially elsewhere). Some efforts have resulted in mechanisms to facilitate interinstitutional cooperation with sharing of resources as a major objective, creating networks and other organizational structures to coordinate the efforts with these objectives in mind. Some were fostered by federal funding explicitly directed at encouraging the development of "multitype" networks at the state level, with resource-sharing as the watchword. Some created the bibliographic utilities, intended in part to facilitate the process of interlibrary lending.

Role of Electronic Access. Now, today, the emphasis on "access" has reached a near crescendo, as the voices of the purveyors of electronic forms of information access add to those of the librarians. The enthusiasts present the vision of electronic information as the wave of the future, and the potential represented by the information superhighway is seen as replacing books and journals with real "information," instantly available, current, and readily processible.

What a vision and what a combination of incentives! "Access" means we will not need to spend money on books, journals, buildings, staff! "Access" means we will have instant information, with all of the technology of computer processing for retrieval, analysis, and presentation! "Access" means that people will be able to communicate directly with "information" as well as with each other, without the need to go to a library and face the problem of finding there what they want! "Access" means speed and efficiency and currency!

However, it also is a fact that access is not free and indeed is very expensive. Compounding the debate is the fact that electronic publication supports both access and ownership. Unfortunately, the issue involves problems in assessing the relative importance of capital investment and operating expenses. A complex problem, therefore, is how should "access" be funded? Should it be funded from the acquisitions budget, thus using capital funds for operational costs, or should it be separately funded? There are no general rules for making that choice; it must be a policy decision of the individual library and its management.

The reality is that *libraries* are still vitally important to the community as collections of materials and not simply as "means for access into the national network," and the gap between electronic potentials and current reality is still so great that librarians must continue to focus their attention on the proper balance today between the benefits and costs of acquisition and access, including those associated with interlibrary cooperation.

Document Delivery. Today, the array of options now includes commercial "document delivery services." Within just the past couple of years, FAX has become a tool of dramatic importance in business and industry; it serves as an essential means both for internal corporate communication and for external information exchange. For libraries the pace has been somewhat slower, but now there is a rapid rate of increase. The potential of digitized data files of texts as the basis for electronic document delivery—on-demand publication, in effect—promises to revolutionize not only that function but the very role of the library and its relationship to users.

The Cost/Benefit Decision

The decision between acquisition and access can be viewed as a weighing of costs and benefits. Formulated as a "cost/effectiveness" evaluation, the equations are quite straightforward and involve an assessment, first, of costs; second, of the relative frequency with which materials will be used; and third, of the effect of access or ownership upon total use of materials. The latter, of course, is especially significant; not only are there delays in access from elsewhere but there is an inherent barrier in not having material directly at hand. Here we will summarize the major elements in the cost effectiveness evalution.

Benefits. The benefits have in part been alluded to already: "No library can own everything," so cooperation is not only valuable but essential. It can lead to better utilization of the money spent for acquisitions by reducing unnecessary duplications among libraries. By sharing resources, by treating the major libraries of the country virtually as a single collection, each library and the constituency it serves has access to more materials than would otherwise be the case. Growth in holdings at individual libraries can be at a slower pace, so there is lessened need for construction of new library buildings.

The Costs to the Library. The costs of access, of sharing, of interinstitutional cooperation, though, are not usually discussed by the enthusiasts. It is almost as if the perception is that the benefits all come free. The reality, of course, is that there are very real costs associated with access. Even in earlier, simpler times, when access meant interlibrary loan (ILL) and use was relatively limited, the major net lenders—especially the universities—found the costs and effects on their own constituencies to be burdensome. They argued repeatedly then and still do today that there should be some mechanism for reimbursement, at least of the direct costs incurred.

In that respect, it is relevant to note that libraries generally have underestimated the costs for these kinds of activities. They frequently will consider only the *direct* costs, ignoring even the most evident of overhead costs (such as salary-related benefits and costs of supervision); that in itself results in estimates that are half of the true costs. The result is that comparisons of access alternatives and of benefits with costs are biased. In fact, the studies that have been made of ILL costs suggest totals, for both borrowing and lending libraries together, on the order of $30 per transaction—*not counting salary-related benefits and overhead*—divided about two-thirds at the borrowing institution and one-third at the lending.[41] Of course, it must be recognized that these studies have generally involved large academic libraries, so they may not reflect the experiences in smaller public libraries.

However, commercial "document delivery services" as replacements for the lending library will be charging fees that will result in roughly comparable total costs. Given those costs specifically associated with access, even a relatively low rate of use easily justifies acquisition instead of access. Indeed, an analysis of benefits versus costs is likely to show that current acquisition policies of major community libraries are close to optimum.

But beyond the costs directly attributable to access are those associated with the mechanisms of cooperation. Memberships in consortia carry their own costs—indirect as well as direct. Indeed, in many respects, the commitment of upper levels of library management to the working with cooperative arrangements represents exceptionally high expenditures of resources. These "general and administrative" costs need to be recognized as decisions are made about access allocations. Furthermore, as increasing numbers of libraries install automated "local systems," each must make decisions concerning input to the national databases in order to maintain those means so needed to facilitate interinstitutional sharing of resources. Again, costs will be incurred, obviously necessary, but also part of the balance in the assessment of benefits versus costs.

The Costs to Users. Those elements of costs are, in principle, ones that can be assessed without essential complication. The costs (and perhaps the benefits) to the constituency served in replacement of acquisition by access are much more difficult to assess but also fundamentally more important. The concern of libraries about maintaining "free access" in replacement of printed indexing and abstracting journals by database access services reflects some of those issues. The potential of reduced use of library resources, if they are unavailable locally or if the access time is seen as a barrier, is even more important.

Even more intangible but potentially most significant is the perception by the community of its quality of life. Competition among communities is real. They compete for business and industry as well as population, using tax incentives but also using the quality of life. It is still true that the *library* is perceived as an important component of that reputation, and any community aspiring to status needs to have a library collection of quality. Companies in business, commerce, and industry look seriously at the quality of the local schools and libraries when considering movement or expansion to new locations. The library board, especially, should emphasize the library's role in attracting such companies, to make sure that community politicians are aware of it.

Centralized versus Local Collection Development. An operational issue that has implications for collection development strategy is the locus of the selection activities themselves. Many larger public library systems use some form of centralized collection development, in which selection decisions are made by centralized bibliographers or book buyers. Using branch protocols or community profiles, they select library materials for all agencies in the system. Other library systems decentralize this activity, making professionals who are providing reference and readers advisory services on site responsible for collection decisions as well, sometimes with guidance from a centralized support office.[42]

SERVICES: ACCESS TO MATERIALS

We turn now from the library's collection to its services. They will be considered in three major groups: (1) access to materials, (2) reference, or access to information resources, and (3) instruction and consultation.

We turn first to access to materials in which the major concern—strategic, tactical, and operational—is with storage of the collection and the means for physical access to it. The major strategic issue, of course, is that collections, for good reasons, still grow, so buildings must be built to house them; the capital costs for construction represent twenty- to fifty-year commitments. The tactical issues, each of which has strategic implications, however, involve choices among a number of alternatives—storage at central libraries, in branches, or at remote facilities; storage on open access shelves or on other kinds of shelving;

storage in alternative media. (The option of dependence on access from elsewhere as a replacement for acquisition has already been discussed.)

Central Library, Branches, or Remote Facilities?

There are different locations at which materials may be stored: branch or neighborhood libraries, central libraries, and remote storage facilities. Here we will review the role of these alternative locations.

Branch libraries have the obvious advantage of bringing materials close to the users, and there is a documented effect of distance upon usage: As the distance from the user to a library increases, the use decreases and the rate of decrease is a function of the cost of transport. If the cost is linear as a function of distance, the usage decays exponentially; if the cost of travel is logarithmic as a function of distance, the use decays quadratically. In either event, the important point is that putting material in a branch makes it more accessible to those served by that branch.

Unfortunately, it also makes the material less accessible to the rest of the community. As a result, usually storage in a branch is limited to materials that are essentially duplicative or whose use is largely limited to the community served by the branch (such as ethnic materials in a branch serving that ethnic group).

Central library storage of materials, whatever the size of the community, has the value of single-point accessibility of the entire collection. It is crucial for general research materials, since there is frequent necessity to follow chains of references from one source to another. The only real disadvantage is the effect of growing collections upon the storage capacity.

Remote storage facilities have the obvious advantages of flexibility and low storage cost, and the obvious disadvantages of relative inaccessibility, with consequent reduced use, and increased costs in operation and in delivery. They can be a strategic response to the space problem, but few public libraries have needed to resort to their use.

Alternatives for Shelving

The alternatives that can be considered for dealing with shelving include traditional open-access shelving, dense shelving, compact shelving, and automated shelving. Assessment among mixtures of these alternative locations will be reviewed here.

Open-stack shelving of bound print volumes at standard density is clearly the most preferred both for the users and for library operations. Materials are readily accessible, easily browsed and examined at the shelf. Serendipitous use is encouraged.

High-density open-stack shelving can be achieved by increasing the shelf density from the standard (no more than 80 percent filled) to as much as 100 percent filled; it can be achieved by increased height of shelving or by decreased aisle space between shelves. Open-stack shelving with densely packed shelves is totally feasible for materials that are essentially fixed in position. They might be historic collections or periodical runs, for example. For any portion of the collection that is growing, though, it is operationally unfeasible. Open-stack shelving with increased shelf height or decreased aisle space between shelves is essentially unacceptable; either makes it impossible for the physically handicapped directly to gain access to materials and either can be exceptionally hazardous.

Compact shelving can be used in any of three modes for organization of materials (i.e., "seamless" with open stacks, used for "lesser used materials," or used for particular materials, such as periodical runs). Any of them, though, results in decreased use of materials and virtual elimination of serendipitous use. In general, compact shelving reduces accessibility, especially by the handicapped; it can result in damage to materials; it can be hazardous if the protective mechanisms are bypassed.

Automated facilities have advantages in dramatic reductions in required space and, especially, in maintenance and in integrity of the stored materials; they have disadvantages in decreased use and increased costs in operation and delivery. One academic library (California State University at Northridge) has installed a highly automated, computer-managed storage facility; it is based on a system for automated warehousing.

Alternative Formats

There are two major categories of alternatives to print formats: microform formats (cartridge and fiche, in particular) and electronic formats (CD-ROM and local databases on-line, in particular). Assessment of the effectiveness of alternative formats in meeting the needs of users is an integral part of the model of user needs presented in Chapter 5.

Relative Roles of Print and Electronic Media. The view of this text is the following: Both print and electronic media are and will continue to be vital; each has particular values and benefits; they are not in general substitutes for each other but in fact are mutually supportive of each other; and the current effect of use of electronic media is to increase the need for and use of print media rather than reducing it.

It is also the case that electronic publication will become increasingly important. The pace of growth can at this time be predicted only in a superficial way, but even dramatic estimates of growth will not mean substantial increases in acquisition of electronic media within the coming ten- or even twenty-year period or in replacement of print by them. Growth of electronic publishing will be seen primarily in periodicals and much less so for monographs.

The pace of growth of electronic publishing is clearly an issue of fundamental importance in assessing its future role. Current data (from Predicasts, for example, in estimates concerning CD-ROM publishing) suggest a rate of growth at about 50 percent per annum for the coming five-year period;[43] given the very small current base, dramatic though that growth would be, the absolute numbers are not spectacular, and one should anticipate a subsequent slowdown in that growth.

Microform replacement is generally seen as disadvantageous, with problems in viewing and copying, problems in use and cost of equipment, and lack of acceptance by users. However, there are some kinds of materials for which it is not only acceptable but desirable and, if it is "the only game in town," users will accept it and use it. Where the microform can directly replace a bound journal, it could well do so.

SERVICES: REFERENCE

On-line Public Access Catalogs (OPACs)

Today, on-line public access catalogs are crucial tools for reader services in community libraries. They greatly increase the ability of patrons to identify materials needed and effectively to utilize collections. Beyond that, however, they can be powerful tools for users to assemble bibliographies and to download data into personal files for manipulation, analysis, and incorporation into databases and documents. They also have value as sources of factual data—such as biographical data (for example, dates of birth and death) for individuals.

Enhanced Bibliographic Records

The local system on-line public access catalog (OPAC) also serves as a central tool in reference services. Efforts to augment the bibliographic data are therefore among the important means for increasing the level of support. The addition of tables of contents and even book indexes, for example, would greatly increase the ability to guide patrons in access to and use of monographs, especially compilations and proceedings. Increased analytics, identification of tables, even current contents of serials—each of these is being experimented with by both individual libraries and the bibliographic utilities.

Local Mounting of Databases

The nearly universal implementation of local system OPACs is now making it feasible for libraries to consider using them to provide access to nationally available databases in addition to the library's own catalog. Subscription pricing arrangements make it possible to offer access to those databases at minimal cost to the users, even free, and as a result greatly increase the amount of use made of them—by factors as much as a hundredfold. Of special value is provision of interconnection between the records of those databases and the holdings records from the library's catalog; that permits users quickly to identify the local availability of retrieved references.

Expert Reference

During this decade, expert systems and generalized expert systems approaches will become operational in libraries. Developed systems will be easily transportable and widely available for libraries for a variety of in-house local systems uses. Of special importance will be implementation of automated ready-reference; it will be operational in virtually every library, providing microcomputer support to the ready-reference function.[44]

The most important role of microcomputers in implementation of local systems is to assure that information services can be easily available on-line and remotely. This already is represented by the dial-in access capabilities of the public library. Locations for access to library information services can include the business office, the laboratory, the schoolroom, and the home. But to make such remote service effective requires that there be easy user interfaces. Hence, strategic management should include in its agenda the development of expert systems (sometimes called artificial intelligence or AI), which would supplement a library patron's personal knowledge of the process and the subject of interest, thus raising the quality level of the overall information-seeking experience. Expert system intelligence, providing ease of use for end users, can best be done at the workstation level.

Hypertext is a relatively simple means for developing an expert system; it involves means within a document for embedded self-indexing (i.e., links from one section in the document to other sections, or even to other documents, in which readers can find related materials, definitions, or amplification). The value of hypertext is that it permits the document to be read in sequences other than the normal page-by-page, linear fashion. Creating such flexibility is a prime example of an expert system and there has been much speculation about the dramatic changes it will make in the means for access to information and in the design of textbooks for more interactive, dynamic education.[45]

Readers' Advisory Services

Readers' advisory services are ordinarily offered as part of the public library reference function. Requests for assistance in finding a good book to read are typically answered at the same public service desk that provides reference service. Some public libraries that emphasize their role as a popular reading center go beyond this fairly passive approach to advising readers. They may market genre fiction of various kinds through displays and special shelving or produce book lists which guide readers to good reading for pleasure.

Limitations to Reference Service

Public libraries may find it necessary to develop policies which indicate strategic boundaries to the reference services they provide. For example, some libraries do not, as a matter of policy, answer questions that can be identified as "homework questions." Others avoid getting involved in answering questions arising from promotional contests. Many public libraries have explicit limitations on the scope of legal or medical questions they will answer.

Organization of Reference Services

With reference services an established tradition in virtually all public libraries, a structure for offering these services is usually well institutionalized. There are, however, many options which library directors might consider. Probably the most ubiquitous structure is to offer reference services through age-segregated departments: adult, children, and perhaps young adult. In this configuration, the patron requests and receives service at an adult reference desk or at a children's reference desk. Specialists in each area provide the service. Larger, research-oriented libraries may organize their collections and reference services for adults into subject departments: fiction, social science, business, and so on. Baltimore County Public Library has pioneered a generalist approach, in which all public service staff provide services to all patrons, regardless of age.

Telecommunications technology may introduce further alternatives for organizing reference service in public libraries. Most of the initiatives currently being developed for digital libraries involve university libraries. However, students at the University of Michigan School of Library and Information Science are experimenting with an interactive public library which provides all of its reference services on-line, through the Internet. Their experiences may suggest new patterns of organizing reference services.

SERVICES: INSTRUCTION AND CONSULTATION

Information Skills Instruction

In the long term, though, it is even more important to develop the skills of the users themselves in access to and, especially, in use of information resources to meet their own needs. The public library will have both the opportunity and the requirement to provide instruction in information skills and consultation in the use of information resources. The development of expert systems can be a component of such information skills instruction, but tools specifically designed to aid that process will also be required, and strategic management could work with reference staff in creating those tools.

Consultation for Information Processing

The ability to retrieve, to analyze, to compare and combine, to process and manipulate, to communicate, is a promise far more important than mere access to information. It is the potential to *use* it. There is increasing use of *personal information managers* that permit the individual to download substantial amounts of data and then to retrieve those data needed most immediately, to establish linkages among those data and between them and other sources. But users frequently need help in doing so.

Typical needs for consulting support are on features of relevant software, on design of database structures, on indexing of data files, on the availability of source data to be downloaded into personal files, in actually downloading data from external sources, on the copyright and licensing requirements. These clearly represent significant needs and ones that will not only continue but increase. The use of personal databases, with downloading of data from the national interlibrary network, from commercial database services, and from CD-ROM files will become standard with users by the end of the decade.

SERVICES: PROGRAMMING

Strategic decisions about programming involve determinations of both the kind and level of programs that the library will offer. Libraries offer programs for a variety of reasons: to extend access to information, to highlight aspects of the collection, to attract people to the library, and to meet cultural or recreational needs of the community. Programs may be home-grown, with library staff providing all of the labor, or they may be subsidized by a programming budget which brings in outside professionals. Often, "Friends of the Library" provides the funding for programs which augment the regular offerings.

As noted previously, programming is an integral part of children's services. The preschool story hour and summer reading program are traditions at most American public libraries. Depending on the library's strategic direction, however, many other kinds of programming for other segments of the population may be both desirable and possible. Public libraries have sponsored programs on bike repair and summer jobs for teenagers; parenting skills and reading readiness for mothers and fathers; book collecting, genealogy, and income tax preparation for adults. Public libraries have held poetry readings, concerts, author visits, book discussions, panel presentations on World War II and on alternative lifestyles. Libraries have sponsored reading marathons and library sleepovers. Apparently almost anything is possible.

Strategic decisions about programming should be focused on the role of programs in the total library product mix of services. Programming should be rational; that is, it should clearly relate to the library's role and purpose in the community. A library craft program for children may be redundant if the parks and recreation department offers a similar service for a similar population. However, it may be highly appropriate if it promotes use of the children's collection or draws new patrons to the library.

Programming is often used as part of library outreach, the library's effort to "reach out" to nontraditional library users. As such, it may be a marketing ploy, or it may represent a new form of service delivery that is particularly appropriate for an underserved population segment. For example, the Chinatown branch of the Los Angeles Public Library held a series of video showings of Chinese operas when it first opened in the late 1970s. These attracted elderly residents to the library, where they enjoyed the social contact as well as the content of the programs. Gradually, the Chinese senior citizens began to use other services of the library as well.

SERVICES: PUBLICATION AND DISTRIBUTION

Desktop Publishing

Throughout the community, there is clear evidence of the need to support desktop publishing. From the perspective of a small entrepreneur, there are evident values in the speed of getting material into distribution, in control of the end product. The most significant evidence of need is the dramatic increase in the use of microcomputer-based word processing, and installation of such capabilities in the public library is a clear recognition of the importance this has. Although desktop publishing is by no means as widespread as is word processing, current estimates are that nationally it will grow at about 40 percent per annum.

A related development is the increasing importance in the use of electronic manuscripts, because of the benefits they provide to the publication and post-publication processing. The Association of American Publishers, recognizing the increasing use by authors of microcomputer-based word processing, established standards for encoding of electronic manuscripts to facilitate the communication between authors, publishers, and printers. Based on SGML (Standard Generalized Markup Language), the standards recognize requirements at each stage in the process of developing, editing, and publishing—from the author to the editor and publisher to the conversion to printed form. They accommodate the array of document types, of structural elements within them (such as equations, tables, graphics), and of data needed not only for publication but for other uses (such as bibliographic access).

The Library as "Publisher"

The technologies of desktop publishing, on-line, full-text storage, and CD-ROM production together provide the opportunity for the public library to be a publisher. On-demand publication is a natural consequence of full-text and digitized image storage; this can include production of publications tailored to meet needs of individual library patrons. Unique resources within collections of the public library can readily and, today, inexpensively be put into CD-ROM format for sale; local history materials could be of special value in such a program. Strategic management could explore the possibilities for such publications and the best means for producing them.

SERVICES: TELECOMMUNICATIONS AND NETWORK ACCESS

Integration of Library/Computer/ Telecommunications

Telecommunications technology enables the public library to provide information services to patrons and other libraries over great distances. The rapid implementation of fiber optic lines means that it will be economical to carry a mix of computer, television, and voice signals efficiently. The metropolitan downtown library should be designated a terminus for fiber optic service by the local telephone company. This presents the library with an enormous communications opportunity and capability to interconnect the downtown library with neighborhood branch libraries. Availability of the capability also suggests that the library should plan on installing a Local Area Network (LAN) of fiber optic lines in its renovated, expanded, or new building to achieve electronic communications connectivity internally and externally.

Even the small-town library should aim for a comparable capability for communication with its peers in neighboring small towns and with the downtown library in the nearest city.

New developments in communications technology are continually emerging from the laboratories. Some examples of potential interest to libraries:

High-Definition Television. This development will provide new capabilities for the library to deliver information to the home or office. At present, home TV screens are unable to display a readable full page of text, but high-definition television will provide this capability.

Integrated Services Digital Networks. The congruence of computer and communications technology has led to new communications networks capable of offering flexible combinations of voice, data, and video services. National and commercial services will soon be available that provide an enriched range of communications services. Users will no longer need to use different networks for different types of calls. Instead, they will use one network and specify the type of call as part of the sign-on. This means that the public library will be able to send and receive all types of electronic signals with the same ease, and at reasonable cost, as if it were using today's telephone network. For the smaller communities, especially, this is an important capability, one well within the available resources, so the directors and boards of small-town libraries should actively explore the means for implementation.

Video Teleconferencing. Advances in teleconferencing systems have dramatically reduced transmission costs of television broadcasts, providing about the same picture quality. The public library could today consider the use of compressed bandwidth teleconferencing as a way to enhance interlibrary communications—especially in reference, education, and research areas—between the downtown library, the neighborhood libraries, and other libraries.

Distance Learning

In the use of telecommunications, distance learning is a development of special importance for collaboration by the public libraries with educators. It provides means by which instruction, through television and a combination of computer and telecommunications technology, can reach students at distant locations. Using distance-learning technology, classrooms can now extend to students in remote sites—in other cities, in other states, and in other nations. A course in advanced mathematics can be taught to high school students in inner-city areas by a professor at a remote university in an interactive mode of instruction. The technology is flexible and offers multiple ways to deliver instruction over a distance. The quality and effectiveness of distance learning are determined by the quality of the educational program and the selection of the appropriate technologies to transmit the instruction.[46]

Smaller public libraries are likely to play important roles in community education projects, such as teaching English as a second language, providing introductions to American culture, or enhancing literacy skills. Their participation in such distance-learning programs can therefore be very helpful and rewarding for their communities.

But there are needs for materials to be available for the student to use in the interactive instructional process and in independent study. The public library is frequently the agency to which the student can best turn to make those materials available. A major requirement for instructional support by the public library is, therefore, to anticipate such expectations.

The Statewide Library Network

The purpose of statewide library networks in the most general sense is to improve access to knowledge for state residents by facilitating the widest possible interchange of information and materials among the state's libraries. The idea of a statewide network of libraries is based on the belief that information is a state resource and that all residents have a right to access this resource from any location in the state. It is furthermore based on the view that the creation of the network will lead to a more prudent use of funds for libraries and enable them to take maximum advantage of new technology. Within any state network, the public library is regarded as a primary resource. It is therefore important for strategic management to play a central role in the future development of the state library network to assure that it is maximally effective. Managers may be required to make strategic decisions about their own libraries' levels of participation in regional and statewide networks. Where networks are designed as partnerships, all agencies are required to contribute in some way, as well as being entitled to receive the benefits of membership. Public libraries will have to weigh the short- and long-term costs and benefits of participation.

Use of On-line Database Services

During the past two decades, the on-line database services have become increasingly important in community library operations. That situation, though, appears to be changing. While in the overall, the predictions are that on-line database services will continue to grow at about 20 percent per annum, that covers the entire range of users.[47] Today, libraries are a relatively small portion of the total market. Given acquisition of many databases in CD-ROM form and the increasing "end-user" direct use of them, use of the on-line database access services in libraries is likely not to increase and indeed may begin to decline during the last half of the decade.

NOTES

1. Baltimore County Public Library's Blue Ribbon Committee, *Give 'Em What They Want! Managing the Public's Library* (Chicago: American Library Association, 1992); James C. Baughman, *Policy Making for Public Library Trustees* (Englewood, Colo.: Libraries Unlimited, 1993); Thomas Childers and Nancy A. Van House, *What's Good? Describing Your Public Library's Effectiveness* (Chicago: American Library Association, 1993); Paul John Cirino, *The Business of Running a Library: A Handbook for Public Library Directors* (Jefferson, N.C.: McFarland, 1991); G. D'Elia, *The Role of the Public Library in Society* (Evanston, Ill.: Urban Libraries Council, 1993); R. Kathleen Molz, *Library Planning and Policy Making: The Legacy of the Public and Private Sectors* (Metuchen, N.J.: Scarecrow Press, 1990); PLA Policy Manual Committee, *PLA Handbook for Writers of Public Library Policies* (Chicago: Public Library Association, 1993); Nancy A. Van House and Thomas A. Childers, *The Public Library Effectiveness Study: The Complete Report* (Chicago: American Library Association, 1993); Holly G. Willett, *Public Library Youth Services: A Public Policy Approach* (Norwood, N.J.: Ablex, 1995).

2. Bill Clinton and Al Gore, *Putting People First: How We Can All Change America* (New York: Times Books, 1992); Charles R. McClure, John Carlo Bertot, and Douglas L. Zweizig, *Public Libraries and the Internet: Study Results, Policy Issues, and Recommendation* (Washington, D.C.: NCLIS, 1994); U.S. House of Representatives, *National Information Infrastructure Act of 1993—HR 1757* (Washington, D.C.: GPO, 1993).

3. Sharon L. Baker, *The Responsive Public Library Collection: How to Develop and Market It* (Englewood, Colo.: Libraries Unlimited, 1993); Mae Benne, *Principles of Children's Services in Public Libraries* (Chicago: American Library Association, 1991); Da-

vid B. Carlson et al., *Adrift in a Sea of Change: California's Public Libraries Struggle to Meet the Information Needs of Multicultural Communities* (Center for Policy Development, 1990); Kathleen M. Heim and Danny P. Wallace, eds., *Adult Services: An Enduring Focus for Public Libraries* (Chicago: American Library Association, 1990); Margaret Ellen Monroe and Kathleen M. Heim, *Partners for lifelong learning: Public libraries & adult education* (Washington, D.C.: Office of Library Programs, U.S. Dept. of Education, Office of Educational Research and Improvement, 1991); Amado M. Padilla, *Public library services for immigrant populations in California: A report to the State Librarian of California* (Sacramento: California State Library Foundation, 1991); *Reaching people: A manual on public education for libraries serving blind and physically handicapped individuals* (Washington, D.C.: National Library Service for the Blind and Physically Handicapped, Library of Congress, 1992); Fannette H. Thomas, *Children's Services in the American Public Library: A Selected Bibliography* (Westport, Conn.: Greenwood Press, 1990); Alan F. Westin and Anne L. Finger, *Using the Public Library in the Computer Age: Present Patterns, Future Possibilities* (Chicago: American Library Association, 1991).

4. Carlton Rochell, *Wheeler and Goldhor's Practical Administration of Public Libraries* (New York: Harper & Row, 1981), chapters 8, 11, 12.

5. Carlton Rochell, *Wheeler and Goldhor's Practical Administration of Public Libraries*, chapter 8; *Intellectual Freedom Manual*, compiled by the Office for Intellectual Freedom of the American Library Association, 4th ed. (Chicago: American Library Association, 1992); John O. Christensen, *Intellectual Freedom and Libraries: A Selective Bibliography* (Monticello, Ill.: Vance Bibliographies, 1991); William Noble, *Bookbanning in America: Who Bans Books? And Why?* (Middlebury, Vt.: P.S. Eriksson, 1990); *Challenged materials: An interpretation of the Library Bill of Rights* (Chicago: ALA), adopted 14 July 1971, amended 1 July 1981 and 10 January 1990; *Diversity in Collection Development: An Interpretation of the Library Bill of Rights* (Chicago: ALA), adopted 14 July 1982, amended 10 January 1990.

6. John F. Kennedy, "The candidates and the arts," *Saturday Review of Literature*, 29 October 1960, p. 44. The full quote is as follows: "These libraries must be open to all—except the censor. We must know all the facts and hear all the alternatives and listen to all the criticisms. Let us welcome controversial books and controversial authors. For the Bill of Rights is the guardian of our security as well as our liberty."

7. Silk Makowski, "Serious about series: Selection criteria for a neglected genre," *VOYA* (February 1994): 349–351.

8. *Brittle Books: Reports of the Committee on Preservation and Access* (Washington, D.C.: Council on Library Resources, 1986); Jan Merrill-Oldham et al., *Preservation Program Models: A Study Project and Report* (Washington, D.C.: ARL, 1991).

9. *Code of Federal Regulations*, 2 April 1982 (pp. 116–178). Executive Order 12356, National Security Information. Establishes the rationale and procedures for military security classification. The legislative authority for doing so lies in 5 U.S. Code 301 which states, "The head of an executive department may prescribe regulations for . . . the custody, use, and preservation of records, papers, and property."

U.S. Congress. House Permanent Select Committee on Intelligence. *H.R. 4165, National Security Act of 1992*. Supt. of Docs., Congressional Sales Office, 1992; *Code of Federal Regulations*, revised as of 1 July 1993, volume 32 (National Defense), Part 158 (pp. 636–643) provides for the periodic review of the classification of documents.

10. David Kahn, *The Codebreakers* (New York: MacMillan, 1967); James Bamford,

The Puzzle Palace: A Report on America's Most Secret Agency (Boston: Houghton-Mifflin, 1982).

11. See, for example, comments by Kenneth B. Allen, Office of Management and Budget (in response to a presentation of the report of the *Public Sector/Private Sector Task Force Report* by Robert M. Hayes), as part of "Reactor panel: views from government, libraries, and the information industry," especially p. 23, in *Minutes of the Ninety-ninth Annual Meeting, the Association of Research Libraries* (Washington, D.C.: ARL, 1982).

12. In the early months of 1994, the reports on the "Clipper" reached a flood stage, with articles appearing in every major newspaper on a daily basis. The debate apparently came to an end in July 1994, when the Clinton administration finally reversed its position and indicated it was willing to consider alternatives. The following are simply a sample from that flood: Peter H. Lewis, "Of privacy and security: The clipper chip debate," *New York Times*, 24 April 1994, F5; William M. Bulkeley, "Cipher probe: Popularity overseas of encryption code has the U.S. worried; grand jury wonders if creator 'exported' the program through the Internet; 'genie is out of the bottle'," *Wall Street Journal*, 28 April 1994, A1; House Science, Space and Technology Committee Sub-committee on Technology, Environment, and Aviation. *Hearings*, 3 May 1994; "Don't worry, be happy: Why Clipper is good for you," *Wired* (June 1994): 132; Amy Harmon, "Cyberprivacy and the 'Clipper'," *Los Angeles Times*, 8 June 1994, D1; Steven Levy, "The cyberpunks vs. Uncle Sam," *New York Times Magazine*, 12 June 1994, pp. 44–51, 60, 70; Jaleen Nelson, "Sledge hammers and scalpels: The FBI digital wiretap bill and its effect on freeflow of information and piracy," *UCLA Law Review* 1139 (1994): 1168; John Markoff, "An administration reversal on wiretapping technology," *New York Times*, 21 July 1994, C1.

13. The FBI "Library Awareness Program" exploded like a bomb as a result of a closed session meeting of the NCLIS: Graceanne A. DeCandido, "FBI presents 'library awareness' to NCLIS at closed meeting," *Library Journal* 113(7) (April 15, 1988): 16; "Surveillance among the library stacks (FBI wants National Security Archive to report on suspicious foreign patrons)," *Science News* 133(24) (11 June 1988): 382; Howard Fields, "People for American Way fund suit against FBI library informant plan," *Publishers Weekly* 233(24) (17 June 1988): 16; Howard Fields, "Librarians challenge FBI on extent of its investigation (reporting of 'foreign-looking' users of certain library materials)," *Publishers Weekly* 234(2) (8 July 1988): 11; "FBI to consider release of 'awareness program' material," *American Libraries* (June 1989): 481; A. J. Anderson, Martha M. Malosky, and Ellen L. Miller, "The FBI wants you—to spy," *Library Journal* 114(11) (15 June 1989): 37–40; Ulrika Ekman Ault, "The FBI's library awareness program: Is big brother reading over your shoulder?" *New York University Law Review* 65(6) (December 1990): 1532–1565; Graceanne A. DeCandido, "FBI investigated librarians who opposed Library Awareness Program," *Library Journal* 114(20) (December 1989): 19; "Funhouse mirror" (FBI library-patron surveillance, editorial), *Progressive* 54(1) (January 1990): 10; Frankie Pelzman, "Washington observer" (FBI's Library Awareness Program), *Wilson Library Bulletin* 64(5) (January 1990): 13–18; "ALA files appeal for full disclosure" (FBI's Library Awareness Program), *Wilson Library Bulletin* 64(6) (February 1990): 11–13; John Swan, "Surveillance in the stacks: The FBI's Library Awareness Program," *Library Journal* 116(1) (January 1991): 162; Christopher Dandeker, "Surveillance in the stacks: The FBI's Library Awareness Program," *Annals of the American Academy of Political and Social Science* 521 (May 1992): 202–204.

14. Alex Ladenson, ed., *American Library Laws* (Chicago: ALA, 1983). California, Florida, and Wisconsin have state legislation all generally reading to the effect that registration and circulation records shall be confidential information, to be revealed only by appropriate court order. John O. Christensen, *Legal Issues in Public and School Libraries: Some Recent References* (Monticello, Ill.: Vance Bibliographies, 1990); Shirley A. Weigand, *Library Records: A Retention and Confidentiality Guide* (Westport, Conn.: Greenwood Press, 1994).

15. Janet Hildebrand, "Is privacy reserved for adults? Children's rights in the public library," *School Library Journal* 37(1) (January 1991): 21–25.

16. California Legislature, Senate Committee on Local Government, *Your guide to open meetings: The Ralph M. Brown Act* (Sacramento: Joint Publications, 1989).

17. Debra Gersh, "Moldea appeals dismissal of $10 million libel suit" (*Moldea v. New York Times Co.*), *Editor & Publisher* 126(28) (10 July 1993): 16; "D.C. Circuit says opinion can be libelous," *National Law Journal* 16(27) (7 March 1994): 6; Christopher Hanson, "Playing 'chicken' with the First Amendment" (the likely impact of a *Moldea v. The New York Times Co.*, on opinion writing), *Columbia Journalism Review* 33(1) (May-June 1994): 21–23; Howard Fields, "In surprise, court reverses itself on Moldea ruling," *Publishers Weekly* 241(19) (9 May 1994): 11–13; "Court enlarges protection for book reviews" (statements in book review are opinion and as such not actionable under libel laws), *News Media & the Law* 18(2) (Spring 1994): 3–4.

18. Michele V. Cloonan, "The censorship of The Adventures of Huckleberry Finn: An investigation," *Top of the News* 41(2) (Winter 1984); Nat Hentoff, *Free Speech for Me but not for Thee: How the American Left and Right Relentlessly Censor Each Other* (New York: Harper Collins Publishers, 1992); Cal Thomas, "Radical left censorship undermines education," in *Opposing Viewpoint Pamphlets*, ed. David L. Bender (St. Paul, Minn.: Greenhaven Press, 1985); Fred L. Pincus, "The left must guard American values," in *Opposing Viewpoint Pamphlets*, ed. David L. Bender (St. Paul, Minn.: Greenhaven Press, 1985).

19. Debra L. Schultz, *To reclaim a legacy of diversity: analyzing the "political correctness" debates in higher education*, a report prepared by the National Council for Research on Women (New York: The Council, 1993); Paul Berman, ed., *Debating P.C.: The Controversy Over Political Correctness on College Campuses* (New York: Laurel, published by Dell, 1992); Jung Min Choi and John W. Murphy, *The Politics and Philosophy of Political Correctness* (Westport, Conn.: Praeger, 1992).

20. "The debate nobody won," *Library Journal* 102(14) (1 Aug 1977): 1573–1580; Clara S. Jones, "Reflections on 'The Speaker'," *Wilson Library Bulletin* 52(1) (September 1977): 51–55; " 'The Speaker' debate goes on: cheers & jeers," *Library Journal* 103(15) (1 September 1978): 1550–51; "Critics of 'The Speaker' scored for censorship," *Library Journal* 104(3) (1 February 1979): 335.

21. See Chapter 6, where this issue is discussed in some detail.

22. Ibid.

23. Betty Carol Sellen and Patricia A. Young, *Feminists, Pornography, and the Law* (Hamden, Conn.: Library Professional Publications, 1987); Greg Byerly, *Pornography, the Conflict Over Sexually Explicit Materials in the United States: An Annotated Bibliography* (New York: Garland, 1980); Herbert N. Foerstel, *Banned in the U.S.A.: A Reference Guide to Book Censorship in Schools and Public Libraries* (Westport, Conn.:

Greenwood Press, 1994); John O. Christensen, *Obscenity, Pornography, and Libraries: A Selective Bibliography* (Monticello, Ill.: Vance Bibliographies, 1991).

24. United States Supreme Court Justice Potter Stewart, re *Jabellis vs. Ohio*, 1964: "I shall not today attempt further to define the kinds of material . . . embraced within that shorthand description . . . But I know it when I see it."

25. Steven Levy, "No place for kids? A parents' guide to sex on the Net," *Newsweek* 126(1) (3 July 1995): 47–50.

26. Charles A. Bunge, "Responsive reference service: Breaking down the age barriers," *School Library Journal* (March 1994): 142–145; "Eye on censorship: Growing challenges to libraries target materials on sexuality," *American Libraries* (November 1993): 902–903; Joan DelFattore, *Why Johnnie Shouldn't Read: Textbook Censorship in America* (New Haven: Yale University Press, 1992); Michael J. Sadowski and Randy Meyer, "New St. Louis policy raises questions of parental control," *School Library Journal* (May 1994): 10–11; "Angry Virginia Beach mom wants her kid's borrowing restricted," *American Libraries* (January 1994): 9; William E. Sheerin, "Absolutism on access and confidentiality: Principled or irresponsible?" *American Libraries* (May 1991): 440–444, refers to permitting parent to choose; "Restraints on children's access controversy," *American Libraries* (July-August 1990): 628–629.

27. Jerry Falwell, "The religious right must guard American values," in *Opposing Viewpoint Pamphlets*, ed. David L. Bender (St. Paul, Minn.: Greenhaven Press, 1985).

28. George Haven Putnam, *The Censorship of the Church of Rome* (New York: B. Blom, 1967).

29. Leslie H. Allen, ed., *Bryan and Darrow at Dayton; the Record and Documents of the "Bible-evolution Trial"* (New York: A. Lee & Company, 1925); L. Sprague De Camp, *The Great Monkey Trial* (Garden City, N.Y.: Doubleday, 1968); Sheldon Norman Grebstein, ed., *Monkey Trial; The State of Tennessee vs. John Thomas Scopes* (Boston: Houghton Mifflin, 1960); Jerry R. Tompkins, ed., *D-days at Dayton: Reflections on the Scopes Trial* (Baton Rouge: Louisiana State University Press, 1965).

30. Ronald Numbers, *The Creationists: The Evolution of Scientific Creationism* (New York: Knopf, 1992). This was extensively reviewed at the time of publication: *Science* 258(5081) (16 October 1992): 487; *New Republic* 208(10) (8 March 1993): 29; *Nature* 360(6405) (17 December 1992): 637; *Christian Century* 110(4) (3 February 1993): 133; *American Journal of Physical Anthropology* 91(1) (May 1993): 135; *American Scientist* 82(1) (January-February 1994): 92; *Sociology of Religion* 55(1) (Spring 1994): 95; *Journal of American Studies* 27(3) (December 1993): 439; Barry W. Lynn, "Vista's school board: Model for disaster," *Church & State* 46(8) (September 1993): 23; "Vista school board takes up 'creation science' issue again" (Vista, California), *Church & State* 46(5) (May 1993): 19–20; Stryker McGuire, "When fundamentalists run the schools (Christian majority on Vista, California, school board)," *Newsweek* 122(19) (8 November 1993): 46.

31. Committee on Science and Creationism, National Academy of Sciences, *Science and creationism: A view from the National Academy of Sciences* (Washington, D.C.: National Academy Press, 1984); Steven N. Shore, "Scientific creationism: The social agenda of a pseudoscience," *Skeptical Inquirer* 17(1) (Fall 1992): 70–73; Ganga Shankar and Gerald D. Skoog, "Emphasis given evolution and creationism by Texas high school biology teachers," *Science Education* 77(2) (April 1993): 221–233; Michele Collison, "Biologist's theory of creation gets him into hot water at San Francisco State U.," *Chronicle of Higher Education* 40(20) (19 January 1994): A20.

32. This will be discussed in detail in Chapter 6.

33. *Predicasts Basebook*, December 1993: Book publishing shipments had an annual growth rate during the prior three years of 8.36%, based on 1978–1980 average. U.S. outlook in 1992, annual growth rate of 2.4%; 1993, annual growth rate of 3.0% 1994, annual growth rate of 3.2% (all in constant 1987 dollars).

34. Linda Stewart, Katherin Chiang, and Bill Coons, eds., *Public Access CD-ROMs in Libraries* (Westport, Conn.: Meckler, 1990); M. Sandra Wood, ed., *CD-ROM Implementation and Networking in Health Sciences Libraries* (New York: Haworth Press, 1993).

35. Carol Hildebrand, "IRS to overhaul system in bid to reduce its reliance on paper" (Internal Revenue Service engaged in $8 billion computer systems overhaul), *Computerworld* 25(24) (June 17, 1991): 8; Thomas Hoffman, "Imaging cures hospital's paper woes: Memorial Sloan-Kettering saving more than $140K/year with a healthy dose of document imaging," *Computerworld* 26(26) (29 June 1992): 74; Susan L. Cisco, "Document imaging finding niche in petroleum industry," *Oil and Gas Journal* 90(45) (9 November 1992): 85–90; Robert N. Beck, "Issues of imaging science for future consideration," *Proceedings of the National Academy of Sciences of the United States* 90(21) (1 November 1993): 9803–9808.

36. "Project JANUS at Columbia University," *Computing News*, a publication of Columbia University Academic Information Systems 5(4) (December 1993).

37. Stu Borman, "AAAS to launch on-line peer-reviewed journal" (American Association for the Advancement of Science: The Online Journal of Current Clinical Trials), *Chemical & Engineering News* 69(39) (30 September 1991): 8; Andrea Keyhani, "The Online Journal of Current Clinical Trials: An innovation in electronic publishing," *Database* 16(1) (February 1993): 14; Beverly Renford and Andrew Ries, "Online Journal of Current Clinical Trials," *The Journal of the American Medical Association* 269(13) (7 April 1993): 1697; "GUIDON improves Internet access to electronic journal" (Online Journal of Current Clinical Trials), *Online* 17(3) (May 1993): 83; David L. Wilson, "A journal's big break" (electronic journal on Medline database), *Chronicle of Higher Education* 40(21) (26 January 1994): A23.

38. David Everett, "Full-text online databases and document delivery in an academic library," *Online* 17(2) (March 1993): 22.

39. This will be discussed in detail in Chapter 6.

40. Ibid.

41. "ARL and RLG to study ILL costs," *Library Journal* 21(7) (17 April 1992): 102.

42. Ann Irvine, "Is centralized collection development better? The results of a survey," *Public Libraries* 34(4) (July/August 1995): 216–218.

43. *Predicasts*, 1990 (estimates concerning CD-ROM publishing).

44. Edwin M. Cortez and Tom Smorch, *Planning Second Generation Automated Library Systems* (Westport, Conn.: Greenwood Press, 1993), p. 70–71.

45. There is one crucial reference for Hypertext, that of the evangelist for it: Theodor H. Nelson, *Literary Machines: The Report on, and of, Project Xanadu Concerning Word Processing, Electronic Publishing, Hypertext, Thinkertoys, Tomorrow's Intellectual Revolution, and Certain Other Topics Including Knowledge, Education, Freedom* (San Antonio, TX: T.H. Nelson, 1987); Myke Gluck, *HyperCard, Hypertext, and Hypermedia for Libraries and Media Centers* (Englewood, Colo.: Libraries Unlimited, 1989); Robert E. Horn, *Mapping Hypertext: The Analysis, Organization, and Display of Knowledge for the Next Generation of On-line Text and Graphics* (Lexington, Mass.: Lexington Institute,

c1989); Emily Berk and Joseph Devlin, eds., *Hypertext/Hypermedia Handbook* (New York: Intertext Publications, McGraw-Hill, c1991); Michael Knee, *Hypertext/Hypermedia: An Annotated Bibliography* (Westport, Conn.: Greenwood Press, 1990); James M. Nyce and Paul Kahn, *From Memex to Hypertext: Vannevar Bush and the Mind's Machine* (Boston: Academic Press, 1991); Philip C. Seyer, *Understanding Hypertext: Concepts and Applications* (Blue Ridge Summit, Penn.: Windcrest, 1991); Ben Schneiderman, *Hypertext Hands-On! An Introduction to a New Way of Organizing and Accessing Information* (Reading, Mass.: Addison-Wesley, 1989); Nigel Woodhead, *Hypertext and Hypermedia: Theory and Applications* (Reading, Mass.: Addison-Wesley, 1991).

46. Alan G. Chute et al., "Distance education futures: Information needs and technology options," *Performance and Instruction* 30 (November-December 1991): 1–6.

47. *Predicasts*, 1990 (concerning database market growth).

PART II
Contexts

4

The Context of Community Problems and Needs

In this chapter and the following two, we will expand on the set of issues of importance to the community library that provide the context for strategic management. They fall into three groups: (1) those that relate to community government, its needs, and its problems, (2) those that relate to the users—the constituencies served—and their needs, and (3) those that relate to the external environment.

This chapter focuses on community government. It is both impossible and inappropriate for this book to deal in detail with the full range of issues in local government, but it is both appropriate and essential that they be identified and briefly characterized so that their effect on strategic management of the community library can be assessed.

COMMUNITY MISSION

The most important determinant of community policies surely is the perception and the reality of mission—as seen by government and by the public. A major theme of this chapter is that, whatever the mission of the community may be, information imperatives apply not only to the library but with at least equal vigor to the community as a whole. In the future, every community will surely need to recognize that information is important to both the society and the individual and that the library is a crucial means for meeting community needs for access to it. But every community will also face the fiscal reality of reduced resources and increasing demands. It is the balancing of these that constitute perhaps the most important of the environments for public library strategic management.

The Major Metropolitan Regions

Some communities are major metropolitan centers, incorporating mixes of manufacturing, business, and commerce; they were the historic base for development of the industrial might of the United States, but they have faced dramatic dislocations as results of structural changes in the economy, in the transition to an information society (in addition to the typical problems when the economy falters or when there has been irrational investment in office buildings). Within the region surrounding a metropolitan center—the "standard metropolitan statistical area" or SMSA—are suburban communities that serve primarily as places where people live rather than work.

Among community missions, those of the major metropolitan regions are surely the most encompassing. They can be seen as political entities, as providers of human services, as supports to intellectual and creative energies, as centers of business and industry, as participants in the international global economy, as ports of entry for immigration and for transition from rural life. They can also be seen as economic agencies, serving their populations with a range of public goods and services.[1]

Within the major metropolitan regions, the local need for public goods is met through interactions among the central city, the surrounding suburban communities, and agencies from other levels of government. Each of them provides public goods and services, largely as determined by local perceptions of needs and priorities. However, state and national governments influence those decisions by providing funds to subsidize some local public goods and services; they even more directly determine them by mandating requirements. Thus, interlevel interactions are important in determining local policies, and the higher levels define the external constraints, the exogenous factors. While to some extent local governments may seek to influence those constraints, they are largely determined by other political forces.

It is useful to compare the economic nature of private goods and public goods, since in one sense, metropolitan regions can be seen as parallel to private sector providers of goods and services. Indeed, there is a national market, evidenced by the fight for economic development between regions of the country. The buyers are those who choose to live in a given community; the sellers are the local governments. The "pure competition model" for private markets uses profit maximization as the criterion measure. The underlying assumptions are first, that no single firm can determine market price; second, that there is easy entrance and exit of providers; third, that competition results in efficiency in production. Do these translate meaningfully for public goods?

Charles Tiebout presented a model of this kind.[2] He proposed that the choice of where to live—the market—served as a focus for competition among metropolitan regions in the bundle of products and services they provide. The bundles include various mixes of infrastructure—streets and roads, parks and libraries, police and fire protection, sewers and water supply—and constitute the product being sold. The Tiebout model assumes mobility and individual variations in tastes or wish for various public goods, and provides a means of balancing that market with costs. The costs for the bundles reflect: direct fees for services (clearly counterparts to private sector funding), subsidies from other levels of government, and local taxes—property taxes, sales taxes, dedicated taxes.

In sum, the Tiebout model assumes:

1. The local market consists of population centers competing with each other and with a national market.

2. People make locational decisions based on the relative merits of available packages of community goods and services and of "quality of life."

3. Local communities will assemble packages that best match the demand for public goods.

4. They must raise the revenue necessary to support those packages.

5. Differences arise from both the decisions concerning mixes of tastes and the ability to fund.

6. The ability to fund is primarily a function of the local tax base.

7. The result is that differences exist among the cost/benefit ratios.

8. Consequently, the locational decisions are influenced not only by the merits of packages but the cost/benefit for them.

9. The community must deal with the relative values of specific portions of the bundle to improving the cost/benefit ratio.

10. Policies will attempt to enhance that ratio and to maximize the tax base.

There are many problems with this model. First, there is no counterpart of "easy entrance and exit of providers"; metropolitan governments are spatial monopolists and cannot simply "come and go." Second, attractive though the concept of the bundles of services may be as an economic analogy, the decision to move is influenced by considerations other than simply economics, among them being "quality of life." Third, local government functions under constraints placed by law, limiting the ability to provide substantially different packages. Fourth, the effects of state subsidy change the costs in ways not under local control. Fifth, buyers are not simply unitary actors but in many cases are parts of large organizational complexes.

Perhaps the most significant problem, though, is the failure of the model to reflect the interaction among governmental entities in the provision of the bundle of services. The suburbs largely depend upon the metropolitan center for major components of their bundle of services, but they all too frequently do not pay for them. The result is that the economic decision does not reflect the underlying costs.

This is clearly represented by the investment in libraries as components of the bundle of services. The major metropolitan centers all have large libraries, many of them with research collections of national importance and all of them with branches serving both inner-city areas and affiliated suburbs. These library systems are crucial to community objectives and reputations, a basis for attracting and supporting business and industry as well as for meeting needs of individuals. The significant point is that, while some libraries for the surrounding suburbs may be branches of the metropolitan library system, others may be parts of a county or regional system or they may be independent. In either event, though, they depend upon the metropolitan central library for resources and materials beyond those for recreation and the simplest of needs in support of education.

Edge Cities

In the past two to three decades, there have appeared newer cities of a range of sizes, called "edge cities," that want to attract business and industry, but on a more limited scale than the metropolitan centers and more focused on high technology, as part of the wave of the information future. Each has been created on the periphery of suburbs around a metropolitan center and is part of the metropolitan region, of course, but they now compete with the center for business and draw on the same suburbs for their work force.

They all need libraries that support their objectives, but do not have enough history to have developed major collections and therefore are dependent on access to resources from elsewhere, and especially from the nearby metropolitan center. Frequently, they are served by branches of county or regional library systems.

Rural, Agricultural, and Tourism Communities

Outside the SMSAs and largely independent of the major metropolitan centers are communities of a wide range of size and mission. Many are based on agriculture, small and widely dispersed; others serve as commercial centers for their surrounding agricultural communities. Some are based on tourism, exploiting natural or even man-made wonders—seashores, mountains or deserts, national monuments or theme parks. The libraries in these communities are likely to be relatively small, limited to a single facility, or at most one or two branches, and with materials focused on recreation and support to school-level education.[3]

It is important to remember that most public libraries in the United States are in such small towns. Out of 8,946 public libraries in this country, more than half—5,465—serve communities with a population under 10,000. Thus, the typical American public library is not the large urban or suburban multibranch system embedded in a complex city or county government bureaucracy. It is instead a small-town library.[4]

COMMUNITIES IN THE COMING DECADES

Communities in the United States face a number of needs and problems during the coming decades, all of them affecting decisions concerning libraries and information resources. Several issues are paramount as determinants of future development: changes in the physical infrastructure of communities, changes in the economics of communities, changes in the nature of the population, changes in the educational system, effects of technology, and changes in patterns of work.

Public Physical Infrastructure

In the decades following the end of World War II, communities placed steadily increasing emphasis upon building infrastructure, especially as the new suburbs exploded on the fringes of major metropolitan centers. During the 1950s and 1960s, federal support to the national highway system and to housing fostered the growth of the suburbs and facilitated the flight of the white middle class from the metropolitan centers. The ratio shifted from a historic pattern of two urban for one suburban to the reverse, one urban for two suburban. The construction of freeways throughout the country had multiple effects, however. It not only facilitated the flight to the suburbs but removed land from the local tax base; physically divided communities, thus creating ghettos and enclaves; and led to the conversion of massive amounts of prime agricultural land to housing.[5]

Private investments accelerated during the 1970s and 1980s, fueled by irrational and even fraudulent speculation, especially of office buildings; this led to the savings and loan debacle, as property values subsequently declined. Significant though that debacle was in depleting available public funds, even more distressing was the burden placed on the public physical infrastructure by such overbuilding. It necessitated parallel public investments in streets, water supply and sewers, airports, police and fire protection; but those investments were in the "edge cities," not in the metropolitan centers where neglect has led to massive deterioration.

Accelerating the erosion of the infrastructure in the major metropolitan areas was the literal destruction of significant portions of communities, some by the razing of substandard housing without adequate replacement, and some by a succession of urban riots in the late 1960s and then, again, in the late 1980s. But whatever may be the concerns about the quality of the existing infrastructure and about needs to rebuild the metropolitan centers, there are no resources to do so. The decades-long commitment to public infrastructure programs now is undergoing dramatic change. There has been a reduction in governmental funding of physical infrastructure which has not been replaced by private sector funding.

At the federal level, the reduction in government funding was the result of a conscious decision made during the 1980s to greatly expand the commitment of resources to national defense. Today, the result of that decision is a three trillion(!) dollar national debt, a commitment to interest payments on that debt that consumes over half of the federal income, and pressures on the remaining discretionary funds that make it virtually impossible to make the commitments required to "clean up the mess." Indeed, the debate is not about how to reduce the unbelievable national debt but about how to reduce just the deficit![6]

Public infrastructures are facilities that have strong links to economic development, high fixed costs, long economic life, system interactions, and requirement for public sector involvement. In the past, the focus has been on physical infrastructure: highways, public transit, waste treatment, water supply, airports. Areas such as communications, libraries, and education have not usually been included even though they fit the criteria. Today, though, it is those areas in which the development of infrastructure is now crucial, and that is what makes it so important for public libraries to play their proper role in the future.

Economics of Communities

The past two decades have seen a steady erosion in the basis of financial support for communities of every kind. In 1992, it reached crisis proportions as state budgets throughout the country were decimated by the recession. In the United States at large, the current perception is that communities face a decade of *decreased resources.*

Special problems arise with respect to metropolitan centers and their capital needs. Buildings and equipment are aging, yet public programs generate new requirements. The housing infrastructure rots and physical infrastructure crumbles. The educational systems fail, and the fatalism of urban gangs escalates, teenage pregnancies explode, substance abuse and the horror of AIDS kill and destroy.[7]

Indeed, the Tiebout model applies well to decisions by individuals to move, and the affluent to flee to the suburbs. Aside from the negative effects of urban decay, there is the positive draw in a perception of superior public goods available in the suburbs, without loss of the advantages of proximity to the metropolitan center (but without paying for it!). In both ways, though, the effect was to dramatically reduce the tax base. But the aged cannot move because they depend on urban services, the poor cannot move because they cannot afford the cost, and urban poverty escalates due to high unemployment rates.

All of this started in the mid-1950s and has grown ever since. In recognition of the problems, federal grants in aid were increased from 10 percent of local spending in the 1950s to 25.3 percent in the late 1970s. But then, beginning with the Carter administration but pursued with a vengeance by the Reagan and

Bush administrations, such policies changed direction. General revenue sharing, instituted by Nixon, was gutted in the early 1980s and eliminated in 1986. Other forms of grants were slashed or eliminated. And while the states tried to fill the gaps, their resources were unable to do so and effectively fell sharply throughout the early 1980s and then leveled off.[8]

A study by the National League of Cities shows that revenues during the past decade increased by 1.3 percent but expenditures by 7.8 percent.[9] The problem is obvious; the means for solution, each difficult or impossible. One approach is to increase revenues—by taxation or by charging fees; this faces almost insurmountable barriers in the lack of willingness of the public to accept them.[10] Another is to increase efficiency and productivity; while laudable, there is just so much that can be done.[11] A third is to compensate for losses by reducing and eliminating various services and public programs—a new era of public budgeting and program management in a context of resource scarcity.[12] Unfortunately, though, state mandates in areas such as health care preclude many of these options. A fourth is to privatize—to have the private sector assume responsibility, either fully or under contract.[13]

In partial recognition of the problems, private and federal agencies have created "indices of fiscal stress."[14] The Brookings Institution calculates an index of "financial liquidity" that seems meaningful. Others though—such as that of the Congressional Budget Office that compares needs with resources, of the Treasury Department that assesses changes in both financial and socioeconomic variables, of the Advisory Commission on Intergovernmental Relations that assesses both absolute tax effort and changes in it over time (almost an analogy to barometric pressure), and of the Urban Institute that measures changes in the level and mix of financial and socioeconomic indicators (such as employment and unemployment, local income, and nature of the population)—on purely mathematical grounds are either trivial or so fraught with measurement faults as to be valueless. A variety of other measures have been marketed by various consulting firms, but they suffer from the same flaws.

The difficulty in developing a useful index or measure of fiscal stress is that one must deal with diverse social purposes, with the inability of policy structures to respond to change from a growth-oriented environment to one of reduced expectations, with the lack of an adequate explanation of the links between a city's economic base and its revenues. Compounding those problems are the real differences among cities, making comparisons almost impossible if not counterproductive.

Why has there been this fiscal decline? There are two competing models. One stresses the socioeconomic factors described above, and the regional and national forces that have led to the flight of the affluent to suburbs and the weakening of the tax base. The other stresses inefficiencies in local government: the effects of patronage and increases in municipal payrolls to meet demands of municipal employees, expansion in bureaucracies due to excessive growth in government, and the prestige deriving from increased size of agencies, the lack of a price mechanism leading to increased quantities of service to meet increased demands not regulated by costs, unsound financial and operational management. How has the problem been handled? Unfortunately, in all too many cases by organized anarchy, in which the decisions are not rational and problems are dealt with by ignoring them, fleeing from them, or resolving them on a haphazard basis. What then are the options available for solution? They fall into two major categories—increase the resources or decrease the costs—for each of which one can take a tactical or a strategic approach. Obvious, isn't it? But let's examine them in more detail, and for each discuss the implications it has for strategic management of the community library faced with the pressures from the community and its government to adopt one or more of them.

The revenue strategies include: First, the revenue option easiest to implement in most communities is to establish "user fees." It usually does not require state permission; beyond adding revenue it may also reduce demand; it makes the costs of government tangible for the constituents. It does raise the spectre of fairness and the fact that fees tend to be regressive, but counterbalancing that is the fact that, if fees are not charged, the affluent are in the best position to exploit the resource and the poor lose out completely. For the community library, this alternative conflicts directly with one of the primary professional imperatives—"free library service for all." Second, there is the possibility of increases in taxes; these usually require state approval, especially income and sales taxes, and are always a political problem; one need only look at the effects of Proposition 13 in California and Prop 2½ in Massachusetts. However, the Pasadena Public Library was able, through very effective strategic management, to gain voter approval for a tax increase.[15] Third, one can draw on reserves and borrow, but clearly there are limits to such answers, and most states have now reached those limits. Finally, there may be the possibility for state or federal aid.

The productivity strategies include: use of technology such as management information systems, improved procedures and work skills, increased motivation through rewards, use of program budgeting and zero-based budgeting, management by objectives, outsourcing (to private sector, other agencies), developing economies of scale. However, the problem of measuring effects is great given the intangibles and multiplicity of outputs. Other means include privatizing, relying on individual citizens as volunteers, cutting costs and reducing service levels. Cutting strategies include: across-the-board cuts, capital improvement cuts, reductions in specific program areas.

Of course, libraries have been affected by such strategies. Internally and on the positive side, they have been exceptionally effective in using the information technologies for improved productivity of internal operations; they have used the best methods of budget planning and management; they have turned to outsourcing, especially for cataloging and book processing; they have turned to volunteers for appropriate services. On the negative side, though, they have sadly experienced the external imposition of forced reductions in services (libraries, along with parks and recreation, being the first to feel the impact of reduced revenues).

Public libraries have traditionally sought additional revenues from private philanthropy; Andrew Carnegie's public library buildings still stand in many communities as a reminder of one particularly influential private donation. Lately, public libraries have also sought corporate sponsorship for both services and facilities. Fast-food chains have sponsored summer reading programs. Telecommunications companies have donated both infrastructure and computers to enable public libraries to use emerging information technologies. Corporations have supported capital improvement projects in exchange for prominent corporate identification in the building. While some criticize the increasing commercialization of public libraries, others see these strategies as essential for providing good service in resource-scarce times.[16]

The Restructuring of Business and Industry

Another major source for the problems has been the succession of economic ups and downs in the national economy. The effects were especially devastating in the "rust belt"—the traditional centers of industrial might on which so many of the major metropolitan centers were built. Aside from the historical fact of economic cycles, the most recent problems are apparently a result of the structural changes occurring in transition of the U.S. economy from its prior basis on industrial production to the new "information economy."

As a result, communities face internal pressures in setting priorities among kinds of infrastructure and between them and direct support to business and industry. Indeed, balance between the community and its business and industry is especially complex, raising questions about what the community is responsible for and what values there are in what it provides.

There is a strange ambivalence today with respect to business and industry. On the one hand, recruitment and retention of business and industry is perhaps the most crucial problem faced by communities, both currently and for the coming decade. On the other hand, there are industries that are fading from the scene and leaving their communities with virtually no economic base. Together, though, they add up to the fact that communities are facing dramatic changes in the industrial base. Later in this chapter we will explore the implications of these changes both for the community as a whole and for the library within it.

Changes in the Population

The population of the community itself is continually changing. For rural communities, a historic and continuing cause of demographic change is the departure of teenagers and young adults, as they go elsewhere for education and for jobs. For the metropolitan centers, the changes are more complex since they serve as "ports of entry"—for migrants from abroad as well as from rural communities; in both cases they provide the means for acculturation into new social and political structures, a process within which the public library plays an especially important role.

Throughout the United States, in communities of all sizes, there is increasing diversity—in age, cultural and ethnic background, skills, and training.[17] Cultural and ethnic diversity is increasingly important, and communities must respond to it as a major and critical component in social change. Certainly, as communities respond to this need, new and different demands will be placed on their libraries and other information resources. They may well require new kinds of information materials and services.

Compounding the problems faced by communities with respect to changes in the populations have been the increasing numbers of mentally ill, homeless, and economically depressed with which they have had to deal. The situation is especially acute in the largest metropolitan centers, because of the numbers of people involved, but it is serious even in small towns. In part, some of the complications arose from the decision to remove many of the mentally ill from institutional care in order to assist them in transition into a more normal environment; the aims were laudatory but the effects have been nearly catastrophic.

That process can be traced back to efforts initiated in the mid-1960s which promoted alternatives to institutionalization of the mentally ill. The Community Health Centers Act of 1963 funded establishment of "comprehensive mental health centers" to provide community-based treatment for mentally ill persons and to facilitate their transition back into normal society. Medicaid and various social security entitlements accelerated the process, providing direct support to mentally disabled persons living in the community. The result was a reduction in mental hospital census from 560,000 in 1955 to 216,000 in 1974 and 100,000 in 1989.[18]

Unfortunately, the result of deinstitutionalization was diffusion not only of the mentally ill into the general population but of administrative responsibilities. By 1977, the proliferation of agencies was so extensive that the General Accounting Office identified it as a prime cause for inadequate care. Various national initiatives during the 1980s—such as "block grants" to the states—simply compounded the problem. Today, it is estimated that, of the 600,000 homeless people in the United States, one-third are severely mentally ill.[19]

But the problem of the homeless in the major metropolitan communities is even greater than just the mentally ill. The overall supply of low-cost rental units declined appreciably during the 1970s and 1980s. In New York alone, the number of single-room occupancy units declined from 127,000 in 1970 to 14,000 in 1982!

Changes in the Educational Infrastructure

Among the most important elements of a community's infrastructure is its system of education, at all levels—elementary and secondary, postsecondary institutions, colleges and universities, adult and continuing education, industrial training and retraining. It is a part of Tiebout's "bundle of products and services" which is the community's means for attracting people, business, and industry.

Elementary and Secondary Education. Unfortunately, the quality of the educational infrastructure, at least at the level of elementary and secondary schools, has become a focus of concern in virtually every community within the United States. For the large metropolitan school systems, especially, the conflicts between rising numbers of students, increasing difficulties in teaching and learning, and reduced financial resources have produced almost intolerable situations.

For decades, the nation's school systems suffered from the demands that they be the means to resolve the problems of racial imbalance.[20] In some cases, those demands properly reflected the reality of school districts deliberately gerrymandered to maintain de facto segregation; in other cases, though, the underlying reality lay not in the schools but in the forces of suburbanization, within which the school itself played only a subsidiary role. In all cases, though, the costs of court-mandated solutions, such as busing, added greatly to the problems, both financially and educationally.

Schools must serve as means not only for education but for acculturation of the continuing flow of immigrants. Such has been the historical role of education, of course, but in recent decades it has had to deal with a vastly greater range of cultures and languages. Today, in cities like Los Angeles, the "majority"—that is, those of essentially European cultural and linguistic heritage— are now literally a minority, with more than 50 percent of the population falling into the wide range of other linguistic, racial, and cultural groups. Again, the problems for schools have grown, both financially and educationally, as they must have educational programs and qualified teachers to deal with such a rich mixture of cultures and languages.

Presumably for reasons of "economy of scale," but also to deal with the problems of racial segregation, many metropolitan school districts have become massive bureaucracies. The organizational distances between those formulating policies and those delivering the education itself are now so great that it is a wonder that education can be effective at all.[21] One wonders whether the scale has become so great that there really are dis-economies and whether racial segregation should not be dealt with in other, more fundamental ways.

Just as other elements of community physical infrastructure have decayed, so has that of the local school systems. Inadequate classrooms, overcrowding, year-round scheduling, deferred maintenance—all have contributed, and the financial resources continue to be inadequate to deal with the needs.

The problems faced by the local school systems have special strategic importance for the community library. They greatly increase the importance of the roles it has as a support to the process of education, as a place for study, and as means for learning how to use information resources. Unfortunately, the long history of efforts to create cooperation between public and school libraries has been one of failure rather than success; since the early days of the Library Services and Construction Act, encouragement of multitype cooperation between those two types at least was an identified objective which almost universally failed to be achieved.[22] But the current crisis means that cooperation between the community library and the local school system has now become an essential strategic objective, not just a desirable one.

In at least one case, the relationship between the public library and the public school has gone beyond cooperation to a new level of collaboration. In 1994, the Los Angeles Public Library and the Los Angeles Unified School District formed a partnership to establish the Electronic Information Magnet High School. Students in this school attend classes at both their home campus and the nearby LAPL Central Library. Reference librarians work with students and teachers to incorporate the latest information resources and technology as well as information literacy skills into the regular academic curriculum.[23]

General dissatisfaction with the quality of public education has also led to an increase in the number of children educated at home—"homeschoolers." It is difficult to pinpoint the exact number of homeschoolers, but estimates range from 350,000 to one million or more, compared with approximately 46.7 million children who attend regular schools. The impact on public libraries has been undeniable; homeschoolers are aggressive library users, relying heavily on local resources for space as well as curriculum materials.[24]

Local Postsecondary Institutions

The local postsecondary institutions—community colleges and trade institutes—are crucial means for the full range of working age population, especially the economically disadvantaged, to gain skills and the educational basis for entering universities and colleges. But they are essentially outgrowths of public school systems and thus partake of all the problems identified above, so the role of the public library in support of the educational objectives of these adult students is potentially even greater than it is for elementary and secondary school children.[25]

Higher Education. The nation's public colleges and universities generally have fared better during the past decades than have the local school systems. They draw their financial support from statewide sources, from tuition, and from research grants and contracts, each of which has been more stable and consistent with objectives and needs than has the local tax base. Whether that situation will continue, of course, is a serious question. Legislatures faced with overwhelming demands are beginning to reexamine their commitments to higher education, shifting more of the burden of financing to tuition. They are making greater demands for accountability, especially with respect to the commitments by universities to undergraduate education, which the legislatures see as the reason for their support but which frequently has been given short shrift, especially by universities committed to research objectives.

The nation's private colleges and universities appear to have fared far better, especially given the well-established bases for financial support through tuition, endowments, and private funding. In a very real sense, the private liberal arts colleges are the best examples of traditional educational goals.

For the local community library, the institutions of higher education, especially the publicly supported ones, represent not so much sources of demand as sources of support. Indeed, most of the statewide "multitype" library networks have been predicated on the perception that the state's university libraries were crucial resources in support of public library services; they have been generally successful in making that perception a reality. During the past three decades, the development of statewide networks, the creation of statewide union catalogs and the inclusion of university OPACs on the menus of public library OPACs, and statewide funding of interlibrary lending services all have provided direct and tangible support to such objectives.

Industrial Training and Retraining. One of the growth industries of the past few decades has been industrial training and retraining. In fact, today the total expenditures for industrial training are virtually equal to the total for all publicly supported education, at every level.[26] They are becoming increasingly important as industry moves into the information economy. Each industry needs a work force that can deal with the technology of today, and the work force must gain those skills if they are to maintain their employability.

Within each community, the growth of such training programs provides an opportunity for the public library to enter into cooperative arrangements with these particular information industries.

STRATEGIC AND TACTICAL MANAGEMENT AT THE COMMUNITY LEVEL

Community Strategic Planning

Every community should have a continuing process of strategic public planning, and the public library must be a central part of it. There should be innumerable public task forces, committees on priorities, and program reviews obtaining data regarding programs and infrastructures and operating policies and processes. Within the library itself, both as part of community planning for information resources and for its own strategic development, there should be an independent strategic planning process, tailored to the perception of needs for library service to the community, developed and monitored by the director and the board.

Since information resources generally and libraries especially are capital-intensive operations, requiring both buildings and equipment, this becomes a critical factor in predicting their progress during the decade. Furthermore, library automation, computing, and telecommunications equipment each represent not just onetime capital demands but ongoing commitments in maintenance and replacement. The allocation of diminished resources certainly will delay implementation of even the most evidently desirable services.

Public Information Infrastructure

But at least there has at last been formal recognition at the national level of the importance of information in the economy. Finally, infrastructure is seen as more than just physical. As discussed in Chapter 3, the "national information superhighway" has become more than rhetoric and has served as a stimulus for both public and private investment. Communications and data networks have become as necessary as roads and bridges. All of the issues discussed above, with respect to the role of physical infrastructure, apply with at least equal vigor to the assessment of the information infrastructure. The national efforts to implement this strategy include the commitment by the Department of Commerce National Technical Information Administration to fund projects to build the information infrastructure, and by the Department of Defense to facilitate its technology conversion program.[27]

The implications with respect to community libraries are clear. Rather than being treated as expenses, they should be regarded as capital resources, as investments in the information infrastructure needed to support structural changes that are occurring in the economy of the country.[28] Since libraries, computer facilities, and other kinds of information resources are vital among the means for attracting industry, the implications are clear. Those communities that commit resources to collections, to service staff, to access services, and to information equipment are the ones that will be successful in attracting business and industry, but the tension between these demands and others in the community, in the context of decreased resources, will be difficult to reconcile. This makes it imperative that the director and board of the library work energetically to keep community leaders aware of the importance of the library to this effort.

Investment in Information Activities

The facts are that investments in technological infrastructure are already being made in communities throughout the United States, by both the private and public sectors. Those investments are in fact far greater than those in the library. Wiring the community and installation of computers for administrative services during the past two decades have represented massive investments. Of even greater importance, though, are two further facts. First, the investment in computer equipment must be repeated, at about five-year intervals, as it rapidly becomes obsolescent if not obsolete; manufacturers cease to provide spare parts or adequate maintenance for equipment that no longer is in widespread use. Second, the investment in equipment is now only a small percentage of the total costs it engenders, perhaps as little as 20 percent; the remaining 80 percent of costs arise from staff, from maintenance, from software, from application, and from space and supporting facilities.

But with respect to information resources broadly defined, the pressures have become so great that substantial increases are likely during the coming decade. To be specific, consider the following:

- The increasing importance of "information" as a part of society and the economy;
- The specific importance of information resources as means for attracting and retaining business and industry;
- Continuing growth in computer use in the community for support to both business and industry and instruction;
- Needs to replace equipment that becomes obsolete, sometimes within months;
- Commitments of expenditures to capital investment in "wiring" the community but with likelihood of substantial cost overruns, and real increases in operating costs by as much as 25 percent to even 50 percent over the initial estimates;
- Needs to acquire materials (such as databases, for example) that cannot be covered by the library's acquisition budgets;
- Needs for services (such as database access) that cannot be covered by the library's operating budgets;
- Growing commitments of staff to running distributed computing facilities and to operations such as "desktop publishing."

In Chapter 10 the relationship between information resources and productivity will be explored in the framework of a model for the effects of transition of local communities into the information economy.

NOTES

1. Jay Forrester, *Urban Dynamics* (Cambridge, Mass.: MIT Press, 1969); Mark Schneider, *The Competitive City: The Political Economy of Suburbia* (Pittsburgh: University of Pittsburgh, 1989).

2. Charles M. Tiebout, "A pure theory of local expenditures," *Journal of Political Economy* 64 (October 1956): 416–424; George F. Break, *Financing Government in a Federal System* (Washington, D.C.: Brookings Institution, c1980). Discusses Tiebout model, pp. 203ff; Mark Schneider, *The Competitive City*.

3. *Statistical Abstract of the United States* (Washington, D.C.: U.S. Department of Commerce, Social and Economic Statistics Administration, Bureau of the Census, 1994).

4. *Statistical Report '95: Public Library Data Service* (Chicago: Public Library Association, 1995).

5. James Milles, *Legal Problems Relating to Scarcity of Agricultural and Urban Housing Land: A Selective Bibliography, 1970–1987* (Monticello, Ill.: Vance Bibliographies, 1988); "Beyond the Williamson Act: Alternatives for more effective preservation of agricultural land in California," *Pacific Law Journal* 15 (1984): 1151–1180; R. N. L. Andrews, ed., *Land in America: Commodity or Natural Resource?* (Lexington,

Mass.: Lexington Books, 1979); J. Baden, "Agricultural land preservation: Threshing the wheat from the chaff," *Institute on Planning, Zoning, and Eminent Domain* (New York: Mathew Bender, 1983); J. Baden, ed., *The Vanishing Farmland Crisis: Critical Views of the Movement to Preserve Agricultural Land* (Lawrence: Kansas University Press, 1984); D. A. Bradbury, "Agricultural law: Suburban sprawl and the right to farm," *Washburn Law Journal* 22 (1983): 448–468; F. Browning, *The Vanishing Land: The Corporate Theft of America* (New York: Harper & Row, 1975); Dolores Hayden, *Redesigning the American Dream: The Future of Housing, Work and Family Life* (New York: W. W. Norton, 1984); J. C. Hite, *Room and Situation: The Political Economy of Land-Use Policy* (Chicago: Nelson-Hall, 1979); J. Meltzer, *Metroplus to Metroplex: The Social and Spatial Planning of Cities* (Baltimore: Johns Hopkins University Press, 1984).

6. *Dealing with the Deficit Now: A Policy Statement* (Washington, D.C.: Board of Trustees of the National Planning Association, 1993); *Reports: on President Clinton's Economic and Deficit-reduction Plan, and Address to a Joint Session of Congress, February 17, 1993* (Washington, D.C.: BNA, 1993); Charles W. Steadman, *The National Debt Conclusion: Establishing the Debt Repayment Plan* (Westport, Conn.: Praeger, 1993).

7. Jay M. Stein, ed., *Public Infrastructure Planning and Management* (Newbury Park, Calif.: Sage Publications, 1988); Michael G. H. McGeary and Laurence E. Lynn, Jr., eds., *Urban Change and Poverty* (Washington, D.C.: National Academy Press, 1988), pp. 44–49, 263–280; Thomas R. Swartz and Frank J. Bonello, eds., *Urban Finance Under Siege* (Armonk, N.Y.: M. E. Sharpe, 1993); Edward C. Banfield, *The Unheavenly City Revisited* (Boston: Little, Brown, 1974); Helen F. Ladd and John Yinger, *America's Ailing Cities: Fiscal Health and the Design of Urban Policy* (Baltimore: Johns Hopkins University Press, 1989).

8. Advisory Committee to the Department of Housing and Urban Development, *Revenue Sharing and the Planning Process: Shifting the Locus of Responsibility for Domestic Problem Solving* (Washington, D.C.: National Academy of Sciences, 1974); *Annual Report of the Office of Revenue Sharing* (Washington, D.C.: GPO, 1974); American Enterprise Institute for Public Policy Research, *The Administration's Plan to Reauthorize Revenue Sharing, 1980, 96th Congress, 2nd session* (Washington, D.C.: American Enterprise Institute for Public Policy Research, 1980); George F. Break, *Intergovernmental Fiscal Relations in the United States* (Washington, D.C.: Brookings Institution, 1967); Thomas R. Swartz and Frank J. Bonello, eds., *Urban Finance Under Siege.*

9. William J. Pammer, Jr., *Managing Fiscal Strain in Major American Cities: Understanding Retrenchment in the Public Sector* (Westport, Conn.: Greenwood, 1990), pp. 16–23; *City Fiscal Conditions* (Washington, D.C.: National League of Cities, 1986); Helen F. Ladd and John Yinger, *America's Ailing Cities*; Thomas R. Swartz and Frank J. Bonello, eds., *Urban Finance Under Siege.*

10. William J. Pammer, Jr., *Managing Fiscal Strain in Major American Cities*, pp. 16–23; Paul B. Downing, "User charges and service fees," in *Crisis and Constraint in Municipal Finance*, ed. James H. Carr (New Brunswick, N.J.: Center for Urban Policy Research, 1984), pp. 83–92.

11. William J. Pammer, Jr., *Managing Fiscal Strain in Major American Cities*, pp. 25–39.

12. Carol W. Lewis and Anthony Logalbo, "Cutback principles and practices," in *Crisis and Constraint in Municipal Finance*, ed. James H. Carr, pp. 83–92; William J. Pammer, Jr., *Managing Fiscal Strain in Major American Cities*, pp. 73–82.

13. Donald Fisk et al., "Private provision of public services: An overview," in *Crisis and Constraint in Municipal Finance*, ed. James H. Carr, pp. 233–242; Timothy Barnekov, Robin Boyle, and Daniel Rich, *Privatism and Urban Policy in Britain and the United States* (New York: Oxford University Press, 1989).

14. J. Richard Aronson, "Municipal indicators," in *Crisis and Constraint in Municipal Finance*, ed. James H. Carr, pp. 3–41; Peggy L. Cuciti, *City Need and the Responsiveness of Federal Grants Programs*. Report for the Subcommittee on the City of the Committee on Banking, Finance and Urban Affairs, House of Representatives, 95th Congress, second session (Washington, D.C.: GPO, 1978) especially pp. 11–14; James M. Howell and Charles F. Stamm, *Urban Fiscal Stress: A Comparative Analysis of 66 U.S. Cities* (Lexington, Mass.: Lexington Books, 1979) (Prior publication by the First National Bank of Boston and Touche Ross & Co.); Richard P. Nathan and Charles Adam, "Understanding central city hardship," *Political Science Quarterly* 91 (Spring 1976): 47–62; Sherwin Rosen, "Wage-based indexes of urban quality of life," in *Current Issues in Urban Economics*, ed. Peter Mieszkowski and Mahlon Straszheim (Baltimore: Johns Hopkins University Press, 1979), pp. 74–104; U.S. Environmental Protection Agency, Office of Research and Monitoring, *The Quality of Life Concept: A Potential New Tool for Decision-Making*, 1973.

15. Citizens' Task Force on Alternative Financing, *Recommendations for Financing the Pasadena Public Library System* (Pasadena, Calif.: Pasadena Public Library Commission), 2 February 1993; John Russell, "If knowledge is power and only the educated are free, we are in trouble," *Pasadena Weekly*, 22 January 1993, 1.

16. Roger L. Kemp, "The creative management of library services," *Public Libraries* 34(4) (July/August 1995): 212–215; "Library of the future? in Calif.," *American Libraries* 26(7) (July/August 1995): 634–636.

17. *Multicultural Review: Dedicated to a Better Understanding of Ethnic, Racial, and Religious Diversity* (Westport, Conn.: GP Subscription Publications, 1992); *Racial and Ethnic Diversity of America's Elderly Population* (Washington, D.C.: U.S. Dept. of Commerce, Economics and Statistics Administrations, Bureau of the Census; U.S. Dept. of Health and Human Services, National Institutes of Health, 1993); *Outcasts on Main Street*, Report of the Federal Task Force on Homelessness and Severe Mental Illness (Washington, D.C.: U.S. Dept. of Health and Human Services), February 1992; Alfred M. Freedman, *Aspects of the Community Mental Health Centers Act* (Bethesda, Md.: National Institute of Mental Health, 1966); Michael G. H. McGeary and Laurence E. Lynn, Jr., eds., *Urban Change and Poverty*; National Institute of Mental Health, *The Community Mental Health Centers Act (1963); A Commentary, Based on Title II of Public law 88–164, "Mental retardation facilities and community mental health centers construction act of 1964"* (Bethesda, Md.: Public Health Service, 1965); U.S. Senate, Committee on Labor and Public Welfare Subcommittee on Health. *Community Mental Health Centers Act; History of the Program and Current Problems and Issues* (Washington, D.C.: GPO, 1973).

18. *Outcasts on Main Street*, p. 16.

19. Ibid., p. 18.

20. Diane Seo, "Students in magnet school go high-tech," *Los Angeles Times*, 19 September 1994, B1.

21. *Homeschoolers and the Public Library: A Resource Guide for Libraries Serving Homeschoolers* (Chicago: Public Library Association, 1995); Don Sager, "Public library service to homeschoolers," *Public Libraries* 34(4) (July/August 1995): 201–205.

22. David J. Armor, *Sociology and School Busing Policy* (Santa Monica, Calif.: Rand Corporation, 1976); Roger DeMont, Larry Hillman, and Gerald Mansergh, eds., *Busing, Taxes, and Desegregation* (Detroit: Metropolitan Detroit Bureau of School Studies, 1973); Lillian B. Rubin, *Busing and Backlash; White against White in a California School District* (Berkeley: University of California Press, 1972); Bernard Schwartz, *Swann's Way: The School Busing Case and the Supreme Court* (New York: Oxford University Press, 1986); Judith F. Buncher, ed., *The School Busing Controversy, 1970–75* (New York: Facts on File, 1975); U.S. House Committee on the Judiciary Subcommittee on Courts, Civil Liberties, and the Administration of Justice, *Limitations on Court-ordered Busing—Neighborhood School Act* (Washington, D.C.: GPO, 1983); U.S. Senate Committee on the Judiciary Subcommittee on the Constitution, *The 14th Amendment and School Busing* (Washington, D.C.: GPO, 1983).

23. Jeffrey Glanz, *Bureaucracy and Professionalism: The Evolution of Public School Supervision* (Rutherford, N.J.: Fairleigh Dickinson University Press, 1991).

24. U.S. House Committee on Education and Labor Subcommittee on Postsecondary Education, *Hearing on the Reauthorization of the Library Services and Construction Act* (Washington, D.C.: GPO, 1989); "Library seeks to host new magnet school," *Los Angeles Times*, 26 March 1994.

25. Anthony P. Carnevale et al., *New Developments in Worker Training: A Legacy for the 1990s* (Madison, Wis.: Industrial Relations Research Association, 1990); Jane Wildhorn, Maryann McGuire and Betsy Ryan, eds., *Return on Vision: Collaborative Ventures in Training and Education* (Los Angeles: Institute of Industrial Relations, Publications Center, 1993); Graceanne A. DeCandido, "Virtual library promulgated by library/education coalition," *Library Journal* 115(7) (15 April 1990): 14.

26. A study in 1986 by the Research Institute of America reported that more than $30 billion was spent in 1986 for formal employee training but that an additional $180 billion was spent for on-the-job training. *Fortune* 127(6) (22 March 1993): 62–64ff uses the figure of $30 billion as the magniture of formal industrial training programs. *Statistical Abstracts of the United States*, 1987, reported that the total expenditure in 1986 for publicly supported education, at all levels, was $212 billion; for private schools, $49 billion.

27. Andrew Kirby, ed., *The Pentagon and the Cities* (Newbury Park, Calif.: Sage Publications, 1992); *Defense Conversion: Redirecting R&D* (Washington, D.C.: Office of Technology Assessment, Congress of the U.S., 1993); Herschel Kanter and Richard H. Van Atta, *Integrating Defense into the Civilian Technology and Industrial Base: Supporting Material for Adjusting to the Drawdown: Report of the Defense Conversion Commission* (Washington, D.C.: Department of Defense, 1993); Andrew Kirby, ed., *The Pentagon and the Cities*, Volume 40, Urban Affairs Annual Reviews; U.S. House Committee on Science, Space, and Technology, *Defense Conversion Initiatives: Progress and Plans* (Washington, D.C.: GPO, 1993); U.S. National Telecommunications and Information Administration, *The NTIA Infrastructure Report: Telecommunications in the Age of Information* (Washington, D.C.: U.S. Dept. of Commerce, NTIA, 1991).

28. Charles R. McClure, John Carlo Bertot, and Douglas L. Zweizig, *Public Libraries and the Internet: Study Results, Policy Issues, and Recommendation* (Washington, D.C.: NCLIS, 1994).

5

The Context of Users and Their Needs

Among the most crucial concerns of strategic management must be the needs of the community of users. Therefore, in this chapter we turn to examination of the users and their needs, both as individuals and as groups.

As we will see, the public library serves an array of constituencies and for them supports general reading, education for students and for independent learning, research by individuals and organizations, public services, and local business and industry. But the communities being served are continually changing, as the nature of the population, of commerce and industry, and of government all undergo change in response to community development. How do we identify these changes in the community and determine what needs to be done to support them with adequate information resources? How should libraries and other information agencies respond to those changes? Those questions have been dealt with repeatedly—by librarians, administrators, enthusiasts, and even the public itself. These are the strategic issues related to the users of the public library.

GENERAL CONTEXT

In Chapter 2 there was a brief summary of factors affecting user needs, of the kinds of users and their uses, of barriers to use, and of characterizing parameters. We will now discuss these in more detail. Before doing so, though, it is valuable to recognize the context that makes a broad definition of users and their needs strategically important: It is a general picture of expanding needs for information services created in part as a result of the overall transition of the U.S. national economy from its historic basis on manufacturing to its growing emphasis on information products and services. Of course, the public library has always recognized the range of kinds of users that will be discussed, so there is nothing new here except perhaps the increased opportunities and demands.

Nature of Users

Demographics of User Groups. It is generally assumed that demographic factors affect the needs of users, the extent to which individuals will use an information resource, and the ways in which they will do so. Age, sex, education, social or economic class, ethnicity, cultural and linguistic background, geographic location—these have all been considered as potentially relevant demographic variables. Indeed, most surveys of public library users will acquire such data and correlate them with the levels of use. And the results are not surprising: The better-educated make greater use of the library; the middle class will use the library more than the poor or even than the very wealthy; men and women will use the library differently; the very young, the very old, and those in between will use the library differently.

The point about demographic variables is that they can be treated statistically. Data are readily available on distributions of them within a community—from the U.S. census, for example—and those data can be correlated with actual usage as the basis for decisions within the library on the best means for serving the community. Such management decisions as branch library location, local collection policies, staffing needs, hours of opening, services provided can all be made with at least a statistical basis in the demographics of the population served.

As useful as demographic statistics are for creating a quantitative profile of the residents of a population area, most specialists in community analysis and needs assessment urge that library managers collect additional data. Roger Greer and Martha Hale, for example, urge that public library decision makers consider the additional factors of community organizations, service- and product-providing agencies, and lifestyles. Virginia A. Walter has provided guidance on analyzing communities from the perspective of young adults. Finally, Cheryl Metoyer-Duran has given valuable insights on analyzing the information needs in ethnolinguistic communities.[1]

Individual Differences. Aside from the demographic characteristics, which are easy to determine and to measure on a statistical basis, individuals will differ in other ways that are much more difficult to assess—motivation, level of knowledge and experience, psychological attitudes such as persistence, orderliness, motivation, willingness to accept help, facility with language(s). These subjective factors clearly affect the nature of needs, the kinds of usage, and the services that will be needed, but to deal with them requires professional insight rather than the use of statistics. There is a considerable body of research on adult information needs which public library managers can turn to for guidance. Unfortunately, it is difficult to generalize from the fine studies that have been done on particular population groups in particular locations at particular points in time. Some of the methodologies that have been used in these studies, however, may be adapted for more intensive levels of effort at community needs assessment by public libraries.[2]

Purposes of Use. To an extent, some individual differences are reflected in the purposes of use, and those can be assessed more objectively. For example, goal-oriented users—exemplified by science, technology, management—will differ from education-oriented users—students and teachers—and from personal interest users. Those who use information to produce information products and services—authors, database developers, report writers—will differ from those who use information for other objectives.

Barriers to Use. A critical barrier is the differential use made of any kind of information resource. Some members of the public, recognizing the value of information to gaining their objectives, will be heavy users of libraries, computers, and other kinds of information resources; other members of the public will make no use of them, perhaps not even recognizing that the library could be of value to them. Inertia will always be a barrier for the individual. The resource may be there, but it takes effort to use it, and by many that effort will not be made.

The Distribution of Activity. First is the amount of activity that each type of usage represents. Reshelving data generally suggests that in public libraries, in-house uses are from one to three times circulation uses. But what do reshelving statistics measure? Which of the usages listed above are involved? This parameter is important to strategic management because it affects the decisions concerning "access allocation"—that is, the level of access to be provided to information materials. In that decision, the distribution of use plays a key role.

Users will differ in their view of the value or importance that information has to them, so there is differential use of any information resource. Those who know the value of an information resource will use it heavily; those with little or no experience will not even think of it. But the great majority of potential users will use it minimally, if at all.

Calvin Mooers, an early pioneer in information science, formulated a law: An information system will tend *not* to be used whenever it is more painful and troublesome to have information than not to have it.[3] Indeed, it appears that individuals in general do not want information even though they may pay lip service to it. The scientists would prefer to do the experiment rather than find out what others have done. The business managers would prefer to make decisions based on intuition. The politicians would prefer to respond from their own perception of priorities.

This means that "market forces," representing decisions of individuals, are not a suitable basis for strategic management of libraries and other information activities. For the good of the community, decisions should be as informed as possible. While the effect of a wrong decision for the individual may be minimal, the cumulative effect of wrong decisions by many individuals could be catastrophic for the community. Thus, information, at least as far as the library is concerned, is a societal investment rather than an individual one.

Language is frequently a barrier to public library use in communities where there are large numbers of new immigrants. Culture itself may be a barrier for these new Americans if they come from a country where there is no tradition of public library service. In general, public libraries are finding that adapting the library to meet these new users' needs is a more effective strategy than expecting the new users to adapt to the library.[4]

Service hours are frequently another barrier to use. Unless libraries offer extended evening and weekend hours, many working adults find it difficult to use their services. When parents are unable to fit the library into their busy schedules, their children are also effectively barred from library use.

Physical access to public libraries created barriers in the past for some handicapped individuals. The passage of the Americans with Disabilities Act, however, has made it necessary for public libraries to comply with rigorous standards for handicapped access and is gradually eliminating this barrier. While the limited funding available for making the required adaptations to the new standards has slowed compliance in many cases, the physical structure and layouts of many library buildings are beginning to reflect a more welcoming and convenient environment for people with disabilities of all kinds.[5]

The Effects of Distance. Distance and the frequency of use of an information resource are inversely related, apparently determined by the cost of transportation.[6] If the cost of transportation is a linear function of distance, then the rate of decay is exponential; if the cost of transportation is logarithmic, the decay is inverse square. The logarithmic case to some extent represents the situation when there is a large start-up cost followed by a lower linear rate (as exemplified by short-distance automobile travel). Perhaps the distance a person is willing to go in order to obtain information is a measure of the value it has. That doesn't result in a "dollar" measure, but it may provide a means for avoiding the reduction of all measures to dollar terms.

In view of this effect, certainly one of the crucial strategic management decisions must be the determination of locations for branch libraries and of the materials that most appropriately are stored at each branch. Such decisions are equally important for the small-town library which is to move to a new location.

Bookmobile service has been one time-honored method of trying to reduce the effect of distance for potential library users. Other public libraries have used the postal system to deliver library materials to distant library users. Recent discussions of the future "libraries without walls" envision electronic service delivery systems that will render physical presence at a public library unnecessary. The proximity of the library and its collections to developing new neighborhoods is especially critical when the population center is shifting, since the needs of older service areas must be balanced with those of newer ones. The objective is to bring materials as close as possible to those most likely to need them. There are now a number of computer-based tools available for analysis of population data and mapping of them as means for aiding those decisions.[7]

The Effects of Response Time. It is clear that it takes time to acquire information from whatever may be the source. If it is to be acquired from primary sources, such as personal observation and validation, it probably takes the most time. If it is acquired through surrogates—others who will acquire and validate—it will take time to train them, time for them to acquire, time for the user to confirm reliability. And time costs both money and delay. But beyond that, in at least some of its applications, information has value as a direct function of immediacy and currency. Historical anecdotes (such as the Rothschild information of the results of the Battle of Waterloo) illustrate the importance of immediacy in such commercial contexts.[8] Of a somewhat different nature, but of equivalent impact, are the various scientific races to discovery, in which immediacy of information played crucial roles.

Another phenomenon related to time is what is called the half-life of information. On the one hand, one expects to see an exponential rate of decay in use. On the other hand, there does seem to be a steady state at a minimal level of use for material, on into the future; such a steady-state condition suggests a continuing value for information over time. Of course, any specific item may never get used or may be very heavily used, so such patterns are characteristic of the entire group. A related phenomenon is the fact that accumulation of information creates value beyond the mere arithmetic sum of the individual values. That value added is almost certainly a function of the reduction in time for access from one item of information to another. Such chained reference is feasible only with large accumulations of information at one place, with sufficient organization and means for access to support chained reference. Currently, for most investigators, chained reference ultimately leads to exhaustion of local resources and recourse must be made to interlibrary loan. The cost in time is severe, but the evidence is that, if the material is needed, the user is prepared to pay that cost. In return the user does want some kind of guaranteed response time. In fact, the user may well be prepared to trade more rapid but less certain response time in favor of less rapid but more certain response time. This parameter is important to strategic management because it affects the decision concerning access allocation, especially as it relates to the needs of the user for rapid response.

The Effects of Cost. The phrase "free access to information" has been traditionally used to describe the commitment of the library community, but there are two quite different issues that the term "free" confuses. The one is "Who pays for it?", the other is "How available is it?" The issue of availability is complicated by ability to pay, so the two issues, while different, are not independent. Both issues, of course, are central to information policy (at the community level as well as the societal level).

The Problem of Equity

The effects of these barriers vary greatly among different groups within the community. There are differences among age groups, economic groups, ethnic and cultural groups, linguistics groups. Those differences are reflected in the nature of use made of information resources, in the relative ability to use them, in the ability to get access or to pay if that is required, in the relative importance of monographs and journals, in the relative importance of print and electronic formats. The result can be a serious problem of equity among different groups of users, of fairness in meeting needs of community groups.

The California State Library recently challenged California public libraries to revolutionize their patterns of service in order to better meet the needs of a radically changing population. Its "Partnerships for Change" initiative, funded with Library Services and Construction Act (LSCA) grants, has enabled many public libraries in California to reassess community needs, form critical partnerships, rethink their services, and embark on new service strategies better suited to meet the information needs of ethnic communities.[9]

PERSONAL USERS

We turn now to considering various categories of users, starting with individual or personal users. In a sense of course, everyone using the library does so as an individual, but here the distinction is between doing so for personal reasons versus doing so for educational, professional, or organizational reasons.

Reading

Most important are the users who want library materials to read—for recreation and amusement, for self-development and education, for enrichment and culture, for enlarging one's horizons and learning about the world, for access to literature and to art, for keeping abreast of current events, and for discovery of the past. They are of all ages and come from all segments of the community. They have been the traditional constituency of the public library, and they will continue to be important users, in many respects perhaps the most important users and surely the vast majority of those who borrow books, taking them home to read.

This is the most self-evident use of a library. After all, aren't books and journals intended to be read? Whether for personal interests or for more goal-oriented uses, books and journals will be taken from the library and read. Their content will, to whatever extent, be absorbed by the reader and become part of the individual's own knowledge, to be used in whatever way they may be.

To deal with the effects of the nonprint media and, especially, of the computer and other information technologies, though, the meaning of the term "reading" needs to be greatly enhanced. Libraries provide their patrons not only with books and journals—the traditional print formats—but "large print" books and talking books for the vision impaired, cassettes and compact disks, and video tapes. In the future, they may well have computer games, software, and full text available for circulation in CD-ROM formats, of special value for interactive recreation. Publication in that form is growing rapidly and, for a variety of reasons as we will discuss, serves many uses more effectively than does even print. In each case, while use of these media certainly is not "reading" in the traditional sense, it is essentially equivalent in the values that one gets from them.

Browsing

Most users, whether casual or intense, use browsing as a primary means for access to desired materials.[10] In this use, books are considered by the patron in a more or less aimless, almost random fashion, walking down the stacks of books, picking out a book because it looks interesting, glancing at it, perhaps deciding that it's worth reading, but perhaps not, and then continuing on in this rather aimless manner with the object of identifying ones that are of interest and to be used either by circulation or in-house. In such usage, many books may be examined and discarded for every one that's actually used. Serendipity serves as the means by which books relevant to needs may be found, virtually by accident. A purpose of the classified shelf arrangement may well be to facilitate such use, by bringing together books that are likely to be related to each other.

Reference

Beyond reading library materials, users of every kind draw upon the resources of the reference collections and the reference and referral services of the library staff. They may need specific information—a date, a name, a fact of whatever kind—which represents reference use of a library or other information source. They may need guidance in identifying materials to read and sources for desired information, and the public library staff, catalog, and other resources provide that guidance. Now added to the traditional services is the increasing public interest in searching electronic resources. The library is a major node on the national network, and must provide access to national databases that serve public needs.

Public libraries are making access to library information services non-location-specific. There is remote access to the library's OPAC from homes, offices, and schools. There is active promotion of telephone service for reference and document delivery, of electronic mail for reference and interlibrary loan; of access to electronic information services through the library's OPAC.

Information Access

Much of the promise of electronic information lies in improved access to information. We see it in the growing use of on-line public access catalogs. That great dying dinosaur, the card catalog, is now rapidly disappearing—millions of cards occupying tens of thousands of trays in thousands of square feet of space—with literally no one there! And next to it, banks of OPAC terminals are all fully occupied, sometimes with lines of users waiting.

Intensive Research

Among "in-house" uses is intensive research use, in which books are successively examined in a process of formulating and testing hypotheses. In such use, data found in one book may lead to a hypothesis that can be tested by data found in other books. In each case, the books are not being "read" in the usual sense of the word. Instead, specific data (using that word in the broadest sense) are found—or perhaps not found—and used to test the hypothesis.

A special case of the intensive research use is chained reference, in which the successive references are followed by rapid access from book to book. Examples of this kind arise in all kinds of research—economic, historical, literary, scientific, and genealogical. Usually, intensive research use will represent the need not only to acquire information but to process it. It is this use that makes electronic information so valuable.

Information Processing

The ability to retrieve, to analyze, to compare and combine, to process and manipulate, to communicate, is a promise far more important than mere access to information. It is the potential to *use* it.[11] It is this use that the computer can serve, provided appropriate data can be obtained from the library to do so. It is this, more than anything else, that makes access to databases so important. Studies of uses made of computers are shown in Figure 5.1.

There is increasing use of *personal information managers* that permit the individual to download substantial amounts of data and then to retrieve those data needed most immediately, to establish linkages among those data and between them and other sources. We see it in the use of computers by scholars in every discipline for the creation and maintenance of databases, for data analysis, and data exploration. The effects of the microcomputer, in particular, have been dramatic in making computer processing an integral part of the day-to-day working patterns, even in the humanities and the arts.

As we move increasingly into computer-based processing of data, the need

Figure 5.1
Distribution of Uses Made of Computers

Activity	Physical Science	Social Sciences	Humanities & Arts
Word processing	58%	63%	62%
Data analysis	55	53	25
Storage of data	42	48	48
Data collection	40	17	24
Searching	28	15	22
Personal databases	18	30	26

to convert existing data sources to digital text (or digital image) form arises throughout the community. Optical character-reading equipment is now well enough developed that it can effectively be used in support of this functional need. Policies need to be established to ensure efficient use of such equipment, including inventory of equipment, announcement of availability, assessment of applicability, and allocation of use.

Expert System Development

"Expert systems" are defined here as the combination of four component elements: (1) an interface for communication with users in the formulation of queries, (2) a decision tree for determining how to interact between the users and the databases, (3) a generic database to support the decision tree, and (4) a factual database. The evidence of the literature is that this will be an important area of research, especially by information entrepreneurs in the community in support of virtually every professional area.

EDUCATIONAL USERS

Those more complex uses—information access, intensive research, data processing, and expert system development—are crucial for several specific categories of users: students, decision makers, professionals, managers of business and industry, and managers in government.

In particular, users will include students at every level of learning, from preschool through secondary school, to college and university, to job training and retraining, to lifelong learning.[12] Their needs are especially acute, as they must prepare themselves for life in a world in which the majority of jobs already are information-based. Collaboration between the public library and educational agencies, both public and private, has become not just desirable but essential. Only in that way can the necessary information resources be readily available for individual use beyond the formal classroom context. A crucial contribution of public libraries to students is information literacy—skills in use of the library itself, in use of on-line databases, in use of the computer as a tool.

One of the most exciting developments arising from the widespread use of microcomputers and, now especially, associated CD-ROM equipment is their value for instruction. Much of the rationale for multimedia projects (such as *The First Emperor*, developed by Professor Chen at Simmons College, and *Columbus*, developed by IBM) is based on the perception that they will enhance the value of computer uses in teaching.

It must be said, though, that the reality is dramatically different from the hopes and wishes involved in these projects. The investment required to produce an innovative, operational instructional package is far greater than that to produce a textbook. And the investment involved in multimedia packages is orders of magnitude greater, similar to entertainment products. The investment by an instructor wishing to use such packages, to incorporate them into a course, is also very great; far more than it is to use an existing textbook as a required reading and the basis for a syllabus. The problem is that the rewards for those investments simply are not there, either financially or in academic advancement.

But as such packages are created, the public library can be a vital means for making them readily accessible to learners at every level, especially to the adults who want to use them for self-development and self-guided education, and for retraining in new careers—applications for which such packages are eminently suitable.

PROFESSIONAL USERS

The users include professionals—scientists, engineers, lawyers, medical practitioners, managers, and administrators. Of course, they are readers of library materials, but beyond that they need access to "information"—the content of books, journals, documents, and databases. It has been estimated that such professionals spend nearly 60 percent of their time communicating and working with information.[13] They incur costs in obtaining information and in using it, but it has been estimated that the direct benefits to them from use of information are as much as ten times those costs. More important than direct benefits, though, are increases in productivity measured by results produced (reports, management publications, research plans and proposals, presentations, consultations, and substantive advice); the time spent doing the work and preparing such results is used much more effectively. Sometimes the needs are specific to their profession, but frequently they involve other fields to which their professional practice may apply. It is clear that the public library is a means for these professionals to get access to the broad range needed and to maximize the benefits of information in their work.

BUSINESS-BASED USERS

Turning to the categories of users in which the greatest rates of growth in use of the public library are likely to occur, we now consider persons in business and commerce. Their use of information reflects their organizational responsibilities (aside from that they may have individually, of course). They need information in support of decision making and in business planning.

Support of Decision Making

It has been said, "information is the crucial ingredient in decision making." Clearly, this is one of the values of libraries. However, it is also more true than not that "Decision makers don't use information to make decisions; they use information to support decisions they have already made." It is a result of the fact that many decisions are essentially political, reflecting orders of priority rather than facts. Any of the alternatives can be supported by data, almost equally, if the decision context is truly complex. The formula which serves as the means for assessing data becomes the embodiment not of the decision process, but of the political views about what is important.

Business Planning

For users in business and industry, information, on a global basis, is essential for product development, marketing, financial management, and operations. The public library is a vital agency in assuring that there will be ready, economic access to information needed by local companies striving to compete in a world-wide economy, especially the small, entrepreneurial businesses.

As a framework to illustrate the growing importance of information to business operations, consider the development of a business plan. It is created to provide a statement of the mission for an organization; to serve as the proposal for obtaining capital investment; to provide a blueprint for future development; to be a guide for subsequent planning and management. It traditionally covers the following issues:

1. The company and the industry
2. The product and related services
3. The technology
4. The market and the market strategy
5. The competition
6. The means for production
7. The management and administration
8. The financial needs, risks, and returns
9. The time schedule

But in response to current information developments, to this traditional organization the company should now add a tenth section:

10. Information resource requirements

The point is that, as we increasingly find ourselves in an information economy, the generic model for a business plan needs to be modified so as to highlight the role of information in support of each of its other components. The entrepreneur should be expected to recognize the needs for information in support of the business objectives, and any potential investor should be given clear evidence in the business plan of the results of that recognition. The following discusses some significant elements of that section.

Information in Development of the Business Plan. What are the sources of information supporting the several sections of the business plan, especially with respect to estimates of market, competition, financial needs, time schedule?

Development of a business plan depends first upon the vision of the entrepreneur in conception of a product or service and of the potentials in a market that will justify investment. It depends upon the managerial skills of the entrepreneur in organizing a framework within which the objectives in creation of the product and in production marketing and distribution of it can be achieved. But it also depends upon *data* on which the estimates of costs (for research and development, for manufacture and production, for marketing and distribution) and of income (from sales) can be derived. As we discuss the role of "information requirements" as part of the business plan itself, there repeatedly will be the implication of parallel needs for corresponding data to support the process in development of it. These data include: industry statistics, product data, state-of-the-art data, market statistics, data on competition, data on vendors and suppliers, specification and standards for needed equipment, data on location and cost of facilities, data on sources of manpower. Among the most important, though, are data on the sources of capital—the potential recipients of the business plan as a proposal.

Beyond the importance to the entrepreneur in development of the business plan, there is comparable, if not greater importance to the potential investor who needs to know that the business plan was based on adequate, reliable, and confirmable data. It therefore should show the basis for estimates; it should show the sources for those data and the means for analysis of them to serve the objectives of the business plan; it should relate them to specific sections of the business plan.

Information in Development of the Product/Service. What is the role of research and development (R&D), of current state-of-the-art knowledge, of sources for raw materials or components? If the product or service requires research and development, the business plan should identify the information requirements to support it. It should specify whether the R&D will be done "in-house" or outside and, if the latter, the availability of means for doing it. It should show clear knowledge of the sources of current state-of-the-art knowledge and of the means for continuing update within the enterprise.

Figure 5.2
Areas for Potential Information Entrepreneurs

```
Research, Development, & Design Services
Training Services
Information Access Service
     · Markets      · Products      · Sources & Suppliers      · Finance
     · Technology & Standards      · Government Policies
Transaction Support Services
     · Accounting Support      · Financial Management      · Brokerage
     · Communication      · Management Information Systems Development
```

Information in Production. What are the information needs for management of purchasing, for staff training, for maintenance of production quality, for inventory management and distribution?

Information in Marketing. What will be the means for monitoring penetration of the market, the effects of competition?

Information in Management. What are the means for providing management information, for measuring the productivity of information support? What are the means for management of the information activities themselves—the special library, computing facilities, telecommunications, database access services?

Business Plans for "Information Industry" Enterprises

The information requirements discussed above, as part of general business plans, can to some extent be met with staff internal to the company—what has been called the "Secondary Information Sector." However, for a number of reasons—access to a number of information sources, economies of scale, necessary management skills, investments specific to information activities but irrelevant to company objectives—there is great value in drawing upon the companies in the business of providing information products and services such as computer software, databases, computer hardware and peripherals, information brokerage, and consultation services. This immediately provides opportunities for information entrepreneurs to fill those needs. They must develop their own business plans, following the general pattern outlined above but with special attention to aspects of particular importance to information enterprises.

These companies, many of them small and just beginning to develop their products and services, are really in most need of information support, so partnership between them and the public library is especially valuable. Those companies represent the real wave of future economic growth as they build new capabilities and as the information superhighway creates new markets (see Figures 5.2 and 5.3).

Information Technology Investment. In particular, information industries today, of all kinds, crucially depend on the use of information technologies. Computer hardware and software are especially important, of course, but the ability to tie in to communication networks, database access services, electronic mail,

Figure 5.3
Elements of Business Planning Specific to Information Industry Companies

- Information Technology Investment
    Hardware, Software, Facilities
    Connection to National, International, & Regional Networks
- Information Staff Skills
    Corporate Management Skills
    Information Management Skills
    Research, Development, & Design Skills
    Marketing Skills
- Information Capital Resources
    Sources of Databases
    Development of Databases
- Accounting Practices
    Capitalization of Information Investments
    Overhead Categories

and new forms of information distribution provides the means to tap the great international resources of information. The business plan for a "Primary Information Sector" company should clearly identify the information technology requirements for the proposed product or service.

Technical Issues in Accessing Information. If these kinds of resources are to be used effectively, there is need for managerial, technical, and professional skills in the use of them. We won't dwell here on the evident needs for managerial skills; they are those which anyone can recount and evaluate, although there are special skills needed for management of information-based enterprises. We should outline some of the technical skills, however (see Figure 5.4).

First, and most important, is technical knowledge of the nature of information itself—the processes by which it is generated, organized, stored and retrieved, analyzed, distributed, and used. Here, we are not talking about the information technologies, but about the information itself. We have only recently, perhaps within the past ten to fifteen years, recognized the necessity of this kind of technical knowledge.

Second is a solid experience with the full range of information resources that are important to corporate operations, decisions, production. Some of these are the internal information, generated by corporate data processing systems, based on data about corporate operations. These are the primary substance of management information systems. But beyond them are the great variety of external information sources—the publications, the databases, the governmental statistics, the scientific and technical information sources. The information resource manager needs to know what kinds of information are available, but even more important is the knowledge of how to identify those that are needed for specific requirements, as they arise.

Third is operating knowledge of the information-processing technologies. These are the means by which information processes are carried out, and the information resource manager needs to have solid understanding of them. Central among them are the technical tools of database management—indexing

Figure 5.4
Necessary Skills

- Managerial Skills
- Technical Knowledge of Information Processes
- Experience with the Range of Information Resources
- Operating Knowledge of Information Technologies
- Technical Knowledge of "Systems Analysis & Design"

structures and vocabularies, file structures, software for search and retrieval of data from files, tools for data analysis and presentation.

Fourth is a technical knowledge of "systems analysis"—the means by which technical decisions can be made about the choices among alternatives that will meet the objectives of the corporation. I must emphasize that this is far more than the traditional "systems and procedures" that have become such standard parts of corporate data processing operations. While the issues of concern in systems and procedures are clearly important and indeed are included in the work of systems analysis, there are much larger problems and more sophisticated methods involved in "information systems analysis and design" than simply systems and procedures in the traditional sense.

GOVERNMENT AND PUBLIC SERVICE AGENCIES

The users include local government and both public and private agencies that provide services to the community. The inclusion of data files from these agencies in the public library OPAC is a major first step in meeting the needs both of these agencies and of the public they serve; the future will see dramatic expansion in the nature of the needs and the ability of the public library to serve them. Relevant to this are efforts to provide electronic access to local government information; clearly, the public library must play a central role in such efforts.

A MODEL FOR USERS, NEEDS, AND FORMATS

As a starting point for development of a model for users and their needs for library materials and services, especially as they may be served by alternative media, two matrices will be defined and represented with illustrative data. The first matrix provides a means for quantifying the relative importance of various kinds of uses of library materials and of library services (see Figure 5.5); the second provides a means for quantifying the relative effectiveness of various media in serving the different kinds of uses (see Figure 5.6).

This technique for modeling is valuable in providing a uniform means for combining data from one's own library with data published or otherwise available from other libraries. For example, the director of a small library can visualize data from a large one, comparing it with local experience; in many cases the patterns of use will be similar even though the amount of activity is sub-

Figure 5.5
Typical Categories of Users, Needs, and Formats

USERS	NEEDS & USES	MATERIALS & SERVICES
General Readers	Reading	Reference Services
Professionals	Browsing	Printed Materials
Other Individual Workers	Database Access	Microform Materials
Business & Industry	Data Processing	CD-ROM Materials
Entrepreneurs	Specific Facts	Microcomputers
Students	General Information	Application Software
Government Agencies		Online Database Services
Private Service Agencies		Online Public Access Catalog

Figure 5.6
Distributions of Uses by Categories of Users: Central Library and Branches

CENTRAL	Reading	Data Access	Reference	Total
General Readers	12%	4%	17%	33%
Students	7%	4%	3%	14%
Work Related	6%	30%	17%	53%
TOTAL	25%	38%	37%	100%

BRANCHES	Reading	Data Access	Reference	Total
General Readers	15%	4%	20%	39%
Students	18%	9%	8%	35%
Work Related	2%	15%	9%	26%
TOTAL	35%	28%	37%	100%

stantially greater. If trends are exhibited in the large library, that may suggest that similar trends may be developing locally, and the director can better prepare to deal with the effects.

Users, Needs, and Formats

The two matrices are based upon categories of users, their needs for library materials and services, and the kinds of formats in which they can obtain them. The following might be typical examples of each:

Matrix 1: Users and Needs. To illustrate Matrix 1, data will be used from surveys of users of the Los Angeles Public Library in 1968 and 1978.[14] In the first survey, users of the LAPL Central Library were asked to identify what kind of users they were and, second, what kinds of uses they had; in the second survey, the same kinds of questions were asked but at a number of branches in addition to the central library. The comparative results showed that the use of the central library was basically unchanged, but that there were substantial differences between the patterns for the central library and the branches. Since the purpose here is merely to illustrate, those results and the number of categories both of users and uses will be much simplified.

Figure 5.7
Values of Alternative Formats for Different Uses

	Reading	Data Access	Reference
Printed Materials	10	3	3
Microform Materials	1	1	1
CD-ROM Materials	1	10	10
Online Database Services		10	10

Of course, there is nothing remarkable about either the matrix model as a means for presentation of results from such surveys or in the differences between patterns for central libraries and branches. The important point is that the matrix provides a convenient means for presenting cross-tabulations of the survey results in a format that permits mathematical manipulation.

Matrix 2: Uses and Formats. The second matrix describes the value of alternative formats in serving particular kinds of needs. For simplicity in illustration, four levels of value will be used—no entry for "Not Applicable," 1 for "Low Value," 3 for "Medium Value," and 10 for "High Value"—but clearly one could use any measuring scale for which appropriate means for measurement are available. In the illustration presented here (Figure 5.7), the values are subjective judgments. Of course, the utility of each format needs to be weighted by the relative percentage of materials available in each format. For example, if acquisition of print materials is from a population of about 50,000 titles, that of microforms is from about 10,000; of CD-ROM from about 1,000; and of on-line databases from about 1,000. In coming years the growth in CD-ROM and on-line text is predicted to be about 50 percent per annum. Although that will certainly not be sustained indefinitely, within the coming five-year period the amount of material available in each of those formats will probably be close to 10,000 titles.

Derived Matrix 3: Users and Formats. In principle, one can mathematically multiply Matrix 1 and Matrix 2 and, by doing so, gain some insight into the relative levels of use of each format. With the examples given above, the resulting level of use by each type of user would be as shown in Figure 5.8.

The point, of course, is that this means for presentation of the results from surveys of users permits one to test the effects of alternative assumptions about the utility of the various formats and the expected rates of growth in publication.

Figure 5.8
Resulting Values of Different Formats for Various Users

CURRENT LEVELS OF USE

Amount	CENTRAL LIBRARY	General Reader	Students	Work Related	Total
50	Printed Material	92	46	101	238
5	Microform Materials	2	1	3	5
1	CD-ROM Material	2	1	5	8
1	Online Databases	2	1	5	8
	BRANCHES	General Reader	Students	Work Related	Total
50	Printed Material	111	116	46	273
5	Microform Materials	2	2	1	5
1	CD-ROM Material	3	2	2	7
1	Online Databases	2	2	2	7

POTENTIAL LEVELS OF USE IN FIVE YEARS

Amount	CENTRAL LIBRARY	General Reader	Students	Work Related	Total
50	Printed Material	92	46	101	238
10	Microform Materials	3	1	5	10
10	CD-ROM Material	22	8	48	78
10	Online Databases	21	7	47	75
	BRANCHES	General Reader	Students	Work Related	Total
50	Printed Material	111	116	46	273
10	Microform Materials	4	4	3	10
10	CD-ROM Material	26	19	24	69
10	Online Databases	24	17	24	65

NOTES

1. Roger C. Greer and Martha L. Hale, "The community analysis process," in *Public Librarianship: A Reader*, ed. Jane Robbins-Carter (Littleton, Colo.: Libraries Unlimited, 1982), pp. 358–366; Cheryl Metoyer-Duran, *Gatekeepers in Ethnolinguistic Communities* (Norwood, N.J.: Ablex, 1993); Virginia A. Walter, *Output Measures and More: Planning and Evaluating Young Adult Services in Public Libraries* (Chicago: American Library Association, 1995).

2. Excellent studies of adult information needs that are relevant to public libraries include: Ching-Chih Chen and Peter Hernon, *Information-Seeking: Assessing and Anticipating User Needs* (New York: Neal-Schuman, 1982); Brenda Dervin and Michael Nilan, "Information needs and uses," *Annual Review of Information Science and Technology* 21 (1986): 3–33; Joan C. Durrance, "Information needs: Old song, new tune," in *Rethinking the Library in the Information Age*, ed. A. Mathews (Washington, D.C.: U.S. Department of Education, 1989), pp. 159–177.

The only study of children's information needs to date is: Virginia A. Walter, "The information needs of children," *Advances in Librarianship* 18 (1994): 111–129.

3. Calvin Mooers, *Zator Technical Bulletin 136* (December 1959).

4. Kathleen De la Pena McCook and Paula Geist, "Hispanic library services in South Florida," *Public Libraries* 34(1) (February 1995): 34–37.

5. Joanne L. Crispin, ed., *The Americans with Disabilities Act: Its Impact on Libraries* (Chicago: American Library Association, 1993); *Directory of Adaptive Technologies to Aid Library Patrons and Staff with Disabilities* (Chicago: American Library

Association, 1994); Donald D. Foos and Nancy C. Pack, *How Libraries Must Comply with the Americans With Disabilities Act* (Phoenix, Ariz.: Oryx, 1992).

6. Robert M. Hayes and Susan Palmer, "The effects of distance upon use of libraries: Case studies based on a survey of users of the Los Angeles Public Library Central Library and branches," *Library and Information Science Research* 5(1) (Spring 1983): 67–100.

7. Christine M. Koontz, "Retail location theory: Can it help solve the public library location dilemma," in *Research Issues in Public Librarianship*, ed. Joy M. Greiner (Westport, Conn.: Greenwood Press, 1994).

The following are commercial packages providing this kind of analysis and mapping: *ATLAS Software* (San Jose, Calif.: Strategic Mapping, Inc., 1992); *COMPASS* (New York: Claritas, NPDC, 1992); *MapInfo* (Ithaca, N.Y.: MapInfo, 1992); *Max-3D: The Information Connection* (Ithaca, N.Y.: National Planning Data Corporation, 1992).

8. See *Chambers Biographical Dictionary* (London: W. R. Chambers, 1984), p. 1153, "(Nathan Rothschild) staked his fortunes on the success of Britain in her duel with Napoleon and, receiving the first news of Waterloo, sold and bought stock which brought him a million of profit."

9. Judith Payne, *Public Libraries Face California's Ethnic and Racial Diversity* (Santa Monica, Calif.: Rand Corporation, 1988).

10. Patricia Willard, "The browser and the library," *Public Library Quarterly* 4(1) (Spring 1983): 55–63.

11. Patricia Willard, "Microcomputer availability to public library clients," *LASIE* 17(2) (September/October 1986): 39–46; Patricia Willard, "Public access personal computers in Australian public libraries," *International Journal of Information and Library Research* 1(3) (1989): 157–174.

12. "Library seeks to host new magnet school," *Los Angeles Times*, 26 March 1994.

13. Bonnie Carroll and Donald W. King, "Value of information," *Drexel Library Quarterly* 21 (Summer 1985): 39–60.

14. Robert M. Hayes, *Evaluation of the Los Angeles Public Library: A Survey of the Users and of the General Public* (Los Angeles: GSLIS/UCLA, 1978); J. Cushman and R. M. Hayes, *Analysis of Usage of the Central Library of the Los Angeles Public Library* (Los Angeles: Institute of Library Research, 1968).

6

The Context
of the Environment

Issues in strategic management external to the community are the least controllable, the most uncertain, and potentially the most dramatic in their effects. This chapter provides an audit of the external environment within which the library and the community function. It reviews elements of the current environment—political culture, social policy (including political, legislative, and legal issues), technological issues, commercial and industrial issues, suppliers, and cooperative networks.

POLITICAL CULTURE

Political culture is the particular cluster of shared values in a society that relate to such issues as authority, justice, and the maintenance of a civil society as they are operationalized as law and government. These values tend to run deep, with roots that extend far back in history. America's basic political values are reflections of the country's revolutionary beginnings and the enlightenment philosophy expressed in the Constitution. Sometimes these values are ambiguous or even contradictory.

What are we to make of our well-known admiration for rugged individualism which exists side by side with our penchant for forming voluntary associations? Some scholars, such as Robert Bellah and his associates, have suggested that Americans join in voluntary associations in order to transcend the loneliness which results from our individualism.[1]

One of the constants of American political culture has been a bias against strong government. As a nation, we have turned to government for solutions to social problems only in times of extreme crisis such as the Depression of the 1930s or wartime. Lyndon Johnson's War on Poverty was an attempt to call on the rhetoric of such crises in order to enlist public support for government intervention in other kinds of problems. The increasing complexity and inter-relatedness of various sectors has also resulted in more government involvement in business and social policy than most Americans feel comfortable with. American tolerance for government ebbs and flows, often in cycles that correlate with economic ups and downs.

Public libraries, as government agencies, often feel the impact of this shifting political culture. When the taxpayers are in revolt against government expenditures in general, there is likely to be less money available for public libraries. However, there have been some positive indicators that voters will support tax increases that are targeted specifically for public libraries. A *Library Journal* survey showed that 72 percent of the referenda for public library capital funds in 1992 were approved. This is a slight dip in the overall average approval rate of 77 percent of capital referenda over the previous eight years. However, levies for increased funding for operations were approved in an overwhelming 50 out of 54 cases in 1994. The study noted that referenda for both types of funding which were held during special elections were more likely to pass than those held during general elections.[2]

Political culture is also manifested in the way that government accomplishes its mission. While there are detractors who argue that the public interest is poorly served in the current climate, there appears to be no retreat from the current trend of market-oriented government. Public library managers, like their counterparts in government organizations of all kinds, are required to conduct their operations ''like a business.'' We noted earlier the increasing emphasis on accountability for results. Elected officials are requiring that bureaucrats demonstrate what kind of a bang they are delivering for the taxpayers' bucks. An emphasis on evaluation and continual improvement has led to public libraries adopting such traditional industrial organization practices as Total Quality Management.[3]

Other manifestations of the current political culture in government bureaucracies include mandates for productivity and new uses of marketing techniques. As noted earlier, public libraries fare quite well in productivity audits. Even the smallest library is able to produce documentation of some of its basic products—books circulated and questions answered—relative to inputs such as materials budget and staff allocations. The library is fortunate that it has a mission which results in tangible services that can be measured and that are generally deemed to be desirable. However, the library director increasingly is called up onto justify the use of relatively better-paid professional staff for the provision of some of these services. Professional standards of service may conflict with local governments' productivity agendas.[4]

A beneficial consequence of productivity awareness in local government is a heightened value placed on innovation. While public libraries are generally perceived as conserving institutions rather than innovative ones, the current political climate may enable them to reinterpret some old roles in new and exciting ways. This is a time in which entrepreneurial strategies in local government are encouraged. A study of the institutionalization of literacy programs in California public libraries in the early 1990s suggested that the library directors who spearheaded the more successful programs had both political and entrepreneurial motivations. These managers perceived the literacy programs as providing the library with political capital, and they also saw these popular, volunteer-driven programs as an opportunity to add a new line to the existing product mix.[5]

Public libraries have embraced the movement toward marketing their services with somewhat more enthusiasm than skill. Most libraries have limited their marketing activities to the public relations or promotion end. These efforts have ranged from the amateurish distribution of photocopied flyers to announce programs, to the highly polished and sophisticated publicity campaigns that have surrounded the openings of the new central libraries in San Antonio and Los Angeles. A few libraries have experimented with new approaches to merchandising their collections, using bookstore-style shelving, for example, to display their new titles cover out. The planning and role-setting process developed by the Public Library Association is, in effect, a methodology for determining the appropriate market niche for a particular public library. At this time, few public libraries engage in detailed market research and market analysis in order to determine their mission, however.[6]

SOCIAL POLICY REGARDING INFORMATION RESOURCES

In areas such as copyright, federal policies on access to governmental information, privatization of governmental functions, and development of the nation's information infrastructure, the actions of Congress and the president create the environment within which community library responsibilities must be carried out. These external factors need to be identified and means created by which the community's needs and obligations can be recognized in the political processes that lead to policy decisions at a national and state level.

Intellectual property rights, accessibility of information, public sector/private sector interactions—these have dramatic impact on the community library's ability to carry out its responsibilities, but the community has minimal effect upon them. It is important to note here that they tend to be treated as problems for the library, but they really are problems for the community because there is where the needs are; the copyright revision provided the library itself with an effective framework within which to operate, and it has successfully done so, but it greatly restricts the abilities of users to use the information.

Copyright

Intellectual property rights are of twofold importance to individuals—as creators and as users of copyrighted material. Indeed, the principle of duality is explicit in the constitutional provision on which copyright legislation is based: "To promote the progress of science and useful arts, by securing for limited times . . . the exclusive right to their respective writings and discoveries." The development of policies to deal with those rights is a matter of current concern in universities throughout the country. Copyright legislation explicitly exempts libraries from liability for copyright infringement by readers, provided notices are posted on the copying machines that alert the readers of their obligations to conform to fair use practices.[7] The impact of technological developments on copyright, however, continues to complicate the strategic situation for libraries.[8]

Recent Court Decisions. The original "look and feel" decision significantly extended the scope of copyright with respect to software, allowing coverage of concepts underlying structure and user interfaces as well as the actual realization of those concepts.[9] Action was brought for infringement of copyright for a computer spreadsheet program. The District Court held that the menu command structure of the computer program, including choice of command terms, the structure and sequence of those terms, their presentation on the screen, and the long prompts, was copyrightable. However, the Court of Appeals reversed that decision, so as a result the Supreme Court decided in mid-1995 to rule on the case; at the time of this writing, the decision is still pending for the 1995/96 Court term.[10]

Severe limitations were placed upon "fair use" of unpublished materials by at least two other court decisions.[11] They arose from the use of such materials in biographies of J. D. Salinger and L. Ron Hubbard. Bills were thereupon introduced in Congress in 1990 and reintroduced in 1991 to make clear that Section 107 of Title 17 of the Copyright Law "applies equally to unpublished as well as published works."[12]

Extension in Application. A bill was introduced in the Senate in 1989—S. 1198, The Visual Artists Rights Act of 1989—"to protect the rights of artists who create single copies or limited editions of . . . works." It embodied "moral rights" provisions intended to establish rights to prohibit intentional distortion, mutilation, or destruction of art works.[13] Part of the objective was to bring U.S. copyright law into closer conformity with international copyright law, in which there is such recognition, especially in "civil law" countries (basically deriving from the Napoleonic Code). The Berne Convention requires its member countries to make certain minimal moral rights available.[14]

Concern about "Electronic Information." In early summer 1994, the commerce department announced plans to release recommendations for rewriting copyright law to protect digital forms of information. It would outlaw the use of picks to open electronic locks copyright owners place on their works. The concern was, especially, by major record labels regarding unauthorized copying and distribution of digital recordings through the Internet. "Existing copyright law doesn't make it clear that it is a violation of the copyright owners' rights to distribute a protected work over the Internet," said Bruce A. Lehman, Assistant Secretary of Commerce. Clinton's National Information Infrastructure Task Force established a blueprint for intellectual property rights on the information superhighway in its report from the working group.[15] A current relevant court case at that time was *Frank Music Corporation v. CompuServe* regarding the transfer of a copyrighted song.[16]

The entertainment and information industries endorsed the draft recommendation for extending copyright law to cover the realms of cyberspace. Kenneth B. Allen, president of the Information Industry Association, was quoted as saying, "Without our industry's products and services, the information superhighway will be an expressway to nowhere."[17]

Government Information

A most central and critical issue, today and for the past decade at least, has been the divergence in views concerning government information. The Public Sector/Private Sector Task Force for the National Commission on Libraries and Information Science examined these issues over ten years ago; recommendations from the report of that task force are still applicable to the situation today.[18]

The principle underlying those recommendations was that information, from whatever source but in particular from the federal government, should be readily, easily, and widely available. Libraries and private sector companies wishing to acquire and provide access to those data, to market and distribute them, to add value to them in packaging or processing, or to combine them with other data should find it easy to do so. The investment made by the government should be regarded as a national capital investment, with prices set to encourage and not discourage use of it. By making government information readily available and by pricing it at the lowest possible level—just the cost of access and reproduction—that result could be expected.

In the decade following, the policies of government have perverted the recommendations. While the policies of the Clinton administration appear to reverse some of those of the prior administration, there are still regulations on the books and operating policies that continue them. Of special concern are three specific policy directions. One is pricing, the second is reduction in availability, and the third is "privatization."

The National Information "Superhighway"

On the positive side, the Clinton administration has committed itself to development of the "information superhighway," the effort to make generally available the National Research and Education Network (NREN).[19] This capability was created initially to facilitate access to the network of supercomputers throughout the nation. That access, though, required such high bandwidth for communication that there is more than enough capacity to absorb all present usages for scholarly communication. Hence, the effort is to make that capacity more generally available. On technical grounds, there are no problems in doing so, though there are potential problems in reliability and response time as the number of users increases. Indeed, the Internet appears to be growing exponentially, both in the number of computers attached to it and in the number of users, though some observers have raised doubts about the reliability of the estimates.[20] From the political and economic standpoint, however, the problems are almost overwhelming. If the debates of a decade ago about public/private sector relationships were difficult, those around NREN will be even more so.

As a direct result of that national leadership, beginning in early 1993 the reporting of Internet events exploded like fireworks. To illustrate, a review of the newspaper citations (covering five major national newspapers: *New York Times, Los Angeles Times, Wall Street Journal, Christian Science Monitor,* and *Washington Post*) for the period from 1 January 1990 through 30 June 1994 showed the following distribution:

	1990	1991	1992	1993	1994
First Six Months	7	2	6	22	127
Second Six Months	1	4	3	72	

From the community library perspective, connectivity through the Internet and eventually through NREN is seen as a real opportunity. While there will be problems in reliability and accessibility, for most users of library services, those will simply be part of normal operations in the use of e-mail.[21] On the other hand, for operational services in the community library, the problems are likely to be far too great to warrant the minor cost savings involved.

Increasing numbers of public libraries are providing Internet access to their patrons at no or low cost. This is coordinated by the state in Maryland, through its SAILOR project, and supported by the California State Library with its InfoPeople program. This is a high visibility service, with at least as much public relations value as actual information value. It gives public libraries a high-tech aura and enables them to make good on their promise to decrease the inequities between the information poor and the information rich.

Public access to Internet also raises some additional problems. The arcane and chaotic nature of the Internet frustrates many new users and has made it necessary for libraries to offer training as well as the computers and the data lines. Several highly publicized instances of children having been exposed to inappropriate materials or actually being molested through Internet contacts has also heightened public demands that children be protected. As this book is being written, there has been at least one attempt in Congress to introduce legislation that would require Internet providers to protect minors from obtaining sexually explicit materials. There are also commercial products emerging that would "filter" harmful material from public access. Public libraries will need to decide whether such filters are violations of their traditional principle of intellectual freedom or whether they are necessary blocks against dangerous materials.[22]

Telecommunications Policy

During the summer of 1995, the Senate and the House of Representatives passed independent but essentially similar versions of a Telecommunications Act of 1995. The result was PL104-104, "The Telecommunications Competition and Deregulation Act of 1995," enacted by Congress in February 1996 and signed by President Clinton on February 8, 1996. This is the first major rewrite of the Communications Act of 1934 and will have dramatic impact on telecommunications, on-line services, and television industries. It will permit long distance telephone companies, local phone companies, cable television operators, and satellite companies to compete in the entire array of markets. Cross-ownership restrictions are relaxed to allow corporations to own more news media outlets in a single market by eliminating limits to the number of radio or television stations a corporation can own.

Without such an overhaul of the nation's telecommunications law, courts and state regulators would be faced with a bewildering array of thorny issues. All of them feature major corporations with diametrically opposing interests. For example, "Baby Bells" want to be allowed to offer video programming, while cable television operators adamantly oppose them. Of course, both claim to have the public interest at heart. PL104-104 has now opened up the competitive playing field to an almost unprecedented extent.

Among the provisions of PL104-104 is one (the Computer Decency Act) that has the intent of limiting access to "indecent materials" through the Internet. It generated several lawsuits and a bill in Congress (S 1567) which would repeal that provision. ALA was a lead plaintiff in one of the lawsuits. In response to that case, the federal courts ruled in mid-1996 that the Computer Decency Act was unconstitutional on First Amendment grounds.[23]

TECHNOLOGY

In November 1994, *Library Journal* reported that 70 percent of the librarians polled cited the need to keep up with technological change as their primary concern.[24] It hardly seems necessary at this point to comment on the role of information technologies in modern information distribution. They pervade every aspect of library operations and services; computer facilities embody them; other kinds of information facilities either use them or represent them. There is need to consider the changes occurring with computers, as they become ever more capable, smaller, yet less expensive. The changes occurring in data storage, in data input and output, in data communications—all need to be considered.[25]

Figure 6.1
Likely Pace in Development of Technologies

	1970	1980	1990	2000
Processor Technologies	Mainframes Minis	Micros Fault tolerant	Supermicros Highly parallel Transputer	5th generation Optical
Storage Technologies	Mag tape/disk	Winchester	Optical Video disk Optical card	Digital audio Erasable optical Digital paper
Human Interface	Menu/command	Icons Pull-down	Common command language	Expert systems Natural language
Human input	Keyboard	Joystick Lightpen Touchscreen	OCR Intelligent OCR Specific Voice	Generic Voice
Output	Monochrome	Color	Windows Graphics Laser printers	Hologram
Workstations	Intelligent terminal		CAD/CAM station PC workstations	Expert System
Software	Specialized	Structured design	Application generators Very high level languages	CASE
Telecomm	Twisted pairs COAX, Microwave	Satellite Fiber optics Packet networks LAN	Bypass Cellular Metro Area Nets	Packet radio ISDN Space platform
Applications	Algorithm	Some heuristics Networking	Special Expert Knowledge based Hypermedia	Machine trans Non-text retrieve

Pace in Development

Figure 6.1 outlines the expected pace in development over the coming decade in each of the major categories of technology.[26]

Implementation

Interaction among these technologies is occurring at several different levels and on a variety of machines to support a variety of user needs. The likely stages of their implementation would appear to be:

1990–1994: Mainframes still key, but increasing implementation of microcomputer-based local area networks; servers supporting use of local CD-ROM files;

1992–1996: Increasing use of high performance microcomputers as distributed, object-oriented, specialized servers; reusable optical disks common;

1994–1998: Low cost, high resolution flat screens; fiber optics;

1996–2000: Optical disk digital libraries integrated into workstations.

User Interfaces

The number of workstations, especially those that are microcomputer-based in local area networks, is expected to increase at 40 to 60 percent per annum. Furthermore, within the decade the processing power they provide will be an order of magnitude greater than it now is; the quality of display and of print output will be an order of magnitude greater; the data communication rates will be an order of magnitude greater; the local storage capacities at least an order of magnitude greater.

The near universal implementation of local systems means that information services can be available on-line and remotely. Locations for access to library information services can include the homes, business offices, local government facilities, and schools. This may require a reorientation of staff thinking and of job functions and organization.

To effect such remote service requires that there be easy user interfaces.[27] Too often local systems, even when acceptable to library staff, are difficult for the user. As a result, more emphasis should be placed on development of intelligent microcomputer interfaces and microcomputer integration as the foundation for the scholar workstation. Microcomputers should be purchased for new installations and as replacements for existing terminals when required. Library systems staff, in cooperation with city/county computer center staff, should develop local micro-based software for distribution to the local community which will assist users in maximizing use of available information resources and provide for navigation among both library and other governmental services.

Local system vendors should be as concerned about user interface issues as they are about technical aspects of their systems. Systems designers must think of the user as they develop automated systems for libraries. In selecting equipment and software for the library, the advice of the local government's computer center staff should be sought, as savings may be achieved through group purchases and compatibility of equipment.

The highly successful PEN system in Santa Monica is one example in which the public library worked with the city government in designing a public access information system for the community. Santa Monica residents may access the library catalog, as well as a number of other local information services, from their modems at home or work.

The Colorado Association of Research Libraries (CARL) has recently brought to market the Kids' Catalog, a graphical user interface to catalog information designed especially for children. Based in part on the research done at the Graduate School of Library and Information Science at UCLA on the Science Library Catalog Project, this product demonstrates the commercial viability of producing more user-friendly electronic catalogs.[28] CARL is currently developing the Peoples' Catalog, which attempts to provide adults with a similar graphical approach to finding catalog information.

Problems

Infrastructure. In some communities there may be a lack of an adequate infrastructure—communications, logistical support, availability of consultation services. If so, this is an almost insurmountable barrier, but recourse to the state library and the assistance it can offer may be helpful in overcoming such obstacles. Indeed, the state libraries might well consider taking responsibility to identify and assist "information underprivileged" communities.

Standards. Failure to conform to standards or, in some cases, a lack of them is a second technological barrier. These are exemplified by departures from standard formats (such as MARC), from standard character codes, from standard programming languages. When local governmental computer centers are involved, the library director should make them aware of the fact that there are standards established for libraries and that there is a need to conform to them. A specific case to illustrate is the Z39.50 standard for communication in client/server contexts, including, for example, the Internet.[29]

Meeting Goals. Failure to meet stated goals in technological development, with respect to both time of delivery and functional capabilities, has been a continuing problem. Clearly, it sets a barrier to future development that depends upon availability of a technology.

Closed Systems. Commitment to "closed systems" has been a most serious technological barrier. The producers of such systems have the evident objective of creating "captive" markets, but the result is a barrier to all future developments, except those that the producers are willing to implement.

COOPERATIVE PROGRAMS

The library community has a long tradition of cooperation. It is represented by interlibrary loan, by the development of cooperative cataloging through the Library of Congress and the bibliographic utilities (OCLC, RLIN, and WLN), the Center for Research Libraries depository center, the preservation program, and a wide range of consortia and networks. These cooperative enterprises have value, as represented by the sharing of resources through interlibrary loan, but they also have costs, both financial and in loss of community prerogatives.

Management of Cooperative Programs

Primary among the costs are those involved in management. Of course, the largest portion of the costs are those that are normal parts of operational and tactical management. But beyond the normal costs are those involved in management of cooperative enterprises. Each of the bibliographic utilities has extensive mechanisms for input from participants to the management process, some of which are not only directly costly but involve exceptional commitments of time donated by the participants.[30]

Integration of Resources

Cooperative efforts require means for identifying materials. To a major extent, of course, that need is met by the bibliographic utilities, as will be discussed. But frequently independent capabilities have been created, especially to link libraries within states. Examples would be the statewide and local library networks exemplified by NYSILL in New York, the North Suburban Library System and Illinet Online in Illinois, CLASS in California, the Morris Automated Information Network in Morris County, New Jersey, and so on.[31]

Much of what is known about the level of interlibrary loan (ILL) activity in public libraries is derived from the data collected annually by the National Center for Education Statistics (NCES). Thomas Waldhart's analysis of that data suggests that public library resource sharing through ILL has grown rapidly in the 1990s.[32] The increase in cooperation among the community libraries in each state and the negotiation of statewide contracts were significant results.[33] Some look toward compilations of larger, regional groups.

Funding for Access and Interlibrary Loan

The historic pattern was for ILL to be treated as a reciprocal good, even though it was recognized that a few libraries were substantial net lenders. As a result, the practice was not to charge for lending services. Beyond that, there are large numbers of reciprocal agreements where libraries formally agree not to charge the participating libraries for ILL services. Where charges have been instituted, a typical charge is $5 per article if there is no reciprocal agreement. It has been suggested that the bibliographic utilities provide an automatic charge, such as $10 per item, for ILL requests processed through their services, in addition to their own fees and as a credit to the lending community. As the burden increases, though, even a fee at that level may not be sufficient to control the proliferation of ILL requests. Commercial document delivery may then become the option of choice.[34]

The Bibliographic Utilities

The several bibliographic utilities (OCLC, RLIN, and WLN) were started with several roles in mind but with one—sharing the costs of retrospective conversion of catalog data—as the initial priority. They have served that function well, to the point that use of them for that purpose by U.S. libraries is steadily declining. That role, while not disappearing, is certainly less important than it was.

Complementary to that role was to provide access to current cataloging both as available from the Library of Congress (as the primary national center for cataloging production) and from interlibrary cooperation. That role continues to be important, although there is an increasing array of alternative sources—CD-ROM versions, tapes available directly from the Library of Congress for mounting on the local system, and data available from other libraries through a number of ad hoc networks.

Another role, at least in the perception of some libraries, was to serve as an interim substitute for a local automated catalog. This surely underlay the motivation for including in some of the utilities records that were library-specific rather than generic. Now, though, with local systems operating in virtually every major community library, that role is surely disappearing.

Perhaps the most comprehensive role of the bibliographic utilities was to serve as the national union catalog, bringing to reality the dream of Charles Jewett of nearly 150 years ago.[35] A national bibliographic database greatly improves the capability of libraries to share resources and to make effective decisions concerning the acquisition, storage, and preservation of materials. Today, we see increasing emphasis placed on access instead of acquisition; this functional objective therefore becomes one of predominant importance. Even this role, though, is being questioned, as some argue that networked interconnections among local systems can serve as a "virtual" national bibliography, permitting libraries to bypass the utilities. Such substitution is fraught with difficulties, and is unlikely to reduce this central role of the utilities.

This has become an added role for the utilities. It is based on the established relationships with libraries, the communications networks and data access systems that are now available to provide access to a wide range of databases, and the means for easy interconnection between the utilities and the local systems in community libraries. This role serves as a broad base for maintaining viability of the bibliographic utilities and for support of them, especially when combined with document delivery services.

The venture of OCLC into electronic publication, made in association with the American Association for the Advancement of Science, raises the potential for an entirely new and exciting role for it and for the other bibliographic utilities.

SOURCES OF INFORMATION

While the role of the publishers may appear to be self-evident, it is important to recognize that publishing is the primary source of information resources that libraries must acquire. Publishing and information service suppliers determine what they will produce and how they will price it based on their own economic interests; while in principle that may reflect the needs of the market, the community and its library are likely to be minor determinants; indeed, given the dependence they have on the sources, they represent a captive market with few alternative sources.

Changing Methods of Publication and Distribution

Primarily as a result of the impact of technology on publishing, there are changes occurring in patterns of publication. The new media—computer databases, on-line access to them, electronic mail and facsimile, distribution of data and images in optical disk formats, desktop publishing—all provide new means for communication of information. How will they affect the traditional print means? At what pace will they develop? What changes will they make in the substance of what is communicated? How do we determine what are real changes in publishing and when those changes will be meaningful to operations of libraries and other information facilities?

Especially difficult for strategic management is predicting the pace at which the suppliers will shift from one mode of distribution to another; the library needs to make plans for acquisition of equipment and facilities largely on the basis of speculation, and the publishers provide little data on which to base those decisions. The well-established relationships for monograph writing, editing, publishing, and distribution have as yet no counterparts in the electronic arena, at least as it relates to the community world. Indeed, the lack of expertise on the part of the publishers in identifying authors as sources for publication, and in marketing, packaging, and distribution may well be the most significant barrier, one that may take decades to resolve.

CD-ROM. Optical disks clearly will affect the nature of journals and perhaps even of books; they are likely to change the kinds of materials published as well as their format and organization.[36] The library community has been at the forefront in development of new formats. In 1986, about 75 percent of CD-ROM publications were specific to library operations (e.g., abstracts and bibliographic data files); in 1988, it was 60 percent; by 1990 it was less than 40 percent.[37] Text files and raw reference data (such as pricing and financial data) are rapidly becoming the dominating kinds of content. For the entire market, including games as well as more substantive information, the number of CD-ROM drives in the country doubled in 1994 (from 5 million to over 10 million) and the sales of CD-ROM titles increased by 77 percent. Clearly, this is a form of publication to be reckoned with.[38]

On-Line and On-Demand Publication. Among the potential services is that of an electronic ''library,'' with on-demand access and publication. It is today largely experiment, promotion, and rhetoric. Still, it represents an important new dimension of private sector services. The OCLC publication of an electronic journal represents this kind of experiment. Another involves scanning journal articles and providing them as electronic document delivery. Some publications have been developed for the networks (today, perhaps 30 journals, 10 refereed,

100 bulletin boards but all moonlighting efforts) and others are derivative from paper journals. Still, the mainstream publishers of books and journals are moving into this form of publication very slowly, very cautiously. That means that there is much uncertainty about when, or even whether, library materials will be available in this form.

Pricing Policies

The economic pressures felt by libraries during the past decade have been exceptional, and the pricing policies of the private sector information industry have been a major element in the crisis. Libraries are clearly seen as captive markets so prices can be set by publishers at whatever the market will bear. The result, though, has been forced policies of "de-acquisition," especially of journals. The argument of the private sector companies appears to be that the availability of their publications from libraries depletes their other markets, since users will go to the library rather than purchase their own. This view does not reflect the reality. Libraries in no way diminish the market, so discriminatory pricing will become self-defeating.

Relationships between Publishers and Libraries

Publishers as Sources. With these developments, the information industries are creating potentially different relationships to the community and to the library. Without question, the central fact is that libraries depend almost completely upon the private sector for their collections and for the tools for access to them. Their collections come overwhelmingly from commercial publishers, with professional societies a secondary source, and governments of all kinds are really minor in the overall. In this respect at least, the library profession sees the private sector as partners. One need merely enter the exhibit area at any meeting of the American Library Association and observe what the librarians do there.

The tools for access also come overwhelmingly from the private sector. The number of exceptions is almost miniscule in comparison. Indeed, one must search carefully to identify any but the most evident examples. Even the most evident one—the cataloging data from the Library of Congress—is accessed through private sector agencies, not public ones. Of course, there is the example of the products and services which the National Library of Medicine has been mandated by congressional legislation to provide. And there is the National Technical Information Service which similarly is mandated by Congress to provide distribution of federal government documents.

The views of the library profession concerning the importance of the private sector with respect to these support tools are evident. Indeed, these are their tools, from wherever they may come. There may be disagreements over rights and privileges; there may be debate over technique and details. But overall, the library profession sees the private sector as an essential partner.

Libraries as Markets. The corollary to the dependence of libraries upon the private sector is the reverse dependence of the private sector on libraries. For a wide range of publications, the libraries of this country represent from one-third to two-thirds of the total market; this is especially the case for scientific, technical, and professional ones acquired by academic libraries. Of even greater importance is that those sales represent the break-even point for the publishers, so that "library sales" cover the risks of the publishers. Libraries therefore are a primary market for major categories of publication.

Libraries frequently provide the information industry with the basis for a pilot test of general markets. An example was the development of the CD-ROM as means for information distribution. In the early days of on-line reference database access, libraries—especially the medical libraries of the country—provided the context for pilot test of such services. And certainly libraries provide a crucial component of the means for distribution of private sector information products and services. With respect to the on-line database services, in particular, they still represent a disproportionate share of total sales.

How does the library profession view this side of the "partnership"? Frankly, with a rather jaundiced eye. The rhetoric of the information industry, of all kinds, has ignored or diminished the importance that libraries have for them. The result is a perception that, if there is a partnership, it certainly is not an equal one. The libraries bear the burdens with little or none of the benefits of partnership. They are merely accepted as simply another market, no more or less important than any other.

SOURCES OF STAFF

The schools of library and information science are the primary sources for professional staff. A matter of vital strategic concern, therefore, has been the closure of library schools during the past decade. The number has been reduced by over 20 percent, and the output of professionally qualified graduates by even more.[39]

Aside from the specific concerns with the status of library schools are the more general ones of qualifications needed for staff.[40] Of special concern is the commitment to imperatives of the profession—preservation of the records of the past, access to those records, equity in access, privacy for the users, service. Also desired are qualities of leadership.

Some public libraries have actively recruited distance education programs in library and information science into their communities in order to maintain a supply of adequately trained professional staff. A still more fundamental problem may be the recruitment of qualified people into the profession. A recent article in the *Los Angeles Times* included the job of public librarian in their list of jobs marked for extinction. Public librarians may have to mount an aggressive public awareness campaign to counteract such misconceptions and to convince people that their profession is a vital and rewarding one, with a future that extends well into the twenty-first century.[41]

NOTES

1. Robert Bellah et al., *Habits of the Heart: Individualism and Commitment in American Life* (Berkeley, Calif.: University of California Press, 1985); Robert Bellah et al., *The Good Society* (New York: Knopf, 1992).

2. Richard B. Hall, "The vote is in: Undeniably operational," *Library Journal* 120(11) (15 June 1995): 40–45; Evan St. Lifer, "Public libraries meet fiscal reality head on," *Library Journal* 120(1) (January 1995): 44–47.

3. Albert C. Hyde, "The proverbs of total quality management: Recharting the path to quality improvement in the public sector," *Public Productivity and Management Review* 16(1) (Fall 1992): 25–38; Warren H. Schmidt and Jerome P. Finnigan, *The Race without a Finish Line: America's Quest for Total Quality* (San Francisco: Jossey-Bass, 1992); Thomas W. Shaughnessy, "Benchmarking, total quality management, and libraries," *Library Administration and Management* 7 (Winter 1993): 7–12; James E. Swiss, "Adapting total quality management (TQM) to government," *Public Administration Review* 52 (July/August 1992): 356–361; Virginia A. Walter, "Evaluating library services and programs," in *Youth Services Librarians as Managers: A How-To Guide*, ed. Kathleen Staerkel et al. (Chicago: American Library Association, 1995), pp. 51–62.

4. David Ammons, "Reputational leaders in local government productivity and innovation," *Public Productivity and Management Review* 15(1) (Fall 1991): 19–43.

5. Peter F. Drucker, *Innovation and Entrepreneurship: Practice and Principles* (New York: HarperCollins, 1985); Virginia A. Walter, "For all the wrong reasons? Implementing volunteer programs in public organizations," *Public Productivity and Management Review* 16(3) (Spring 1993): 271–282; Dennis Young, *If Not for Profit, for What? A Behavioral Theory of the Nonprofit Sector* (New York: Lexington Books, 1983).

6. Cosette Kies, *Marketing and Public Relations for Libraries* (Metuchen, N.J.: Scarecrow Press, 1987); Benedict A. Leerburger, *Promoting and Marketing the Library*, rev. ed. (Boston: Hall, 1989); Virginia A. Walter, "Research you can use: Marketing to children," *Journal of Youth Services* 7(3) (Spring 1994): 283–288; Darlene Weingand, *Marketing/Planning Library and Information Services* (Littleton, Colo.: Libraries Unlimited, 1989); Elizabeth J. Wood, *Strategic Marketing for Libraries: A Handbook* (Westport, Conn.: Greenwood, 1989).

7. *United States Code*, 1988 Edition. Title 17, Section 107 defines fair use. Section 108 defines the rights of libraries to make copies under specific conditions. In particular: "(d) The rights of reproduction and distribution under this section apply to a copy, made from the collection of a library or archives, where the user makes his or her request or from that of another library or archives, of no more than one article or other contribution to a copyrighted collection or periodical issue, or to a copy or phonorecord of any other copyrighted work, if—(1) the copy or phonorecord becomes the property of the user, and the library or archive has had no notice that the copy or phonorecord would be used for any purpose other than private study, scholarship or research; and (2) the library or archive displays prominently, at the place where orders are accepted, and includes in its order form, a warning of copyright in accordance with requirements that the Registrar of Copyrights shall require by regulation."

8. Henriette D. Avram, "Copyright in the electronic environment," *Educom Review* 24(3) (Fall 1989): 31–33; Jose-Marie Griffiths and Donald W. King, *Intellectual Property Rights in an Age of Electronics and Information* (Washington, D.C.: Office of Technology Assessment, U.S. Congress, 1986); *Intellectual Property Rights and Fair Use: Strengthening Scholarly Communication in the 1990s.* Proceedings of the 9th Annual Conference of Research Library Directors. Dublin, Ohio: OCLC, 1991; Jeff Leeds, "Cyberspace copyright proposal draws praise," *Los Angeles Times*, 8 July 1994, D1; Teresa Riordan, "Writing copyright law for an information age," *New York Times*, 7 July 1994, C1; Jeff Leeds, "Cyberspace copyright proposal draws praise"; Teresa Riordan, "Writing copyright law for an information age."

9. The case in point was: *Lotus Development Corp., Plaintiff v. Paperback Software International.*

10. Julie Pitta, "Judge overturns copyright ruling against Borland," *Los Angeles Times*, 10 March 1995, 114; "Lotus plans to appeal case against Borland to Supreme Court," *Wall Street Journal*, 24 March 1995.

11. The two cases in point were: *Salinger v. Random House, Inc.* and *New Era Pubs. Int'l ApS v. Henry Holt & Co.*

12. PL 102–492, approved 24 October 1992. Addendum to Section 107 of the Copyright Act of 1976 to clarify the application to unpublished materials of fair use standards allowing limited use of copyrighted materials. Related to HR 4412; also to S 2370 (101st Congress), HR 4263 (101st Congress).

13. U.S. Congress, House Committee on the Judiciary, *Berne Convention Implementation Act of 1987.* Hearings before the Subcommittee: June 17, July 23, September 16 and 30, 1987, February 9 and 10, 1988 (Washington, D.C.: GPO, 1988); U.S. Congress, Senate Committee on the Judiciary, *The Berne Convention*: Hearings before the Subcommittee: February 18 and March 3, 1988 (Washington, D.C.: GPO, 1988); U.S. Congress, Senate Committee on the Judiciary, *Moral Rights in Our Copyright Laws*: Hearings before the Subcommittee: June 20, September 20, and October 24, 1989 (Washington, D.C.: GPO, 1990); David Nimmer, *The Berne Convention Implementation Act of 1988* (New York: Matthew Bender, 1989).

14. Sam Ricketson, *The Berne Convention for the Protection of Literary and Artistic Works: 1886–1986* (London: Centre for Commercial Law Studies, Queen Mary College, Kluwer, 1987); W. A. Smits, *United States Adherence to the oBerne Convention: A Missed Opportunity for Moral Rights Protection?* (Ph.D. dissertation, UCLA, 1989).

15. Teresa Riordan, "Writing copyright law for an information age"; Bruce A. Lehman, *Intellectual Property and the National Information Infrastructure.* The Report of the Working Group on Intellectual Property Rights. Washington, D.C., September 1995.

16. Junda Woo, "Publisher sues CompuServe over a song," *Wall Street Journal*, 16 December 1993.

17. Jeff Leeds, "Cyberspace copyright proposal draws praise."

18. *Public Sector/Private Sector Interaction in Providing Information Services: Report to the NCLIS from the Public Sector/Private Sector Task Force* (Washington, D.C.: NCLIS, 1982); Robert M. Hayes, "A commentary on the NCLIS Public Sector/Private Sector Task Force and its Report," *Minutes of the Ninety-Ninth Annual Meeting, The Association of Research Libraries* (Washington, D.C.: ARL, 1982), pp. 12–41.

19. "ARL, Cause, Educom form new information resources coalition, "*Manage IT* 1(2) (April 1990): 1–2; Bill Clinton and Al Gore, *Putting People First: How We Can All Change America* (New York: Times Books, 1992); U.S. National Telecommunica-

tions and Information Administration, *The NTIA Infrastructure Report: Telecommunications in the Age of Information* (Washington, D.C.: U.S. Dept. of Commerce, NTIA, 1991); Nancy Cline, "Information resources and the national network," *Educom Review* 25(2) (Summer 1990): 30–34; Richard M. Dougherty, "An ideal win-win situation: The national electronic highway," *American Libraries* (February 1991): 182; Albert Gore, "Remarks on the NREN," *Educom Review* 25(2) (Summer 1990): 12–16; Paul G. Huray and David B. Nelson, "The federal high-performance computing program," *Educom Review* 25(2) (Summer 1990): 17–24; Erik Jul, "Project to analyze Internet information is underway," *OCLC Newsletter* (March/April 1992): 13–15; Clifford A. Lynch, "Library automation and the national network," *Educom Review* 24(3) (Fall 1989): 21–26; Clifford Lynch, "Telecommunications and libraries," *DLA Bulletin* 6(1) (Fall 1986): 1, 3; Michael M. Roberts, "The NREN and commercial services," *Educom Review* 24(4) (Winter 1989): 10–11; Susan M. Rogers, "Educational applications of the NREN," *Educom Review* 25(2) (Summer 1990): 25–29; U.S. House of Representatives, *National Information Infrastructure Act of 1993*—HR 1757 (Washington, D.C.: GPO, 1993).

20. Peter H. Lewis, "Doubts are raised on actual number of Internet's users," *New York Times*, 10 August 1994, 1.

21. Brendan P. Kehoe, *Zen and the Art of the Internet* (Chester, Pa.: Widener University, January 1992).

22. Bruce Flanders, "A delicate balance: Keeping children out of the gutters along the information highway," *School Library Journal* (October 1994): 32–35; Jean Armous Polly and Steve Cisler, "Should public libraries connect?" *Library Journal* 119(6) (15 March 1994): 24–26; Nat Hentoff, "The Senate's cybercensors" (Communications Decency Act, part of telecommunications bill), *Washington Post*, 1 July 1995; Lawrence J. Magid, "Porn ban risks on-line censorship" (proposed Senate Bill S-314), *Los Angeles Times*, 15 March 1995.

23. Ralph Vartabedian, "Landmark reform of communications laws OKd in House" (the House of Representatives passes the Communications Act of 1995), *Los Angeles Times*, 5 August 1995; Mike Mills, "House approves phone, cable bill; act would open market for local calls, end TV system rate curbs," *Washington Post*, 5 August 1995; Jube Shiver, Jr., "Sweeping reform of communications laws clears Senate" (bill allows greater competition within long-distance carrier, local phone and cable TV markets), *Los Angeles Times*, 16 June 1995; Alexandra Marks, "The telecom revolution: At what price?" (analysis of the proposed Telecommunications Act of 1995), *Christian Science Monitor*, 7 August 1995; "Telecom act draws mixed reviews from librarians: ALA file challenge," *American Libraries*, 27(3) (March 1996): 8–9.

24. "Technology is dramatically changing the way librarians work," *Library Journal* 119(21) (1 November 1994): 49.

25. Caroline Arms, "Libraries and electronic information: The technological context, part two," *Educom Review* 24(3) (Fall 1989): 34–43; James Herman et al., "Shaping the 1990s," *Computerworld* 23(48) (27 November 1989): 77–85; Susan Hockey, "The role of electronic information in higher education: The faculty perspective," *OCLC Academic Libraries Directors' Conference*, 1992; Shirley Hyatt, "New era communications gives libraries new options," *OCLC Newsletter* (May/June 1992): 15–19; Philippe Kahn, "Forces shaping academic software development," *Educom Review* 24(4) (Winter 1989): 24–25; S. B. Kiesler and L. S. Sproull, eds., *Computing and Change on Campus* (New York: Cambridge University Press, 1987); F. W. Lancaster, "Whither libraries? or, wither libraries," *College and Research Libraries* 39(5) (September 1978); John Martyn et al.,

Information UK 2000 (London: British Library Research, Bowker-Saur, 1990); Jack A. Meadows, "Higher education and the influence of information technology: Research," in *The Electronic Campus—An Information Strategy.* Proceedings of the Conference in Banbury, England, 28–30 October 1988; Raymond K. Neff, "Merging libraries and computer centers: Manifest destiny or manifestly deranged?" *Educom Bulletin* (Winter 1985): 8–12, 16; *NTIA Information Services Report* (Washington, D.C.: Department of Commerce, August 1988); Thomas J. Galvin, "Research library performance in the delivery of electronic information," *OCLC Newsletter* (March/April 1992): 20–21; Wallace C. Olsen, *Toward an Integrated Information System* (Ithaca, N.Y.: Cornell University Press, April 1986); "Technology assessment at OCLC," *OCLC Newsletter* 179 (May/June 1989); James Thompson, *The End of Libraries* (London: Bingley Press, 1982).

26. Rowland C. W. Brown, "Brushstrokes in flight: A strategic overview of trends in technology in higher education," in *The Electronic Campus—An Information Strategy.* Proceedings of the Conference in Banbury, England, 28–30 October 1988.

27. Ronald Baecker and William Buxton, *Readings in Human-Computer Interaction: A Multidisciplinary Approach* (Los Altos, Calif.: Morgan Kaufmann, 1987); Mike Berger, "The patron meets the Melvyl catalog: A short history of the Melvyl patron interface," *DLA Bulletin* 12(10) (Spring 1992): 6–7, 24–26; Moran Card, Allen Newell, and Thomas P. Moran, *The Psychology of Human-Computer Interaction* (Hillsdale, N.J.: Lawrence Erlbaum Associates, 1983); John M. Carroll, *Interfacing Thought: Cognitive Aspects of Human-Computer Interaction* (Cambridge, Mass.: Bradford/MIT Press, June 1987); Stephen Draper and Donald Norman, *User Centered System Design* (Hillsdale, N.J.: Lawrence Erlbaum Associates, 1986); Roger W. Ehrich and Robert C. Williges, *Human-Computer Dialogue Design* (New York: Elsevier Science, January 1986); Tom Gilb and Gerald M. Weinberg, *Humanized Input: Techniques for Reliable Keyboard Input* (Wellesley Hills, Mass.: QED Information Sciences, Inc., 1977); Erik Jul, "Ben Schneiderman speaks on user interface design," *OCLC Newsletter* (May/June 1992): 10–11; Michael J. McGill, "Z39.50 benefits for designers and users," *Educom Review* 24(3) (Fall 1989): 27–30; "Z39.50: lousy sports car, great library standard," *American Libraries* (October 1990): 903; *OCLC Gateway Project*, 15 January 1992; Jane N. Mosier and Sidney L. Smith, *Guidelines for Designing User Interface Software*, August 1986; Raymond Nickerson, *Using Computers: Human Factors in Information Systems* (Cambridge, Mass.: Bradford/MIT Press, 1986); Ben Schneiderman, *Designing the User Interface: Strategies for Effective Human-Computer Interaction* (Reading, Mass.: Addison-Wesley, 1986); Edward A. Tomeski and Harold Lazarus, *People-Oriented Computer Systems* (New York: Van Nostrand, 1975), chapters 1–4.

28. Christine L. Borgman et al., "Children's searching behavior on browsing and keyword online catalogs: The Science Library Catalog Project," *Journal of the American Society for Information Science*, in press; Paula Busey and Tom Doerr, "Kid's Catalog: An information retrieval system for children," *Journal of Youth Services in Libraries* 7(1) (Fall 1993): 77–84; Virginia A. Walter et al., "The Science Library Catalog: A springboard for information literacy," *School Library Media Quarterly*, in press.

29. Maribeth Ward, "Expanding access to information with Z39.50," *American Libraries* (July/August 1994): 639–641.

30. Robert M. Hayes, "Distributed library networks: programs and problems," in *The Responsibility of the University Library Collection in Meeting the Needs of its Campus and Local Community* (La Jolla: Friends of the UCSD Library, 1976); Allen Kent and

Thomas J. Galvin, *The Structure and Governance of Library Networks* (New York: Marcel Dekker, 1979).

31. John W. Head and Gerard McCabe, eds., *Insider's Guide to Library Automation* (Westport, Conn.: Greenwood Press, 1993).

32. Thomas J. Waldhart, "Resource sharing by public libraries," *Public Libraries* 34 (4) (July/August 1995): 220–223.

33. Mark Kibbey and Nancy H. Evans, "The network is the library," *Educom Review* 24(3) (Fall 1989): 15–20; *Libraries & Technology: A Strategic Plan for the Use of Advanced Technologies for Library Resource Sharing in New York State* (Albany, N.Y.: N.Y. State Library, 1987); Beryl Glitz, "The California multitype library network: An update," *Pacific Southwest Regional Medical Library Service* (January/February 1991): 1, 4.

34. Charles B. Lowry, "Resource sharing or cost shifting?—the unequal burden of cooperative cataloging and ILL in network," *College and Research Libraries* (January 1990): 11–19; *Interlibrary Loan Discussion Panel: Final Report* (Dublin, Ohio: OCLC, October 1990); Kenyon Stubbs, "Introduction," *ARL Statistics, 1990–91* (Washington, D.C.: ARL, 1992) (shows increase in ILL borrowing of 47% from 1985/86 through 1990/91, a compounded rate of 8%. However, OCLC data showed a *doubling* of ILL borrowing from 1985/86 through 1990/91, a compounded rate of 15%!); "ARL and RLG to study ILL costs," *Library Hotline* 21(17) (17 April 1992): 102; *ARL/RLG Interlibrary Loan Cost Study: Worksheet* (Washington, D.C.: ARL, 1992).

35. Charles Coffin Jewett, *On the Construction of Catalogues of Libraries, and their Publication by Means of Separate, Stereotyped Titles*, 2d ed. (Washington, D.C.: Smithsonian Institution, 1853).

36. Doug Iles, "CD-ROM enters mainstream IS," *Computerworld* (5 June 1989): 75–80; David C. Miller, *Special Report: Publishers, Libraries, & CD-ROM* (Benicia, Calif.: DCM Associates, March 1987) (Prepared for Fred Meyer Charitable Trust); David C. Miller, *The New Optical Media in the Library and the Academy Tomorrow* (Benicia, Calif.: DCM Associates, August 1986) (Prepared for Fred Meyer Charitable Trust); David C. Miller, *The New Optical Media Mid-1986: A Status Report* (Benicia, Calif.: DCM Associates, August 1986) (Prepared for Fred Meyer Charitable Trust); William Paisley and Matilda Butler, "The first wave: CD-ROM adoption in offices and libraries," *Microcomputers for Information Management* 4(2) (June 1987): 109–127.

37. "CD-ROM database sales should hit about 2.2 mil by 1996 vs. 1.4 mil in 1991," *Computing World* (March 1992): 9; "Market share of CD-ROM information products tabulated by type of product for 1988 and 1990," *Computerworld* (30 January 1989): 77; "Database vendors revenues projection," *Information* (part 1) (October 1989): 6; "Sales of electronic databases to grow 20% in 1989 vs. 1988," *New York Times*, 30 December 1988, 23.

38. *Publishers Weekly* 241(29) (18 July 1994): 17.

39. John Seelmeyer, "The anatomy of a library school shutdown," *American Libraries* (February 1985): 95–96, 113; "State budget woes threaten U. of South Fla. library school," *American Libraries* (November 1991): 926; Russell Shank (Chair) et al., *Report of the ALA Special Committee on Library School Closings* (Chicago: ALA, June 1991); Trevor Haywood, *Changing Faculty Environments* (Birmingham: Birmingham Polytechnic, July 1991); Maurice P. Marchant, "The closing of the library school at Brigham Young University," *American Libraries* (January 1992): 32–36.

40. Jose-Marie Griffiths and Donald W. King, *New directions in Library and Infor-*

mation Science Education (White Plains, N.Y.: Published by Knowledge Industry Publications for the American Society for Information Science, 1986); *Strategic Vision for Professional Librarians*, Strategic Vision Discussion Group, Steering Committee. December 1991; Warren J. Haas, "Library schools in research universities," *35th Annual Report 1991* (Washington, D.C.: Council on Library Resources, 1992): 27–33; Tom Gaughan, "Taking the pulse of library education," *American Libraries* (January 1992): 24–25, 120; Charles R. McClure and Carol A. Hert, "Specialization in library/information science education: Issues, scenarios, and the need for action," *Proceedings of the Conference on Specialization in Library/Information Science Education* (Ann Arbor: SLIS, University of Michigan, November 6–8, 1991).

41. Emily Gest, "The jobs of the past, the jobs of the future," *Los Angeles Times Magazine*, 20 August 1995, 26–27.

PART III

Techniques for Assessment

7

Assessing the Strategic Position

In this chapter we turn to assessment of the strategic position of the community library with respect to the critical elements both externally and internally—effectiveness of library tactical management, the quality of the collection and of its management, operational performance, the values to the community and to the constituency served, and effects of the external environment.

INFORMATION GATHERING AND STRATEGIC DATA FILES

There are needs for computer-based tools and services to support library management at all three levels: strategic (i.e., concerned with response to external environment), tactical (i.e., concerned with internal allocation of resources), and operational (i.e., concerned with efficient use of resources). At the end of this chapter the relevant generic data management packages are summarized; in addition, two commercially available packages of value to strategic management will be described.

Managers may maximize their organization's strategic position by making good use of available information. Strategic management thus requires the maintenance and interpretation of enormous amounts of data. The constantly changing and interrelated pieces of relevant information may be managed most effectively in electronic data files. Some of the essential information focuses on internal operations data:

- Internal Administrative Structure and Operational Matrix
- Budgeting
- Costs of Operation
- Staff
- Equipment
- Collection
- Usage

Given the potentially massive amount of data that can be generated from operations, though, it is essential that the scan be carefully managed so as to select only the most significant for the purposes of strategic management. Chapter 9 will provide a framework in which to identify the relevant data, organized around a model for costing library operations, but encompassing the full scope of quantitative aspects.

Some of the data concern the community. Again, the scan must be selective, but there is as yet no model to guide the identification of what is crucial or for organizing it. Clearly, such a model needs to be developed.

- Administrative
- Population
- Educational Programs
- Community Agencies
- Business and Industry

The external environment encompasses a wide array of contexts, so the scan must deal with a comparable array of sources. Primary among them is the literature related to each component of the environment. The data-gathering process needs to identify those literatures, extract the most important data from them, index and abstract those data according to their strategic impact, and provide for periodic assessment of their import.

- Funding Sources
- Consortial Contexts
- Suppliers
- Legislation
- Technological Developments

Persons

Good, updated information on persons may be the most important data in the strategic library director's portfolio of strategic management tools. The library manager interacts with many persons who have a stake in the library's operation: trustees, elected officials and their staffs, key colleagues in other government departments, influential citizens, formal and informal community leaders, community gatekeepers, Friends of the Library, library volunteers, representatives of the media, business people, clergy, educators, known library supporters and detractors, and professional colleagues from outside the community. Managing these relationships is complex. An electronic data file can help to organize this effort and also provides the means for creating customized mailing lists as needed.

A data file on persons serves as a means for management of planning efforts, for identifying the roles of individuals, and for communication with them. Each record in the file should include data for name, title, address, telephone number, and links to all other files (community programs, facilities, projects, and external environment). The linkages to other files, in a relational database structure, permit bringing together relevant data for each person that is contained in them, without redundancy or inconsistency.

Among the fields that can be included in this file are assessments of political positions—identification of "players" and of the bases for their interests (including defined responsibilities, existing capital commitments, personal priorities, and interpersonal relations). These data provide the basis for assessing the technical effects of political positions with respect to design decisions and resource commitments, and for assessing means for their resolution. Admittedly, this concept is sensitive and fraught with potential difficulties. If properly handled, though, it provides a most important component of strategic management.

Community Agencies

The purpose of the community agencies data file is to provide means for identifying individual units (schools, public safety, welfare, community development, business and industry, and others). Each record should include data for name, responsibility, budget, staff. Links with the other data files (facilities, projects, persons, and external environment) again permit bringing together relevant data; of special importance is the linkage to the persons file, in the identification of the responsible manager.

External Environment

It may be more difficult to convert information about the external environment to electronic data files. This information is often in the form of planning documents from the centralized local government, census data, newspaper articles, and ephemera of all kinds. The most useful approach might be to index the materials that are relevant to understanding and assessing the external environment in order to be able to retrieve relevant materials as needed. Although somewhat time-consuming, it is also useful in the long run to create digests of the accumulated information about the external environment that has been amassed and to disseminate it to other key members of the library staff. A planning session can then be devoted to discussing the implications of the data for the library and developing alternative scenarios for the library's strategic position.

The data file on the external environment has the purpose to tie in data about relevant literature, technological forecasts, political and societal forces, the status of publishing, and so on. The records provide both bibliographic references and technical details. Again, links to the other files provide means for relating relevant data.

ASSESSMENT OF MANAGEMENT

We turn now to the use of these data files for evaluation of the library's strategic position, first with respect to management.

Structure and Control

Chapter 2 discussed the relevant aspects in assessment of the structure of the library and the means for control—management style, decision-making processes, centralized or decentralized administration, hierarchy or matrix structure, functional or programmatic organization. For the specific situation, of course, those aspects need to be evaluated as objectively as possible so as to identify aspects that are deficient and need change or are exemplary and need support.

Budget and Finance

We have noted in previous chapters the difficulties of making financial predictions in the volatile public sector. The public library is dependent for its annual operating budget on the economic health of its community and on the prevailing political winds. Nevertheless, there are some useful strategic calculations in which a public manager can engage. Financial modeling can at least help the public library director predict the consequences of various budgeting scenarios. The objective of financial planning models is to provide means for assessing the effects of alternative financial policies and of external environments upon the financial structure. Historical financial data, especially for sources and uses of funds, provide the input. A budget model then permits the testing of alternative policies and alternative assumptions about the internal and external factors. Typically, such a model will consist of equations that relate variables (such as costs of processing, costs of acquisition, cash flow as a percentage of costs, means for depreciation of capital investments, liabilities, assets).

There are two stages in the development of effective models for projection of expenditures. The first is the cost model itself; this sets a relation, usually linear, between specific operating parameters and the associated cost projection. In Chapter 9 we will present a detailed model for costing of library operations and services, identifying relevant operational parameters within it.

The second is a set of management considerations, which provide the context for budget projections and for setting confidence limits on the results. The following discusses examples of such management considerations, classified into internal and external managerial elements.

Internal Managerial Elements. These include administrative categories of budget, time periods of support, and levels of funding. The resulting projections serve as the means for overall control of budget. Categories of budget are affected by internal and external policies on appropriate uses of funds and by the level of existing commitments. Time periods are affected by delays in cycle and by whether the funding is recurring or nonrecurring.

Given the projected budgets, based on the programmatic parameters and related managerial elements, library management will then allocate the totality of funds to each administrative unit. They can treat the total budget for each unit as a control figure. The following aspects affect the managerial decisions: carry-forward budgets, carry-forward liens, reimbursables, prudency in management (to avoid overruns), accumulation of funds (to make major purchases). The freedom to use funds in these ways or the extent to which it is circumscribed is crucial to strategic funds management.

External Considerations. There are a number of external considerations that affect the budgeting and expenditure processes: inflation, funding delays, funding mandates, external management decisions and controls, delays in personnel processes.

Risks

The assessment of risks—financial risks, programmatic risks, market risks, administrative risks—is a necessity if strategic management is to proceed with awareness. The assessment of financial risk is relatively straightforward since the data are quantifiable, though that by no means says that it is easy. It requires that projections of costs and income be treated not as fixed quantities but as subject to statistical variation. The financial model should incorporate distributions reflecting such variation; the appendix to this chapter describes one commercial package, an "add-in" to spreadsheets (i.e., a capability added to those built into them), that provides that kind of capability.

More difficult to assess are the nonquantifiable risks. Later in this chapter, we will discuss means for programmatic assessment of collections, collection management, and operational performance. For larger public libraries, with respect to the collections and their management, the state of embrittlement clearly is a matter of risk. Assessment of the market risks (e.g., repercussions from the community) surely are a central part of decisions concerning collection development and operations. But making such assessments today is essentially qualitative, without evident means for modeling even in a descriptive way.

In the same vein, the risks involved in administrative decisions should be assessed, but there are few models to guide assessment of them.

ASSESSMENT OF MARKET AND POSITION

We turn now to a number of existing models that have been developed for the business world, first discussing them in that context and then commenting on the extent to which they are applicable to community libraries.[1] They are descriptive matrices used to display and assess the strength of business position, market, and competition for various products and services. The purpose is to provide an objective basis for resource allocation among constituent business units.

Community Library Context

The interpretation for their application to community libraries will be made at the level of the organization as a whole. But they are equally meaningful for assessment of an individual product or service, so the reader should visualize application in that way as well. To provide a framework for doing so, let's briefly review the community library products and services and the markets for them.

Products and Services. Community library products include (1) acquisition and related services, (2) bibliographic control and related services, (3) management of automated information systems, (4) information management and access services, (5) document delivery services, (6) publication both in bulk and on demand, (7) information staff management and training services, (8) information analysis services, (9) database design and management services, and (10) programs (such as those for children's services).

Markets. The markets for those services from the community library include the general reader, students, persons from business and industry, staffs of community government and public service agencies, information brokers, persons in professional practice, and other libraries.

The BCG Growth-share Matrix

This matrix model (identified with the Boston Consulting Group, hence the acronym) was developed during the 1960s as a simple method for analysis of the strategic position of companies.

The Business Interpretation. Underlying the BCG model are two assumptions: Growth in a market implies it is desirable to invest in it; gaining a large share of a market implies a strong position. Growth is used as the primary determinant because it is argued that in growing markets it is easier to gain market share; a

Figure 7.1
Categories of Business Units

Growth of Market

		High	Low
Share	High	Stars	Cash Cows
of			
Market	Low	Problems	Dogs

given market share increases in value as the market grows; demand is likely to exceed supply, supporting higher prices and profits. Market share is used as the measure of strength because firms with a large share enjoy advantages of size— economies of scale, dominance, strong bargaining positions. They will gain experience faster and can therefore reduce their costs more rapidly, exploiting what is called the "experience curve."

These rationales derive from analyses (called PIMS, for "profit impact of market strategy") of a database generated by General Electric in the early 1960s; it covered over 2,000 business units in over 200 firms. One analysis showed a virtually linear relationship between market share and return on investment. Another showed that highly capital-intensive companies do not have high return on investment (precisely because of the high capital investment, but also because of high competition).

The model easily divides business units into four categories (see Figure 7.1), based on high or low growth versus high or low share. The most superficial strategy is to move cash from the Cows to the Problems. A more complex strategy is to examine the Dogs to determine whether a shift of focus might not move them into the higher share categories; generally, though, the view is that it is best to liquidate them.

There are serious problems with the BCG model. The model is sensitive to the measure used—past growth versus predicted future growth—and the basis for classification into high or low. The model is sensitive to definition of product and market—scope, focus, already served or newly to be served, categories of customers. The analyses are sensitive to subjective judgments.

Community Library Interpretation. Is it meaningful to apply the BCG model to community libraries? On the surface, it would seem that the answer is a resounding NO. Virtually every aspect seems alien and inappropriate, if not totally contrary to experience. Specifically, markets for community library products and services are essentially stable, at best growing at rates comparable to general population growth. The "experience curve" has been almost fully traversed by community libraries; as a result, they already are efficient throughout their operations. Community libraries are, by their very nature, exceptionally capital-intensive; indeed, the investment in collections and in the means for access represents about one-third of their yearly budget, a commitment much greater than even the high technology industries.

Figure 7.2
Potential Strategies—Industry Attractiveness Model

Industry Attractiveness

		High	Medium	Low
	High	Invest	Invest	Selective
Business Position	Medium	Invest	Selective	Divest
	Low	Selective	Divest	Divest

The last point is especially relevant. The share of the market for community library products and services, as measured by statistics of use, is high in comparison with that for computers and commercial services. Given the low growth rate, the BCG matrix would suggest regarding them as "cash cows," but the PIMS analysis shows that there will not be high return on investment in capital-intensive industries, whatever the market share.

Industry Attractiveness/Business Position Matrix

A second descriptive matrix generalizes from the BCG model. A mix of measures is used to identify "industry attractiveness"—size, growth, customer satisfaction, competition, price levels, profitability, technology, governmental regulation, economic sensitivity. These are all evaluated in terms of return on investment. In the same vein, a mix of measures is used to characterize "business position"—size, growth, share, customer loyalty, profit margins, distribution, technology skills, patents, marketing, flexibility, organization.

The Business Interpretation. The basic model, of course, isn't different, and the resulting strategies are generally variants of those for the BCG model (see Figure 7.2).

Community Library Interpretation. This model is far more appropriate than the BCG model, since the mix of measures begins to incorporate some that are very meaningful to community libraries.

The market size is easy to determine and can be evaluated for consistency with expenditures (as reflected in percentage of community budget, for example); its growth rate is easy to determine and relevant to decisions. The customer satisfaction is measurable in many ways, and for most community libraries is very high. There is little direct or indirect competition. Price levels and profitability, while not directly applicable, are representable by expenditures. Technology has been well absorbed by community libraries, in exceptionally effective and efficient ways. Governmental regulation is a problem in the areas that have been discussed in Chapter 6, but it affects any competition at least to the same extent. There is great economic sensitivity, especially in the current environment.

With respect to business positions, community libraries are not large com-

Figure 7.3
Potential Strategies—Directional Policy Model

Industry Attractiveness

		High	Medium	Low
Business Position	High	Leader	Grow	Generate Cash
	Medium	Try harder	Proceed Carefully	Phased Withdraw
	Low	Quit	Phased Withdraw	Withdraw

ponents of the community; their budgets will probably be less than 1 percent of total community expenditures. The share of the community market and customer loyalty are both high. The means for distribution are highly effective, as are the technology skills. There is the strength of professional identity, a proprietary position virtually equivalent to a patent. The tools for marketing of services are excellent. There is strength and flexibility in organization. In other words, the range of measures for both market and position are relevant and measurable. The current assessment for community libraries must be *high* on both Industry Attractiveness and Business Position, which argues for Invest.

Directional Policy Matrix

The Business Interpretation. Another modification of the BCG model adds refinements—more quantification and specificity in recommendations. For the first, weights are developed to translate the qualitative assessments of the BCG and ''industry attractiveness/business position'' models into quantitative measures. For the second, the three alternatives (Invest, Selective, Divest) are replaced as shown in Figure 7.3.

Community Library Interpretation. Since this model builds upon the ''industry attractiveness/business position'' model, it also can be applied to community libraries. Of course, the use of weights to emphasize the relative importance of the several component measures for the two dimensions adds greatly to the richness of representation. It does mean, though, that essentially qualitative issues will be almost artificially translated into quantitative ones. The weights of necessity will be subjective and even political. The value, though, is that this model provides means for dealing with those kinds of issues.

Three-Dimensional Model: Attractiveness, Position, Competition

Another generalization of the BCG model adds a third dimension—the level of competition—to those of market and position. At its simplest, it presents an array of eight cells (see Figure 7.4).

The Not-for-Profit Interpretation. For each cell, there is traditional wisdom

Figure 7.4
Potential Strategies—Three-Dimensional Model

Market Attraction

		High			Low	
		Competition			Competition	
		High	Low		High	Low
Business Position	High	1	2	High	5	6
	Low	3	4	Low	7	8

about the appropriate choice of options in the business community. Of more immediate importance here, though, are the interpretations that apply to not-for-profit agencies in general, since community libraries would appear to fall into that group.[2]

In not-for-profit agencies, the "competition" arises from alternative agencies that either provide similar services or are in principle capable of doing so. For example, a welfare agency may provide job counseling services, but the local school district and community college may be able to do so as well; it may provide referral services, but the local public library may do so as well.

The appropriate strategies to adopt for each of the eight cells shown above are as follows:

Cell 1: Negotiate from strength with the alternative agency, dividing programs as most appropriate to the missions of both agencies. It is of some interest to note that this strategy is *not* one generally available to commerce and industry because of the constraints of the Sherman Antitrust Act; indeed, it may not be available to some not-for-profit organizations.

Cell 2: This is obviously the ideal position. The imperative is to consolidate the position and to expand as aggressively as possible in order to preclude potential entry of competitors in the future.

Cell 3: Under these conditions, there really is no reason for the agency to consider the service or to continue it if already providing it. Divestment of services in which the agency is noncompetitive is usually a painful choice, but it may result in strengthening the agency in the remaining areas of service.

Cell 4: If the programs are truly attractive, the obvious strategy is to commit the resources to create strength and move the agency into Cell 2. If the resources for doing so are not available, the alternative strategy is to assist other agencies in developing strengths.

Cell 5: With low market attractiveness, competing strengths become nonproductive, so the strategy is to deliberately transfer programs together with expertise to the strongest competing agency, assisting them as may be most effective.

Cell 6: This may well be the most difficult of the strategic contexts, since the agency with strength may be the only means for meeting very real needs. The strategy must be to make a most careful evaluation of mission and of the degree to which the activity is central to it.

Cell 7: The strategy is clear: Get out fast, though responsibly. The activity may be important enough to warrant assuring that it is transferred to the strong alternative agency in an orderly, effective manner.

Cell 8: What are we doing here? Clearly, someone has failed to assess the importance of an activity, the resources needed to serve it, the demand for it.

Community Library Interpretation. This model looks exceptionally valuable for application to community libraries, especially as the assessments of market and position use an enriched set of criteria for evaluation. The importance of information in the community implies that the market attraction is *high*, and the strength of community libraries in general implies that their business position is *high*. The result is that the order of priorities for consideration of alternatives should be cells 1, 2, 3, 4. Of course, the assessments of market, position, and competition will need to be made by each particular library.

ASSESSMENT OF COMMUNITY LIBRARY OPERATIONS

Collections and Collection Management

We now turn from models developed in the business world to those that are more specific to community libraries.[3] They provide means for assessment of the relationships among products and services, missions, and markets.

The book collection of a library, the data files of an indexing or abstracting service, the contents of an archive—these are the basic capital resources for any information system.

Measurement and evaluation of the individual collection, of the policies for its development, and of its management are basic to management decisions about what will be acquired, what means are appropriate for organization of them and access to them, where the materials will be stored, what materials need to be preserved, and in what form. Assessment of the collections of groups of libraries or other information communities are essential in large-scale management decisions.[4]

There are several models for collection assessment and evaluation:

Formula Approaches. The use of formulas, the most well-known of which is the Clapp-Jordan formula for academic libraries, is one approach.[5] It identifies variables that characterize the programmatic objectives of a collection (such as numbers of students, faculty, degree programs, etc., for an academic library); it then uses weights for each variable, summing across the set of them to obtain a measure of desired levels of either holdings or additions. Only the largest public research libraries are likely to engage in any comparable approaches to collection evaluation.

User-based Methods. Evaluation methods that tie collections with users are more appropriate for most public libraries. These seek answers to questions such as: How do we know what people are looking for but not finding? Are we really buying the best items available on a given subject? Are we covering more than one or two points of view? building balanced collections according to the interests and needs of as many people as possible? purchasing materials that will outlive the season? Will they be valuable next year? These methods gather information about users—through a survey, a community profile, and an in-house survey.[6]

Output Measures for Public Libraries and its more specialized companion volumes, *Output Measures for Public Library Service to Children* and *Output Measures and More: Planning and Evaluating Public Library Services for Young Adults* provide a number of standardized and tested ways to measure usage of the collection. These include a selection of "fill rates," which measure availability of materials as well as variants of the traditional circulation, in-house usage, and turnover measures.[7]

Operational Performance

The performance of a library or other information system is defined here to be the efficiency (i.e., "cost/effectiveness") in its operation. The significant issues relate to the means for measuring effectiveness and cost. Of special importance is the distinction between those aspects of performance that can be quantified and those that are essentially qualitative.

Delivery of Public Services. The various PLA manuals on output measures present a number of options for quantifying the outputs of public services such as reference and readers' advisory, programs and youth participation. With the addition of good input data, such as salary information, one can develop cost/effectiveness models of these services as well. In the city of Sunnyvale, California, for example, where the city council has adopted a cost-accounting budgeting system, elected officials make public funding decisions based on knowing the relative costs of mounting a weekly series of preschool story hours and sweeping the streets once a week.

Technical Services. Chapter 9 provides a model that can be used for assessment of technical services performance as well as costs.

ASSESSMENT OF COMMUNITY VALUE

A community library functions within the larger community context. It requires tangible expenditures in capital investments (in the collection, in the buildings to house it, and in the equipment needed for processing) and in the operating expenses for staff and services. But the benefits are largely intangible and uncertain, accruing in the long-term future, and not at the time expenditures are made. How does one balance these? There must be some basis for determining the value to the community that will justify the investment it makes in providing information.[8]

Ultimately, a public library's existence depends on its value to the community. Some of this is symbolic or metaphoric value: The presence of a "good" public library demonstrates the community's commitment to cultural and educational values. Therefore, some members of the public will support the public library even though they never use it themselves. Intangible though this is, library directors should not underestimate the "motherhood and apple pie" nature of the institution they manage. What they should guard against, however, is the danger of becoming an "overinstitutionalized" community agency which is valued only for hollow, symbolic values, not for its real, everyday impact on the lives of people.

One effective library director, Marilyn Gell Mason of the Cleveland Public Library, explained that the goal for any public library is to obtain adequate public funding in a volatile political arena. She goes on to say, "The political strategies for achieving this goal include the provision of the highest quality service possible, the effective presentation of budget requests, an understanding of political pressure points, and the ability to mobilize an effective demonstration of power" (p. 115).[9]

The strategies which Mason outlines can be operationalized in a number of ways, many of which have already been discussed in this book. The quality of the library's services can be monitored through techniques such as Total Quality Management or PLA's output measures. Effective use of internal operational data may produce better budget requests. The habit of directing one's vision to the external environment as discussed throughout this book will enhance a director's understanding of political pressure points. It will also enable the director to build coalitions and marshal public support when necessary.[10]

ASSESSMENT OF THE EXTERNAL ENVIRONMENT

Chapter 6 summarizes factors relevant to the assessment of the external environment. While there do not appear to be any models for quantifying or assessing the impact of each environmental factor on the public library, it is still worthwhile to attempt to systematically consider these factors in relation to the library's strategic position in the community. For example, increasing numbers of working mothers combined with stable child care facilities may mean that the library is faced with large numbers of unattended latchkey children in the after-school hours. A nonstrategic response to the latchkey children might be to develop policies and practices banning them from the library. While this might, in fact, be the appropriate decision, a more strategic response would be to first assess the political capital and community support that would accrue from such an array of alternative approaches to the latchkey children. An assessment of such environmental factors, combined with a rational assessment of the library's resources, should determine the library's actions.[11]

APPENDIX

Generic Computing Software

Spreadsheet software is a powerful tool for making the various assessments identified in this chapter.

Database software is crucial to the maintenance of the basis data files identified at the beginning of this chapter.

Specific Commercial Computer Software

InfoMapper is a software package that provides means for maintaining databases in a manner especially appropriate to strategic management.[12] It uses an array of database structures together with means for organization of the stored data and reporting from them. The result is an exceptionally valuable tool, worthy of consideration by anyone with responsibility for management of strategic planning. The reports that can be derived permit the information resource manager to identify who does or does not use materials that would be of value to their respective responsibilities. As a result, areas of lack, of overlap and duplication, or of potential sharing of information can be made evident.

Basic data about information resources, the users, and the relationships between them are entered to provide the basic record from which all other operations and results are developed. The range of resources is unlimited, encompassing internal documents (technical and administrative reports, correspondence, files, etc.) and external sources from print publications to electronic databases and on-line services.

@RISK dramatically extends the ability to use Lotus 1-2-3 spreadsheets for "what if" analyses.[13] It does so by providing means for assessing effects on critical dependent variables of statistical variability in data from which they are derived. It thus brings to the microcomputer a powerful, even essential tool for risk analysis.

The program provides an array of thirty-four @functions to supplement those that are standard in Lotus 1-2-3 spreadsheets. Each @function represents a statistical distribution for the data in the cell in which it is stored. In normal spreadsheet operation, the value delivered by the @function is the "expected value" (or mean) for the distribution, so that the effect is identical to that resulting from storage of the expected value itself.

The power that is available, though, is spectacular. *@RISK* provides means for automatically sampling the distributions stored in cells so that the effects of their statistical variability upon a criterion variable can rapidly be determined. The commands available permit the user to control simulation of large numbers of such sampling and then to show graphically what the resulting distribution for the criterion variable(s) would be. The result is a dramatic picture of the risks implied by potential variability in source data.

Appropriate @functions for distributions are recorded in cells of the spreadsheet. For example, they might represent the expected distributions of "Sales" and "Costs," or of "Bond Price" and "Prime Rate." The distribution of a derived value for "Net Revenue" could then result from a calculation based on the combination of distributions for "Sales" and "Costs"; that for determining "Present Value" of a bond, from a calculation based on the combination of distributions for "Bond Price" and "Prime Rate."

Once the appropriate distributions have been entered and @RISK has been attached, simulations can then be run that sample from the distributions and determine the resulting value for the dependent variable. With a single @RISK command specified from the @RISK menu (in standard Lotus 1-2-3 structure), the user can call for a simulation and specify the type of sampling, the number of samples (i.e., iterations) to be taken, and the variable(s) to be evaluated. The results can then be viewed in graphical form as a distribution of the dependent variable together with the usual array of statistics for that distribution, including identification of the expected value, or mean, and of various percentiles. The user thus has a clear picture of the range of values and can qualitatively assess the risk implications.

NOTES

1. Each of the course textbooks listed in note 1 of Chapter 1 has a section devoted to discussion of these models. The following identifies the respective chapter numbers: Aaker, chapter 10; Boulton, chapters 4-7; Certo & Peter, chapter 4; Glueck, chapter 5; Hax & Majluf, chapter 15; Justis, chapter 3.

2. Ian C. Macmillan, "Competitive strategies for not-for-profit agencies," in *Advances in Strategic Management, Volume 1*, ed. Robert Lamb (Greenwich, Conn.: JAI Press, 1983), pp. 61–82.

3. Richard M. Dougherty and Fred J. Heinritz, *Scientific Management of Library Operations* (Metuchen, N.J.: Scarecrow Press, 1982).

4. American Library Association, *Guidelines for Collection Development* (Chicago: American Library Association, 1979); H. W. Axford, "Collection management: a new dimension," *Journal of Community Librarianship* 6 (1981): 324–329; Sheila T. Dowd, "The Formulation of A Collection Development Policy Statement," *Collection Development in Libraries: A Treatise* (Greenwich, Conn.: JAI Press, 1980), pp. 67–87; Martin Faigel, "Methods and issues in collection evaluation today," *Library Acquisitions: Practice and Theory* 9(1) (1985): 21–35; *Guide to Evaluation of Library Collections* (Chicago: American Library Association, 1989); N. K. Kaske, "Evaluation of current collection utilization methodologies and findings," *Collection Management* 3(2–3) (1979): 197–199; F. Wilfrid Lancaster, *The Measurement and Evaluation of Library Services* (Washington, D.C.: Information Resources Press, 1977).

5. Verner W. Clapp and Robert T. Jordan, "Quantitative criteria for adequacy of community library collections," *College and Research Libraries* 50 (March 1989): 153–163; Melvin Voigt, "Acquisition rates in university libraries," *College and Research Libraries* 36 (July 1975): 263–271. (The formula presented in this article, with minor

modification and called the Voigt-Susskind Formula, has been the basis for allocations within the University of California for more than a decade.)

6. William Aguilar, "The application of relative use and interlibrary demand in collection development," *Collection Management* 8(1) (1986): 15–24; Robert Broadus, "Use studies of library collections," *Library Resources and Technical Services* 24(4) (1980): 317–324; Robert W. Burns, Jr., "Library use as a performance measure: Its background and rationale," *Journal of Community Librarianship* 4(1) (1978): 4–11; Dorothy E. Christiansen, C. Roger Davis, and Jutta Reed-Scott, "Guidelines to collection evaluation through use and user studies," *Library Resources and Technical Services* 27(4) (October/December): 432–440; Steven S. Church, "User criteria for evaluation of library services," *Journal of Library Administration* 2(1) (1981): 35–46; F. Wilfrid Lancaster, "Evaluating collections by their use," *Collection Management* 4(1–2) (1982): 15–43; Manuel D. Lopez, "The Lopez or Citation technique of in-depth collection evaluation explicated," *College and Research Libraries* 44(3) (1983): 251–255; Christopher Millson-Martula, "Use studies and serials rationalization: A review," *The Serials Librarian* 15(1–2) (1988): 121–136; Philip M. Morse, "Measures of library effectiveness," *Library Quarterly* 42(1) (January 1972): 15–30; Susan K. Nutter, "Online systems and the management of collections: Use and implications," *Advances in Library Automation and Networking* 1: 125–149; Beverly Obert, "Collection development through student surveys and collection analysis," *Illinois Libraries* 70(1) (1988): 46–53; Charles B. Osburn, "Non-use and user studies in collection development," *Collection Management* 4(1–2) (1982): 45–53; Bart Sarloe, "Achieving client-centered collection development in small and medium-sized community libraries," *College & Research Libraries* 50 (May 1989): 344–353.

7. Nancy A. Van House et al., *Output Measures for Public Libraries*, 2d ed. (Chicago: American Library Association, 1987); Virginia A. Walter, *Output Measures and More: Planning and Evaluating Public Library Services for Young Adults* (Chicago: American Library Association, 1995); Virginia A. Walter, *Output Measures for Public Library Service to Children* (Chicago: American Library Association, 1992).

8. Robert M. Hayes, "The management of library resources: The balance between capital and staff in providing services," *Library Research* 1(2) (Summer 1979): 119–142; Robert M. Hayes and Timothy Erickson, "Added value as a function of purchases of information services," *The Information Society* 1(4) (December 1982): 307–338.

9. Marilyn Gell Mason, "Politics and the public library: A management guide," in *Politics and the Support of Libraries*, ed. E. J. Josey and Kenneth D. Shearer (New York: Neal-Schuman, 1990), pp. 112–123.

10. E. J. Josey, "Building Coalitions to Support Library and Information Services," in *Politics and the Support of Libraries*, pp. 241–250.

11. Frances Smardo Dowd, *Latchkey Children in the Library and Community: Issues, Strategies, and Programs* (Phoenix: Oryx, 1991).

12. Robert M. Hayes, "InfoMapper," *Information Today* 9(8) (September 1992).

13. Robert M. Hayes, "@RISK," *Information Today* 9(8) (September 1992).

8

Visualizing the Future

Busy managers rarely have the time to sit and think about the future. Yet that is precisely what strategic management requires. Strategic management looks outward and forward, often building on what is known about the past as it anticipates the future. In this chapter, we suggest some methods for forecasting. Admittedly, this can be as much art as science. In lieu of consulting a crystal ball, we suggest some quantitative and qualitative techniques for visualizing alternative future scenarios for the public library.

Beyond the value of these methods in providing guidance to strategic management of the public library is the opportunity they each provide for involving the community in the issues that must be considered. The result is that both individuals and groups gain a sense of participation, an increased awareness of the importance of the library, and a feeling of involvement in the process of decision making. Thus, even the process of collaborative construction of future scenarios for the library can add to the library's value in the community.[1]

QUANTITATIVE FORECASTING

It is beyond the scope of this volume to provide technical details about the rich array of mathematical techniques for quantitative forecasting. For those, the reader will need to turn to appropriate texts.[2] However, there is value in providing a brief descriptive overview of the means that are available.

Methods

Extrapolation from Past to Future. The most evident means for quantitative forecasting is Time Series Projection. It uses historical data to identify alternative models—trends, moving averages and smoothing, seasonal variations. The appendix describes one available commercial computer package providing extensive capabilities for time series analysis.

Simulation. A simulation depends upon having a model of relationships among variables that characterize the system or situation being studied. For example, the relevant variables may include ones that represent the internal resources of the library—its collection, its staff, its computer equipment—from which the model can derive measures of production. They may include ones that reflect the policies of the library—for collection development, for access allocation decisions, for delivery of services—from which the model can derive effects of different policies. They may reflect the nature of the market or constituencies served—their needs, the frequency of request, the required response times—from which the model can predict the effects of differing market demands.

Chapter 9 provides a basis for simulations of at least parts of these variables—especially those related to internal operations and to policies. The Lotus 1-2-3 add-in, *@RISK*, described at the end of Chapter 7, provides a powerful means for implementing simulations within spreadsheets.

Sources of Data

Predicasts. This is a valuable source of data for input to models for decision making.[3] It draws upon sources in which predictions are made about future events.

Co-Works Foundation Pack. The commercial package described in the appendix to this chapter provides access to a wide range of economic and demographic time series.

Reported Library Statistics. The public and state library groups each provide yearly reports of representative data about their respective libraries.[4] As will be illustrated in Chapter 9, these can be used both for formulation of models and for testing of them.

Statistics of Use. The most evident data are statistics derivable from actual operations of a library. There are two flaws or deficiencies. First, they represent only the users, not the nonusers. Second, they reflect the specifics of the information system rather than those of the users; as a result they embody the perceptions of the users about what they can expect rather than of what they need. Despite those deficiencies, though, statistics do provide an objective set of data on which to base estimates of user needs and characteristics.

Monitoring and Analysis of Use Logs. Of special value with respect to data about use is the fact that automated systems provide easy means for monitoring operations, acquiring data in the form of "usage logs" (limited only by the requirements of privacy for the individual user).

Problems

Reliability of Data. All sources of data are subject to inaccuracy in measurement, inconsistency, and general unreliability. The problems with published data in this respect have been thoroughly identified, but in many respects "they are the only game in town" so, if one wants to play, one has to accept the unreliability.[5]

Stability of Models. A technical problem of special importance, but one not generally recognized, is the likelihood that models will be ill-conditioned and, as a result, unstable. To illustrate the effects of such instability, consider the following simple example. Suppose the library consists of four collections (e.g., branches) and that there are four groups of users (e.g., ethnic groups); suppose we have historical data showing the level of use of each collection by each group of users. Such a situation is likely to be represented by a set of linear equations, $A(x) = b$ (see Figure 8.1), where A might represent the historical pattern of use, the distribution of resources among the set of libraries might be given by x, and the use by each ethnic group by b. It can then be used to determine the x that will best serve a given b. But suppose that the measurement of the values for $b = (32,23,33,31)$ is slightly in error and that $b^1 = (32.1,22.9,33.1,30.9)$ is used instead of the real values for b. The model will then produce as its answer a dramatically different result (see Figure 8.2).

Another problem arises from errors in the model. Suppose that the values in the matrix A, representing the decision model, are slightly in error (see Figure 8.3). This problem is potentially even more catastrophic than those due to error in measurement of variables, since one tends to accept the model as given and to be concerned only with assuring that variables are reliably measured.

QUALITATIVE FORECASTING

Questionnaires, Interviews, and Surveys

These are self-evident means for determining needs, independent of data about the library itself, though usually they may focus on the library as the context for assessment of needs.

Typically, questionnaires, interviews, and surveys will ask respondents to identify and assess the relative importance of a number of alternative sources for needed information.[6] In Chapter 5 a matrix model was presented as a means for organizing the responses. In virtually every case, the response to such a question will identify, in order of use, friends, professional advisors, and current reading. Libraries will be ranked anywhere from number four to number seven.

Figure 8.1
An Example of an Ill-Conditioned Matrix

$$
\begin{array}{cc}
A & x = b \\
\begin{bmatrix} 10 & 7 & 8 & 7 \\ 7 & 5 & 6 & 5 \\ 8 & 6 & 10 & 9 \\ 7 & 5 & 9 & 10 \end{bmatrix} & \begin{bmatrix} x_1 \\ x_2 \\ x_3 \\ x_4 \end{bmatrix} \begin{bmatrix} b_1 \\ b_2 \\ b_3 \\ b_4 \end{bmatrix}
\end{array}
\qquad
\begin{array}{cc}
A & x = b \\
\begin{bmatrix} 10 & 7 & 8 & 7 \\ 7 & 5 & 6 & 5 \\ 8 & 6 & 10 & 9 \\ 7 & 5 & 9 & 10 \end{bmatrix} & \begin{bmatrix} 1 \\ 1 \\ 1 \\ 1 \end{bmatrix} \begin{bmatrix} 32 \\ 23 \\ 33 \\ 31 \end{bmatrix}
\end{array}
$$

And such a result should not be surprising, though usually the librarian is disappointed if not shocked to be considered so infrequently.

These methods are simple to use and can be very effective, especially for the small public library. A well-prepared questionnaire distributed in the community can not only provide insight into expectations but can encourage participation. It can help resolve issues related to needs for new services and materials. The critical incident method for interviewing encourages people to talk about their own experience in ways that will involve them in positive interaction with the public library.

High school students can be enlisted as volunteers to hand-carry the forms to retirement centers, where the elderly citizens will appreciate the interest shown by their involvement.

Key Informant Interviews. Key informant interviews are, as the name implies, ones with people whose opinions are likely to be key or particularly relevant to the topic you are researching. These are not randomly selected people, but individuals who are selected specifically for their expertise or position. If the library is trying to understand possible trends in homelessness in the community, for example, key informants to interview might include social workers, employment counselors, and mental health professionals. These same informants might be able to offer guidance for policies and practices that would respond positively to the information need and lifestyles of homeless people.[7]

Focus Groups. Focus groups have long been used in applied social science and market research as a means of generating usable data from a small group of individuals. A focus group is an in-depth interview of a sample group of eight to twelve people that represent a larger target group. The interview is focused on a single topic. A public library trying to envision the future impact of a new industrial park, for example, might conduct a focus group with representative tenants to determine what they expect their business information needs to be.[8]

Future Studies

Three techniques for what are called "Future Studies"—simulations, scenarios, and Delphi studies—will be discussed later in this chapter. Of special value is the use of these methods to involve the community in library planning. The scenario method, for example, should have appeal to the entire range of ages, and it provides a means for interaction among different groups in very positive

Figure 8.2
The Effect of Errors in the Result Vector

$$
\begin{array}{ccc}
A & x' & = \quad b'
\end{array}
$$

$$
\begin{bmatrix}
10 & 7 & 8 & 7 \\
7 & 5 & 6 & 5 \\
8 & 6 & 10 & 9 \\
7 & 5 & 9 & 10
\end{bmatrix}
\begin{bmatrix}
9.2 \\
-12.6 \\
4.5 \\
-1.1
\end{bmatrix}
\begin{bmatrix}
32.1 \\
22.9 \\
33.1 \\
30.9
\end{bmatrix}
$$

and creative ways; simulations can be exciting as means for exploring the effects of alternative decisions; the Delphi Technique can be a powerful tool in identifying important differences.

In using these methods, the public library might be able to gain the cooperation of other community services. For example, teachers in local high schools might use them as class assignments, in social studies or mathematics classes. The city council will find each of the methods valuable in eliciting community involvement in setting goals and objectives for information services.

Critical Incident Technique. The "critical incident technique" (CIT) is an especially effective form of interview. In it, the interviewer asks the respondent to think of a *specific* incident (the critical incident) in which an information need was particularly significant. It then explores three aspects of the critical incident: the "antecedent" context for the need, the means by which the need was or was not satisfied, and the outcome.

The respondent is asked to supply information of a demographic nature, providing details about himself or herself, about position and responsibilities, about knowledge and experience. The CIT then involves a series of carefully structured questions designed to elicit data on which the nature of needs can be identified and classified; that provides the means for exploring antecedents or the context for the critical incident. The CIT then asks about the means for getting the needed information. Again, a list of typical sources may be provided, also openended so as to encourage additions or redefinitions. Questions will explore whether the respondent used the sources directly or used an intermediary of some kind.

Finally, the CIT examines the effect of the information obtained upon resolution of the antecedent need. Did it meet the needs? If so, in what way, and if not, why not? What was the outcome for the critical incident and what role did the information received play in that outcome?

Of course, as with any of the methods for determining user needs for information, data acquisition through the CIT interview is only the first stage. The set of interviews must then be analyzed, and a taxonomy of needs will be derived.

Simulations. While simulations appear to be quantitative, they provide powerful means for qualitative study of the future. In particular, they permit one to explore hypothetical futures, to determine the implications of alternative models, to evaluate the effects of variation in data, to assess the effects of different

Figure 8.3
The Effect of Errors in the Matrix Itself

$$
A'' \qquad\qquad x'' = b
$$

$$
\begin{bmatrix}
10.00 & 7.00 & 8.10 & 7.00 \\
7.08 & 5.04 & 6.00 & 5.00 \\
8.00 & 5.98 & 9.89 & 9.00 \\
6.99 & 4.99 & 9.00 & 9.98
\end{bmatrix}
\begin{bmatrix}
-81 \\
137 \\
-34 \\
22
\end{bmatrix}
\begin{bmatrix}
32 \\
23 \\
33 \\
31
\end{bmatrix}
$$

policies. A spreadsheet provides a simple example of such uses in its ability to make "what if" assessments. A more powerful example with spreadsheets is represented by the use of the add-in *@RISK* for risk analysis.

One important strategic management use of simulation is for contingency planning. It allows the manager to see what the effects of change, for example, in funding or in demand, will be and to explore alternative responses to them. Another is for assessment of operational effectiveness, to assess the extent to which objectives are, or are not, being met by simulating the intended performance and comparing the results with the actual.

Scenarios. Another method for obtaining data from the persons with a stake in the design and implementation of a system is the use of "scenarios."[9] While usually applied in efforts to predict the future, as is the Delphi method (to be discussed later), it is equally applicable to policy-making contexts.

The objective is to identify a number of alternative systems, each of which is strategically plausible and makes good operational sense. The alternatives are not expected or intended to be mutually exclusive, but each should depict a radically different set of priorities, objectives, methods for solution, choice of technology, and so on. The effects on users, on management, on operations would presumably be different under each of them. The objective, then, is to determine how actions and choices made by the participants can be affected by each of them and, in the implementation, how each of them can influence the design and development of the system.

Teams are formed from persons who represent the groups or individuals with a stake in the outcome of the design and development process. Each team postulates a strategy and related scenario or descriptive narrative of what will, in its view, meet the needs it has identified. Each team then presents its listing of needs, its postulated strategy, its set of events, and its scenario to the entire group of teams. In this way, all participants gain a wide view of the set of alternatives, of the priorities with which various aspects are viewed.

The final stage is an analysis of the substance from the several scenarios. The result is a basis for assessment of the impact of any final choice upon each of the positions identified. There may be a final reconciliation of views, with the group as a plenary body rather than as team participants.

The Delphi Technique. The "Delphi Technique" is a procedure using sequential questionnaires by which the opinions of experts can be brought to bear on issues that are essentially nonfactual. Its original use was for establishing predictions about the future, with the view that the opinions of experts, especially if they represented a spectrum of informed knowledge, could be combined into useful statistical consensus.[10] That use is still of value in the strategic management of public libraries as a means for assessing the external technological and publishing environment. It is also of value in assessment of political positions. Positions will vary in the extent to which they are supportive of the library strategic interests or resistive to them. They will differ in their effects—their basis, nature, degree of certainty, and degree of importance.

The use of questionnaires rather than open forum discussion is intended to avoid the effects of dominant personalities, of people that could sway or affect the opinions of others simply on the basis of force of argument. Another value of a sequence of questionnaires is the possibility they provide for the experts to assimilate the views of others, to rationalize their arguments, to incorporate the evidence of the results from one questionnaire in responding to the next one. The underlying rationale is that even experts are uncertain in their views when faced with nonfactual issues and will modify those views based on rational— or perhaps even not so rational—responses to what other experts appear to conclude about the same or related issues.

The process is facilitated and the effects are amplified if face-to-face discussion occurs between successive questionnaires. In that way, discussion can be based upon the statistical results from prior questionnaires, and later ones can benefit from the arguments presented during the discussion, but will be sufficiently removed from the impact of personality to permit the individual's own knowledge and experience to be dominant in the answers.

With that as the general frame of reference for the Delphi process, it seems eminently suitable for dealing with issues of policy formulation, perhaps even more appropriate for them than for the more usual applications to predictions (since, in a sense, predictions become matters of fact, not opinion, while matters of policy remain forever nonfactual). Beyond that, however, it provides a means for dealing with political factors in the process of strategic management.

APPENDIX

Co-Works Time Series Library provides a source of time series data together with powerful display and analysis tools. It functions as a Lotus 1-2-3 application program for the display and analysis functions. It can draw upon associated files of over 500 existing individual time series related to economic and demographic data for the United States and regions of the world.[11]

NOTES

1. George D'Elia, Eleanor Jo Rodger, and Carole Williams, "Involving patrons in the role-setting process," *Public Libraries* 30(6) (November/December 1991).

2. Spyros Makridakis and Steven C. Wheelwright, *The Handbook of Forecasting*

(New York: Wiley, 1987); Spyros Makridakis and Steven C. Wheelwright, *Forecasting Methods for Management*, 5th ed. (New York: John Wiley, 1989); Fred S. Roberts, *Measurement Theory with Applications to Decision Making, Utility, and the Social Sciences* (Reading, Mass.: Addison-Wesley, 1979). Encyclopedia of mathematics and its applications, vol. 7; Thomas L. Saaty, *Mathematical Methods of Operations Research* (New York: McGraw-Hill, 1959); Thomaas L. Saaty, *Thinking with Models: Mathematical Models in the Physical, Biological, and Social Sciences* (New York: Pergamon Press, 1981); John W. Tukey, *Exploratory Data Analysis* (Reading, Mass.: Addison-Wesley, 1977).

3. *Predicasts F & S Index United States* (Cleveland: Predicasts, Inc., 1980–); *Predicasts Forecasts* (Cleveland: Predicasts, Inc., 1980–); *Predicasts, Inc. World Casts: Product* (Cleveland: Predicasts, Inc.); *PROMT, Predicasts Overview of Markets and Technology* (Cleveland: Predicasts, Inc.).

4. A number of agencies and organizations collect and publish data about public libraries. The National Center for Educational Statistics produces an annual report of aggregate statistics. State libraries collect and disseminate selected data about individual library operations and performance. Another useful tool is the annual statistical report from PLA's Public Library Data Service. The latter is a compilation of data which is submitted voluntarily by public libraries all over the country; it is a good sample of libraries serving communities over 100,000; smaller libraries are less well represented.

5. Robert M. Hayes et al., "An application of the Cobb-Douglas model to the Association of Research Libraries," *Library and Information Science Research* 5(3) (Fall 1983): 291–326; George Piternick, "ARL statistics—handle with care," *College and Research Libraries* 38 (September 1977): 419–423.

6. Russell Ackoff, *The Design of Social Research* (Chicago: University of Chicago Press, 1953); Abraham Bookstein, "Questionnaire research in a library setting," *Journal of Public Librarianship* 1(1) (1985): 24–28; Meredith Butler and Bonnie Gratch, "Planning a user study: The process defined," *College and Research Libraries* 43(4) (1982): 320–330; Peter Checkland, *Systems Thinking, Systems Practice* (Chichester, England: John Wiley & Sons, 1981); K. Colin, George N. Lindsey, and Daniel Callahan, "Toward usable user studies," *Journal of the American Society for Information Science* 31 (1980): 347–356; Colin Harris, "Surveying the user and user studies," *Information and Library Manager* 5(3) (1985): 9–14; James S. Kidston, "The validity of questionnaire responses," *Library Quarterly* 55(2) (1985): 133–150; Lowell Martin, "User studies and library planning," *Library Trends* 24 (January 1976): 483–495; Barbara B. Moran, "Construction of the questionnaire in survey research," *Public Libraries* 24(2) (1985): 75–76; Ronald R. Powell, *The relationship of library user studies to performance measures: A review of the literature* (Chicago: University of Illinois, 1985); *User Surveys. SPEC Kit 148* (Washington, D.C.: Association of Research Libraries, Office of Management Studies, Systems and Procedures Exchange Center, 1988); *User Surveys and Evaluation of Library Services. SPEC Kit 71* (Washington, D.C.: Association of Research Libraries, Office of Management Studies, Systems Procedures and Exchange Center, 1981); *User Surveys in ARL Libraries. SPEC Kit 101* (Washington, D.C.: Association of Research Libraries, Office of Management Studies, Systems Procedures and Exchange Center, 1984); Constance A. Mellon, *Naturalistic Inquiry for Library Science: Methods and Applications for Research, Evaluation, and Teaching* (Westport, Conn.: Greenwood, 1990); Matthew B. Miles and A. Michael Huberman, *Qualitative Data Analysis*, 2d ed.

(Thousand Oaks, Calif.: Sage, 1994); Michael Quinn Patton, *How to Use Qualitative Methods in Evaluation* (Newbury Park, Calif.: Sage, 1987).

7. The following citations are not specific to key informant interviews, but rather good general guides to interviewing techniques.

Jane B. Robbins, "Interviewing," in *Tell It! Evaluation Sourcebook and Training Manual*, ed. Douglas Zweizig et al. (Madison: School of Library and Information Studies, University of Wisconsin–Madison, 1994); I. E. Seidman, *Interviewing as Qualitative Research: A Guide for Researchers in Education and the Social Sciences* (New York: Teachers College Press, 1991).

8. Thomas L. Greenbaum, *The Practical Handbook and Guide to Focus Group Research* (Lexington, Mass.: D.C. Heath, 1988); Debra Wilcox Johnson, "Focus Groups," in *Tell It! Evaluation Sourcebook and Training Manual*, pp. 161–170; Richard A. Krueger, *Focus Groups* (Newbury Park, Calif.: Sage, 1988).

9. Michel Godet, *Scenarios and Strategic Management* (London: Butterworths, 1987); James Herman et al., "Shaping the 1990s: A new way of looking at the future helps industry participants develop their visions of the next five years," *Computerworld* (27 November 1989): 77–85.

10. Olaf Helmer, *Looking Forward: A Guide to Futures Research* (Beverly Hills, Calif.: Sage, 1983); Olaf Helmer, *The Delphi Method for Systematizing Judgements about the Future* (Los Angeles: UCLA Institute of Government and Public Affairs, 1966).

11. Nicholas Delonas, "The time series machine," *Lotus* (November 1991).

9

Costing Library Operations and Services

Among the most crucial elements of strategic management is a clear picture of costs of library operations and information services.[1] Unfortunately, data reported in the literature vary widely and use widely divergent bases—units of work, inclusion or exclusion of overhead, means for determining data (time and motion study versus full accounting).[2] The result is that there are very few solid, easily replicable methods to support this essential function. In this chapter, we attempt to deal with this lack by presenting a formal approach to costing of library operations and services. The model presented is largely based on one that was developed for academic libraries, but with modifications to reflect the differences and special needs of public libraries.

COSTS OF LIBRARY PROGRAMMING, SERVICES, AND OPERATIONS

Three major categories of library costs need to be distinguished, since they represent substantially different sets of costing problems. First are those costs associated with essentially internal operations; those include what are frequently called technical services (i.e., acquisitions, cataloging, record keeping for serials, physical handling and management of materials), but they also include reader service functions (circulation of materials in particular). Here the workloads are usually controllable and easy to measure; the assignment of staff can be determined almost directly from those workloads.

Second are those costs associated with traditional services to readers; those include use of materials and, especially of reference services. For these areas, workloads are not controllable, since they depend upon the readers themselves and they are not at all easy to measure; the assignment of staff must be based on experience and anticipation of demand.

Third are those costs associated with programming: planning, preparing, publicizing, and presenting programs such as story hours, book talks, author visits, film and video programs, poetry readings, panel discussions, puppet shows, concerts, and so on. This is not peripheral but is a major aspect of a public library's services. A related function is outreach—time spent out in the community, creating goodwill for the library and establishing relationships with significant groups, organizations, and individuals. This is especially significant in public libraries which want to encourage groups that may be underserved, but it is increasingly being seen as a necessary function for all public libraries and all groups they serve. For these functions the costs are largely determined by the commitment of highly qualified professional staff, with special skills in relating to specific groups—children, the elderly, cultural and ethnic communities, those whose native language are other than English, and so on.

The model presented in this chapter is focused on the first two categories of cost. Of course, it would be desirable for programming to be integrated into it, but the problem in doing so is the almost limitless diversity and the lack of data on which to base any general principles. There is one article that deals with costs of children's programming, but that is all that has been identified in this crucial component of public library operations and costs.[3]

FUNDAMENTAL APPROACH TO COSTING

The fundamental approach used in this cost analysis is an ex post facto cost accounting.[4] That is, cost data reported in a wide variety of ways are reduced to a common cost accounting structure. This approach is in contrast to the typical "time and motion study," in which careful measurements are made of the time actually taken for each of a sequence of operations, and to a "total cost" approach, in which reported costs for an operation are taken as a whole and simply divided by the total workload. Finally, it is in contrast to a true cost accounting, in which data are recorded and analyzed in standard cost categories at the time they are incurred.

It is important to recognize the differences among these approaches, since they result in dramatically different estimates of cost that are difficult to reconcile. The most accurate and complete is a true cost accounting based on records at the time costs are incurred and properly allocated. The most detailed will be the time and motion study, but it will usually account for only the most specific costs. At the other extreme, the total cost approach provides no detail and no means for analysis of functions; it is the least accurate of the methods and may grossly misestimate the costs, both under and over, in ways that make it impossible to calibrate. The ad hoc cost accounting approach presented here is an effort to establish a standard means for dealing with quoted costs that will include all components in a framework that permits analysis.

The use of *volunteers* must be considered in estimating the costs of public library operations and services. Historically, they have been of great value to the library, not only providing needed staff but representing a recognition of the importance of the library to the community. Today, though, given the financial strains, they are a vital part of the staffing in public libraries of every size—in the major metropolitan centers, in the neighborhood branches, in the county and regional systems, in the smallest of rural communities.[5]

While it may appear that no costs are involved in the use of volunteers (because no wages are paid), there really are significant costs and they must be recognized. First, and in many respects most important, the time of the volunteer is a real cost; the fact that it is being contributed in no way reduces that cost, it simply changes the source for funding it. It is important not only to recognize the value of that time but to assess what costs would be incurred if paid staff were needed to perform the same work, as they may well be at other times or other places. Second, there are costs associated with the use of volunteers that will, of necessity, be incurred by the library, such as supervision especially, supplies, space, insurance—those costs that in the model presented in this chapter are treated as part of overhead or general administration; the only effective means for assessing those costs is by an adequate accounting of the time donated by the volunteers. The labor is not free, though it may appear to be so, but supervision and related costs are by no means free and they must be paid for.

How then should the services of volunteers be represented in estimation of costs? The answer is simple: Their time should be accounted for as though it were the time of regular, paid staff at the appropriate proportionate FTE (i.e., "full-time equivalent"); their salaries should be accounted for at the level of equivalent regular, paid staff with an appropriate balancing addition to the library's budget. As we move through the successive components of the costing model, therefore, volunteer labor should be considered as though it were part of the regular, paid staff of the library.

ESTIMATES OF DIRECT LABOR

Workload Factors

The model uses a matrix of "workload factors" as the means for estimation of the staff required to handle a defined workload, measured in appropriate "units of work." For each of a set of library functions and subsidiary processes, such units of work have been defined. The workload factors then are expressed as percentages of FTE (yearly full-time equivalent) staff for the performance of

1,000 (K) units of work for each library function and subsidiary process. An equivalent and somewhat more concrete way of expressing the workload factors is the following: One FTE per thousand transactions is equal to 100 minutes per transaction. Thus, .25 FTE per thousand is equivalent to 25 minutes per transaction. This equivalence is a result of the fact that there are almost exactly 100,000 minutes in a working year (i.e., 42 weeks at 40 hours per week at 60 minutes per hour is 100,800 minutes).

The default values currently used in the model are, with few exceptions, identical with those first published in 1974. Since the past twenty years have seen a dramatic change in both technical services and reader services due to use of the computer, the question is whether those default values should not have changed. The evidence from application of the model to data from hundreds of libraries over the past thirty years is that automation does not fundamentally change the efficiency of human operations. What does change is the mix of tasks performed. That is best illustrated by cataloging, in which the mix of original cataloging and copy cataloging has dramatically changed in the past twenty years. The effect of bibliographic utilities has been profound and has led to dramatic reductions in the staffing of technical services.

Even more important, though, is the effect on services and on the users. It permits the library to provide services otherwise inconceivable, vastly increasing the value of the users, and improving its productivity. The result has been increases of staff requirements for providing information services and for educating users in the opportunities provided by the new information technology. It is this that makes the new technology worthwhile.

The model is focused on traditional library functions in acquisition, cataloging, and use of information media, whatever their form may be. But there may be activities within a library that are not well represented by them; there may be special projects that, while parallel to traditional functions, must be separately accounted for; there may be structural effects that are not well represented by the model's workload factors. Each of these should be considered when using the model for assessment of staffing and costs.

Figure 9.1 presents the workload factors providing standard estimates for direct labor in "FTE" per 1,000 transactions, FTE representing the "full-time equivalent" of a working year of 42×40 = 1,680 hours. (The remaining ten weeks of the calendar year provide for holidays, vacation, sick leave, and personal leave.)

The workload factors fall into two major categories—technical services, for which the default values for public libraries are identical with those for academic libraries (though the workloads themselves will be quite different), and reader services, for which the default values as well as the workloads for public libraries are different from those for academic libraries.

It is important to note that the estimates for "Reference" are expressed in

Figure 9.1
Workload Factors (Illustrative Values for Direct Labor)

Category	Level of Staff	Yearly FTE	Units
Acquisitions			
Selection	Professional	0.25 FTE per 1000	titles
Ordering	Clerical	0.20 FTE per 1000	titles
Invoicing	Clerical	0.20 FTE per 1000	titles
Cataloging			
Original	Professional	1.60 FTE per 1000	titles
Copy	Clerical	0.20 FTE per 1000	titles
Maintenance	Clerical, Student	0.25 FTE per 1000	titles
Circulation			
Records	Student	0.06 FTE per 1000	items
Shelving	Student	0.04 FTE per 1000	items
Serials			
Receiving	Student	0.10 FTE per 1000	serials
Records	Student	0.10 FTE per 1000	serials
Physical Handling			
Receiving	Student	0.02 FTE per 1000	items
Labeling, etc.	Student	0.06 FTE per 1000	items
Preservation & Binding			
Identification	Student	0.06 FTE per 1000	items
Assessment	Professional	0.12 FTE per 1000	items
Bibliographic	Clerical	0.40 FTE per 1000	items
Preparation	Student	0.40 FTE per 1000	volumes
Reproduction	Technician	1.50 FTE per 1000	volumes
Treatment (3)	Technician	1.50 FTE per 1000	volumes
Binding	Technician	0.25 FTE per 1000	volumes
ILL Borrowing			
Bibliographic	Professional	0.20 FTE per 1000	borrows
Handling	Student	0.10 FTE per 1000	borrows
Records	Clerical	0.20 FTE per 1000	borrows
ILL Lending			
Bibliographic	Professional	0.05 FTE per 1000	lends
Handling	Student	0.10 FTE per 1000	lends
Records	Clerical	0.20 FTE per 1000	lends
Reference (other than ILL)			
Bibliographic	Professional	0.50 FTE per 1000	hours
Ready	Clerical	0.50 FTE per 1000	hours

units of work different from those for other kinds of processes. "Hours of Desk Service," as shown here, may be the appropriate unit of measure, and in testing of a spreadsheet model it will be used, but with many reservations about doing so. Similarly, the units of work for "Information Skills"—exemplified by bibliographic instruction—are different from those of other kinds of processes. "Size of population served" has been taken as the measure, and it seems appropriate.

Data from Observation of Library Operations

The generic estimates of workload factors were the result of an iterative process, carried out over many years, in which estimates at a given point in time were matched with actual and/or reported costs for a visited library and operations within it as of that time. If estimates matched library costs to within 10 percent, they were regarded as further confirmed. But if the estimated costs differed substantially (i.e., by more than 10 percent) from the reported ones, they were carefully examined for possible reasons for the differences. Were they caused by flaws in the means for estimation? If so, should they result in changes in the basis for estimation? Did they reflect differences in operations rather than flaws in the means for estimation? If so, should they result in additions to the bases for estimation? Did they reflect real differences in efficiencies? If so, how should the efficiencies be treated?

Data Reported in the Literature

There is an extensive array of published data.[6] On the surface, they appear to be so inconsistent and unreliable as to be valueless. However, by careful evaluation of the basis on which the values are reported—units of work, basis for assessment of time, and so on—it was possible to reconcile differences and produce results that could be calibrated with those from other sources.

Time and Motion Study

Some published data are based on time and motion studies, but to use such data requires recognition of the difference between those results and direct labor time (which the workload factors represent). The crucial point is that the usual time and motion study will not include the wide range of times that are not specifically related to the process under study. A rule of thumb was finally derived for determining direct time from time and motion study data: 1.5/1. That is, if the time and motion time for an operation was measured at 30 minutes, the direct time was taken at 45 minutes.

Analogy

Another means used for developing workload factors was analogy, with the view that comparable tasks should take comparable times. This permits several different sources of data to be compared, even though they may seem to deal with different functions.

Rules of Thumb for Manual Operations

Underlying the workload factors also were a number of rules of thumb for manual operations.[7] However, they are separable from the workload factors and have application in much broader contexts.

Keyboarding. A manual operation is "keyboarding" (which years ago we called typing, then keypunching). How much time does it take to keyboard a given amount of data? As a base rate, we have estimates for typing—60 to 100 words per minute as a time and motion study rate, but sustainable for fairly long periods of time. That would imply rates of keyboarding (counting a word as six characters plus a space) of 25,000 to 42,000 keystrokes per hour. Using my factor of 1.5 for conversion from time and motion study to direct time, that's equivalent to 17,000 to 28,000 keystrokes per hour for eight hours of direct time. That rate assumes keyboarding of straight text, from clean copy, without any decision making or interpretation.

However, typing turns out not to be a good basis for estimating data entry into computer systems, whether by punched cards or by CRT terminals. Here, the experience is more on the order of 10,000 to 13,000 keystrokes per hour of direct time. Again, that rate assumes straight text, from clean copy, without decision making or interpretation. It also assumes a production context, rather than a start and stop context. For a start and stop context, the rate is on the order of 3,000 to 5,000 keystrokes per hour. Similar reductions will be experienced if there are problems with the source data, if many decisions need to be made, if data are largely numerical or tabular.

Error Rates. Persons make errors in keyboarding data. Some errors will be detected at the time they are made and will be corrected immediately; the rule-of-thumb keyboarding rates indicated above include time for such immediate correction. I have no idea what the rate of such immediately detected errors is; it probably varies widely from individual to individual and depends upon context.

For errors that must be detected by proofing (i.e., errors that are not corrected during the original typing), the rule of thumb is 1/1000—one error per thousand keystrokes. There have been studies of the nature of such errors for different kinds of data—numerical and textual. A typical error is interchange; another is doubling one character rather than an adjacent double. (Incidentally, a separate kind of error, not represented in the rule of thumb, is spelling error or grammatical error.) Data from OCLC suggests that the error rate after proofing is on the order of 1/3000—that is, normal proofing will pick up about two errors in three.

Sorting and Filing. Storage of records into manual files usually involves a two-stage process in which a batch of records is sorted into filing sequence and the batch is then merged into the file. For these operations, the following two graphs (Figure 9.2) provide bases for estimation.

The primary content of these graphs is provided by the following equations:

$$\text{Sorting } \log(T_1) = .2 + .2*\log(B) + \log(B), \text{ or } T_1 = 1.6*B^{.2}*B$$
$$\text{Filing } \log(T_2) = .8 + .2*\log(F/B) + \log B, \text{ or } T_2 = 0.9*(F/B)^{.2}*B$$

where T_1 and T_2 are total times, in seconds, respectively to sort and file a batch

Figure 9.2
Estimates of Time per Item for Sorting and Filing

SORTING TIME, per Item in a Batch
as a Function of (Batch Size)

log(Time per Item) = .25 + .25*log {(Batch Size)}

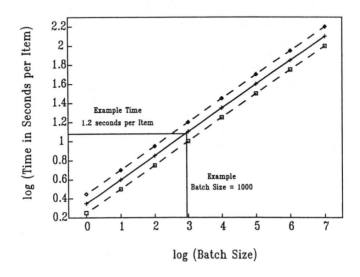

log (Batch Size)

FILING TIME, per Item in a Batch
as a Function of (File Size)/(Batch Size)

log (Time per Item) = .75 + .25*log {(File Size)/(Batch Size)}

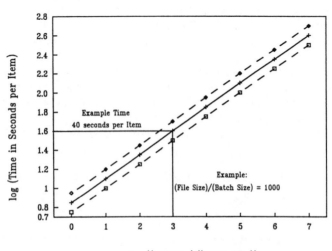

log {(File Size)/(Batch Size)}

of size B into a file of size F. To illustrate, consider the task of filing 100 cards into a catalog of 100,000 cards: B = 100, F/B = 1,000.

$$T_1 = 400 \text{ seconds, } T_2 = 1,380 \text{ seconds}$$

Actual times are subject to wide variation around these nominal values, by a factor from .8 to 1.2; for the example, the range of likely times would be from 320 to 480 seconds for sorting and from 1,100 to 1,650 seconds for filing.

The logarithmic relation between time and batch size for sorting is well recognized in machine sorting; the logarithmic relation between time and the ratio of file size to batch size for filing is not recognized and may not be valid. However, these rules of thumb have served well for estimating time for these kinds of tasks.

Searching Time. The time for searching a file for an item whose ID is known (i.e., whose position in the file is known) is taken as the equivalent of filing a batch of one item:

$$\text{Searching } \log(T_2) = .8 + .2*\log(F), \text{ or } T_2 = 0.9*(F)^{.2}$$

Thus, for the example of a catalog of 100,000 cards, the time to find one item would be about 63 seconds, or 1 minute (ranging from 50 seconds to 75 seconds).

OVERHEAD

The next major component of the cost accounting model is "overhead." In general, overhead or, as it is frequently called, "indirect," includes those costs that cannot be directly attributed to "productive work." That in no way means that such costs are not necessary or significant. It simply means that it would be difficult or irrational to attempt to associate them directly with productive work. Supervision, for example, is clearly necessary, but it in no way in itself produces catalog entries, binds volumes, films pages, or does the actual work, whatever it may be. Holidays, vacations, and sick leaves are necessary components of a compensation package, but usually no productive work is accomplished during such time.

The purpose of "overhead" or "indirect costs" is to account for these kinds of costs. A typical rule for doing so is "proportional to direct labor costs," and that is the rule used here. The resulting generic values for overhead are presented in Figure 9.3.

This figure provides two alternative means for presentation of the overhead accounts. It is important to recognize both the differences between the two and the essential equivalence of them. One, which treats "total salary" as the foundation, is typically used in not-for-profit institutions; the other, which treats

Figure 9.3
Alternative Methods for Overhead Allocation

Category	Percentage of Total Salaries	Non-profit Allocation	Commercial Allocation
Total Salaries	1.00 T		
Direct Salaries	0.67 T	1.00 T	0.67 T = 1.00 D
Indirect Salaries . . .	0.33 T		0.67 T = 1.00 D
Salary Benefits	0.14 T	0.14 T	
Overhead Expenses . . .	0.20 T	0.20 T	
Sub-Total		S = 1.34 T	1.34 T = 2.00 D
General & Administrative	0.10 S =	0.13 T	0.13 T = 0.20 D
Total		1.47 T	1.47 T = 2.20 D

"direct salary" as the foundation, is typically used in commercial contexts. Whichever may be used, the total costs (leaving aside allocation of profit or amortization of capital costs) must be the same, if efficiencies are the same. And, with all due respect to the much vaunted efficiency of private enterprise, there is nothing inherent in the tasks here that implies greater efficiency as a result of different means for accounting for costs. For a variety of reasons, though, the commercial accounting model seems to provide a firmer basis for control of operations. Therefore, it is the one used here.

In the following subsections, each of the major categories of overhead will be described and then the relevant data from the site visits will be summarized. It is to be noted that the functions of overhead are as necessary and important to production as are the direct functions.

Personnel Indirect Time

Supervision and Clerical Support. Clearly, any operation must have supervision, and that usually implies clerical support (not clericals as part of direct labor, but in administrative functions). Even a "one person" operation requires planning and scheduling of work, reporting and evaluation of performance, correspondence, and record keeping; in such contexts, supervision and clerical support must be treated as a portion of the single person's time. But in many-person contexts, these overhead items are critical and should be carefully and separately accounted for.

What is the portion of time required for the functions of supervision? Military and industrial experience, over centuries, has established a standard "span of control," represented at the simplest level by the squad—a group of eight to twelve persons under a noncommissioned officer as supervisor. That ratio, of $\frac{1}{8}$ to $\frac{1}{12}$, appears to be quite common and, given no other data, was the original basis for my hypothetical overhead rates, as presented above. The history of examination of libraries generally confirmed the validity of that ratio of supervisors to direct staff FTE.

However, the data from several libraries visited can be used to obtain more immediate factual estimates, both for supervision in general and specific to preservation tasks. Except for the smallest of groups, the ratio was uniformly 12 percent (plus or minus 0.5 percent)—a ratio of roughly one supervisor to eight staff, not far from the military and industrial experience in span of control. In the very small groups, the description of duties clearly shows that persons identified as "supervisors" spend a high portion of time in direct, productive labor, and there is no reason to treat the ratio of supervision time to direct labor time in such circumstances as substantially different from ⅛.

That ratio, though, doesn't recognize the fact that the supervisors are universally paid at higher salaries. As a result, the proportion of salary dollars is dramatically different, being nearly double—about 20 percent. Again, the proportion was quite uniform, differing by at most 0.5 percent either way from 20 percent.

Unallocated Time. In every operation there is time of staff, who may be in principle assigned to direct work, which should be assigned to indirect or overhead time—here called "unallocated" time (i.e., not allocated to direct, productive work). For example, staff attend meetings; they participate in orientation; they must deal with visitors that ask for data about operations and costs; they attend union meetings; they go to professional society meetings; they participate in training programs. There are innumerable demands on staff time that fall into this category.

Unfortunately, there are no practices in libraries to account for it. The kinds of activities involved may or may not be recognized as reducing the time for direct, productive work. Surely, some, such as time to attend professional society meetings, are recognized; but even for them, there is no evident record of the total time commitment. Others, such as time for training and for internal meetings, appear simply to be accepted as part of the workload, even though they clearly are not specific to the workload tasks. Of all of the categories of overhead, it is the one most likely to result in dramatic increases in indirect costs and in reduction in productivity. Given that, it would seem valuable to establish at least some benchmarks for acceptable ranges of values.

Benefit Days. A major set of benefits, of course, are the days for holidays, vacations, sick leaves, personal leaves, and sabbaticals. There are wide variations among these categories, but the modal cluster is clear and narrow. First, the range for holidays is typically from 10 to 13 days, but the evident mode is 11 days per year. Given 260 days total per year (52 weeks at 5 days per week) as the total salary period, at 11 days per year holidays represent 4.2 percent of total salary.

Second, a likely range for vacation time is from 15 to 25 days per year, with a mean at 22 days (about four weeks). For 260 days total per year, that represents 8.4 percent of total salary.

Figure 9.4
Summary of Benefit Days

Category	Days	Percentage of Year
Holidays	11	4.2 %
Vacation	22	8.4 %
Sick Leave	16	6.1 %
Total	49	18.7 %

Third, sick leave and personal leave are usually treated as part of a combined package by most, if not all, institutions even though, in principle, they should not be substitutable. Combined, they cluster around 16 days per year which, for 260 days total, represents 6.1 percent of total salary. Of course, the extent to which these are in fact used varies much more than holidays and vacations, so the actual cost of sick leave and personal leave may be different from the stated policies.

As Figure 9.4 shows, adding all of these together produces a total of 18.7 percent of total salary that must be paid for benefit days for full-time employees.

Benefits

The total range for salary-related benefits is very wide but the modal cluster is clearly defined at just about 25.5 percent of total salary, as is the average. Furthermore, the basis for the quoted values varies from statements in documents on benefits policy to ratios of expenditures. The latter will result, as will be demonstrated below, in substantially lower actual percentages because of the lessened benefits for hourly employees. In any event, the average of 25.5 percent is most representative of the benefits policies.

The categories of benefits (and representative percentages of total salary), though not all of them were necessarily defined by any one institution as part of their benefits package, are shown in Figure 9.5. In each case, the figure reflects the employer's contribution, not that of the employee.

Overhead Supplies

This overhead item is difficult to estimate. Supplies and expenses are treated as a central budget in libraries and not allocated to individual departments in any manner that permits association with either functional activities or even general costs. The result is that there is no basis for estimation of their contribution to overhead, so the model uses a nominal 5 percent of total salary for this category.

Figure 9.5
Categories of Benefits

Social Security	7.50 % salary
Disability	1.00 % salary
Unemployment	0.50 % salary
Fica	3.00 % salary
Life insurance	0.50 % salary
Medical insurance	4.00 % salary
Tuition	1.00 % salary
Retirement	8.00 % salary
Total	25.50 % salary

Space, Maintenance, Utilities

These overhead items are exceptionally difficult to account for. The cost for construction is uncertain; the time period for amortization is undefined; the space allocable to specific functions is uncertain. The cost for maintenance depends upon the nature of the space occupied but is never clearly defined; the basis for quoting the cost of maintenance varies widely among institutions; the extent to which it in fact is provided is uncertain. The charges for utilities are usually buried in institutional budgets; they vary widely and unaccountably by the type of space occupied.

However, estimates are quite focused around a modal value of $150 per square foot. If we use an amortization period of 20 years, that's $7.50 per square foot per year. Estimates of the costs of maintenance are quite narrowly clustered around $5.00 per square foot per year. Finally, data for space occupied by various functions suggests that each person requires about 250 square feet (including both space actually occupied and the necessary "public space"). The result is a cost per year, per person, of $3,125. That is about 14 percent of the average current salary.

Community Overhead

A final potential overhead item is the community overhead. However, important though it is, there are great variabilities in it, great dependence upon the basis for allocation and institutional specifics, and much overlap with the library's own budget. As a result, no effort has been made to estimate either the magnitude of community overhead or the basis for allocation of it.

GENERAL AND ADMINISTRATIVE

Functions

The operation of a major public library requires central administration of a high order, covering a wide range of responsibilities that, by their nature, make no direct contribution to the production of library services or to operations. They are nevertheless essential functions, without which the library could not operate. To be specific, the following typically are included in these "general and administrative" functions:

• Leadership. This clearly is the most significant function in public library administration. It sets objectives, the priorities, the style for the library. It determines how and where resources are needed and will be committed. It creates the working relationship with the institution served by the library.

• Personnel Administration. The functions of hiring, evaluating, promoting, maintaining records on, and in general providing all that is necessary for personnel administration are a fundamental general and administrative (G&A) responsibility. To some extent, the public library may call on the larger community administration for assistance, but in all of the public libraries visited, the library itself provided for all significant aspects of personnel administration.

• Budgeting and Accounting. As multimillion-dollar operations, the public libraries must maintain complete and dedicated services for financial management. Book funds, personnel funds, project funds—all must be carefully and completely accounted for. These must be handled at the G&A level.

• Public Relations and Publicity. Every major library maintains an extensive program of communications, publicity, and public relations. This kind of G&A activity is essential for development of financial support of the library, but it is even more essential to the community because of the central role of the public library in the community's well-being.

• Collection Development. The central library administration plays a substantive role with respect to collection development.

• Other Kinds of Support. None of the libraries visited included any legal counsel services within the library's administration. Instead, each depended upon the legal counsel of the community. Nor were any other specific functions identified as a part of G&A.

Should G&A Be Included in Costing?

With this definition of "general and administrative functions," the question of whether their costs should be included in the cost assessment must be considered. Some would argue that these are costs that will be incurred by the library whether a new system were involved or not. They see G&A costs as fixed and would treat system management costs as "marginal costs," without any allocation of G&A.

The position of this chapter is that G&A costs must be considered and properly allocated, proportionally to the direct and indirect costs involved. The rationales are as follows:

• A new systems project will almost certainly involve a disproportionate time of the central library administration. Initiatives must be developed, proposals must be prepared, funds must be obtained, accounts must be established to manage the funds, personnel must be added, projects must be managed. And all of these take the time of the most expensive staff of the library's operation. They are all add-on tasks, diverting those staff from other priority responsibilities. Those costs are not marginal but real diversions of costs and should be clearly and carefully accounted for.

- If independent operations—such as fee-based services to business and industry—are established to carry out any of the tasks involved, G&A costs will be incurred and will need to be paid for, not as marginal costs but as operational costs. If such alternatives are to be properly evaluated and properly budgeted, they should be compared with equivalent G&A costs in current library operations.

G&A Costs

Among the categories of information this is the most difficult to obtain as unequivocal, uniform data. In some cases, the central administration is defined to include heads of branches or operational departments in ways impossible to separate out. In other cases, the central administration, as defined, may not include all of the G&A functions; yet, it may not be clear where those functions were provided.

However, available data show that G&A—the community librarian's office, to be specific—averages about 15 percent of total operating costs (not counting costs of acquisitions). The range was fairly narrow, and the figure is not dramatically different from the hypothetical one in Figure 9.3.

IMPLEMENTATION OF THE COSTING MODEL AS A SPREADSHEET

The costing model described in this chapter can very easily be put into a spreadsheet for use by individual libraries needing to assess their costs for strategic management purposes. The data involved fall into four categories:

1. Data measuring the workload for each function and subfunction. These data presumably would be derived from operating statistics for acquisitions, cataloging, circulation, and so on. They would then be entered in the spreadsheet for multiplication by the associated workload factors.

2. Data measuring costs. These would relate to salaries and wages of the several levels of staff, to acquisitions, to direct expenses.

3. Data measuring elements of overhead. These would include percentages for supervisory staff, clerical support, estimated unallocated time, benefit time, other benefits, space and utility costs, other indirect expenses.

4. Data representing changes in the values for workload factors. These may be needed to reflect the specifics for the particular library.

Such a spreadsheet with values appropriate to academic libraries has been embodied in a commercial product called *LCM—The Library Costing Model*, which has been sold to several libraries in the United States, Canada, Australia, and Japan.[8]

Changes in the Public Library Version

A prototype Public Library Version of *LCM* has been created. Its central structure, technical processing workload factors, and overhead factors are identical with those for academic libraries. For the reader services functions (circulation and reference, in particular), though, changes are needed in order to deal with the significant differences in public library services compared with those in academic libraries. For the public library version, the changes from the model for academic libraries fall into just two categories. First, there are a few calculations as the basis for estimating workloads in cases for which the workload data are not available; of course, if actual values for the calculated variables are available, they would be used instead. Second, there are changes in the workload factors themselves for Circulation and for Reference.

The first calculation is of Volumes Acquired, since published source data do not present that datum:

$$\text{Volumes Acquired} = (\text{Materials Expenditures})/\$20$$

The basis for that calculation is the available data on average cost per volume. Unfortunately, a comparable calculation for "Titles Acquired" doesn't work because great multiples of copies of a title are acquired, so one must do something else.

The second calculation is of Central Library "Departments" (for those libraries that have central libraries):

$$\text{Departments} = (\text{Holdings} - 50,000*\text{Branches})/150,000$$

This is based on a regression of Holdings against Central Libraries (i.e., whether the library had one or not) and Branches that yielded 50,000 volumes per branch; the choice of 150,000 as the denominator is essentially arbitrary. The rationale underlying this calculation is that it provides a means both to establish the size of the central library collection and to determine a set of functional parameters: (1) number of titles acquired, (2) number of reference stations, (3) amount of reshelving.

The third calculation is for Titles Acquired:

$$\text{Titles Acquired} = \$68,209*\text{Departments}/\$30, \text{ with Central Library, if} > 3,000$$
$$\text{Titles Acquired} = \text{Holdings}/(300), \text{ with NO Central Library, if} > 3,000$$
$$\text{Titles Acquired} = 3,000 \text{ otherwise}$$

This is based on a regression of "Materials Expenditures" against the number of departments and the number of branches which, with R-squared = .72, yielded values of $68,209 for each department and $77,455 for each branch. The rationale is that titles are acquired by the central library, based primarily on the subject coverages of its departments, and that additional copies are acquired for the branches, on a highly selective basis. The choice of 3,000 as the minimum number of titles is arbitrary.

The fourth is for Reference Services:

Central Library Reference Stations = 4*Departments+(Central Circ)/500,000
Branch Library Reference Stations = Branches/4+(Branch Circ)/500,000
Information Skills Instruction = Circulation/500,000

(the reference stations being at 3,000 hours per year each)

This is based on pure conjecture, but the rationale is that central library reference desks require relatively large numbers of staff and that they will tend to be organized around subject departments. Note that, as before, each reference station involves up to 3,000 hours of staffing (i.e., 1.5 FTE) to cover 8 A.M. to 12 P.M.; that may be an overestimate, but it's what is used so as to be as minimal as possible in changing parameters. However, to accommodate small libraries with relatively low circulation, the number of reference hours is calculated as follows: If

(Circulation/100,000) < (Branches + Central + Subject-Departments)
multiply 3,000 by
(Circulation/100,000)/(Branches + Central + Subject-Departments)

The fifth is for Reshelving:

Central Reshelving = 2.4*(Circulation)*(Departments/
(3*Departments+Branches))
Branch Reshelving = 1.2*(Circulation)*(Branches/
(3*Departments+Branches))

This is based on reported data that show ratios as follows:

(Central In-house Use) = 2.4*(Circulation)
(Branch In-house Use) = 1.2*(Circulation)

It assumes that distribution of Circulation will be roughly based on relative size of Holdings in the ratio of 150,000 for Departments to 50,000 for Branches (as used for determining the number of departments).

Turning to the changes in workload factors, only those for Circulation (both

Record Keeping and Reshelving) have been changed. First, the following shows the prior Workload Factors for Circulation:

	Professional	Clerical	Hourly
Records		0.0300	0.0300
Reshelving			0.0200

The Circulation Reshelving subfunction is replaced by two reshelving subfunctions, one for the Central Library (if there is one) and the other for the Branches. Second, the Workload Factors themselves are modified:

	Professional	Clerical	Hourly
Records		0.008	0.008
Reshelving, Central			0.009
Reshelving, Branch			0.006

The rationale for reducing the factor for Record Keeping from 0.03 to 0.0125 is that the record-keeping functions for circulation in public libraries are significantly simpler than those in academic libraries. The rationale for "Reshelving, Central" and "Reshelving, Branch" is that time for reshelving is a complex function of circulation size, batch size for filing, and collection size. Basically, though, the smaller the collection, the shorter the filing time for the same size of batch. The figure of 0.004 reflects the fact that branch collections are substantially smaller than central library collections.

Application of the Public Library Model to Composite Libraries

The prototype has been tested on data from the "Public Library Statistical Report '90" for the 66 largest public libraries (those serving populations from about 150,000 to over 1,000,000). The data are as reported for 1990 so it is important to note that there have been rather dramatic reductions since then;[9] in particular, 14 of these 66 largest libraries—over 20 percent—are in California, and they have been badly hit by the recession during the past five years. Figure 9.6 shows the averages for the relevant parameters for groupings of them into a set of composite libraries and for the average over all of them.

Application of the public library version of the costing model, as described above, to these data produces the following results (see Figure 9.7); columns labeled "Model" are the results from the model; those labeled "Actual," the averages as shown above; and those labeled "Diff Ratio," the difference between the two divided by the smaller.

A separate analysis has been made of all 168 California public libraries (again from "Public Library Statistical Report '90"). The results for the large libraries are consistent with the composites shown above. For the broad range of libraries,

Figure 9.6
Averages of Relevant Parameters for Composite Libraries

NAME	POPULATION SERVED	BOOK HOLDINGS	CURRENT SERIALS	EXPENSES			
				MATERIAL	SALARY	OTHER	TOTAL
Largest-10	2289124	5449800	11183	6678853	24972635	9298218	46463971
Second-10	1024448	1904196	5497	2090352	7678951	4056218	15594485
Third-10	772478	1895032	5409	2653324	9009447	2879321	16680854
Fourth-10	669351	1401457	3886	2431433	7993039	2716725	14563382
Fifth-10	558230	1830338	4734	2791425	8195727	2898972	15184348
Sixth-10	453990	1396141	2840	1267123	4154686	2258133	8788647
Seventh-6	171967	532157	1077	429711	1768624	576856	3074321
AVERAGE	848513	2058446	4947	2620317	9110444	3526349	17192858

NAME	STAFF			SERVICES			
	PROF	NON-PROF	TOTAL	BRANCHES	CIRCUL'N	ILL-LOAN	ILL-BORR
Largest-10	304	745	1049	57	8435420	14503	1343
Second-10	101	228	329	24	4798299	13891	449
Third-10	122	279	401	23	4893681	4610	550
Fourth-10	90	251	341	19	5314244	8197	1315
Fifth-10	95	252	347	20	4007553	9181	330
Sixth-10	55	159	213	15	2339771	9920	2830
Seventh-6	23	54	84	7	769400	2432	135
AVERAGE	113	282	394	23	4365481	8962	993

Figure 9.7
Comparison of Staffing Estimates from Model with Averages for Composite Libraries

ENTRY	Professional FT		Diff Ratio	Total FTE		Diff Ratio
	Model	Actual		Model	Actual	
1 Largest-10	366	304	0.20	853	1049	-0.23
2 Second-10	103	101	0.02	328	329	0.00
3 Third-10	109	122	-0.12	346	401	-0.16
4 Fourth-10	94	90	0.04	337	341	-0.01
5 Fifth-10	113	95	0.19	330	347	-0.05
6 Sixth-10	74	55	0.36	199	213	-0.07
7 Seventh-6	20	23	-0.14	59	84	-0.43
AVERAGE	116	113	0.03	341	394	-0.16

though, the spread is somewhat wider, with only 50 percent of the difference ratios for Total FTE falling within +20 percent and −20 percent.

Figure 9.8 shows the estimate by the model of the distribution of the staff across the set of library technical processing and service functions, as one of the derivative results that can be obtained from the Costing Model. These dis-

Figure 9.8
Distributions of Staff as Estimated by the Model

Entry	–Tech Processes– Coll Mgt	Catalog	—————Reader Services————— Circulate	Reference	ILL(B&L)	General & Admin
1 Largest–10	128	127	282	245	8	63
2 Second–10	40	27	152	77	7	24
3 Third–10	50	35	155	77	3	26
4 Fourth–10	45	30	167	66	5	25
5 Fifth–10	52	37	131	81	5	24
6 Sixth–10	25	16	77	60	7	15
7 Seventh–6	9	5	24	16	1	4
AVERAGE	50	35	141	85	5	25

Figure 9.9
Distributions of Staff between Central Processing and Branches

AVERAGE LIBRARY	Prof	Non–P	Hrly	Total		
Central Tech Proc	15	25	10	50		
Central Depts	45	55	55	155	=	26/Dept
Branches	55	75	60	190	=	8/Branch
Total	115	155	125	395		

tributions of staff among various categories of function permit one even to estimate the distributions of staff between central library operations and branches. To do so, it must be recognized that a major part of the "Coll Mgt" functions are in selection and usually that involves reference staff from both central library subject departments and the branches. Figure 9.9 shows the resulting distributions (rounded from those estimated by the model).

Overall, the staffing of a central library department would seem to be between 25 and 30 FTE; that for a branch, on the order of 6 to 8. As will be discussed next, the reported data from a specific public library shows 110 in central library departments to be divided, for the model, among 5 departments—an average of 22 per department; for branches, 169 FTE are divided among 22 branches—an average of 7.6 per branch.

Application of the Model to a Specific Public Library

The following two tables show the application of the model, as described above, to actual data (in 1994) for a specific library; they illustrate two of the kinds of results provided by the Library Costing Model. The first compares the Professional and Total Staffing FTE as estimated by the model with the reported actual; the second provides a distribution of the FTE estimates for the model by functions.

Entry	Professional FTE		Diff	Total Staffing FTE		Diff
	Model	Actual	Ratio	Model	Actual	Ratio
Total-1994	123.37	118.23	0.04	402.96	386.50	0.04
Central-1994	63.69	69.08	-0.08	147.19	238.79	-0.62

Note that the model's estimate of Total Staffing FTE is substantially less than the Actual, but recognize that the Actual includes staff required to handle the workloads generated by the branches—for central processing in collection management, cataloging, central processing of circulation data, and ILL.

Entry	Technical Services		Reader Services			General
	Coll Mgt	Catalog	Circulate	Reference	ILL(B&L)	& Admin
Total-1994	24.60	11.15	223.26	105.60	8.50	29.85
Central-1994	12.87	10.00	50.83	53.90	8.68	10.90

The latter is especially useful as means for both calibrating and using the model, since it provides a basis for direct comparison of staffing tables for each function. The data provided from the public library is shown in the following table by the entry ACTUAL; the data for Central 1994 are derived by taking the Technical Services staff for the Total System, the Reader Services staff for the Central Library alone, the General and Administrative staff for the entire System, the Borrower Support as 25 percent of the Circulation, and Structural (elements not covered by the model) as 4 for special programs and 29 for fleet services. Comparison of the two is close and provides sufficient confirmation of the applicability of the model to consider its use.

Model Central Assignments

Entry	Technical Services		Reader Services			General
	Coll Mgt	Catalog	Circulate	Reference	ILL(B&L)	& Admin
Central 1994	24.60	11.15	50.83	53.90	8.68	29.85
ACTUAL	34.43		110.00			33.00

Entry	Borrower Support	Central Structural	Total	Branches	Volunteers	System Total
Central	34.49	33.00	246.50	189.65		436.14
ACTUAL	28.18	33.00	238.61	169.16	28.00	435.77

NOTES

1. Lauren Kelly, "Budgeting in nonprofit organizations," *Drexel Library Quarterly* 21(3) (Summer 1985): 3–18; Ann Prentice, "Budgeting and accounting: A selected bibliography," *Drexel Library Quarterly* 21(3) (Summer 1985): 106–112; Gordon Williams et al., *Library Cost Models: Owning versus Borrowing Serial Publications* (Washington, D.C.: Office of Science Information Service, National Science Foundation, 1968).

2. Charles P. Bourne and Madeleine Kasson, *Preliminary Report on the Review and Development of Standard Cost Data for Selected Library Technical Processing Functions* (Palo Alto, Calif.: Information General Corp., 1969); *Pre/Post Implementation Time and Methods Study of Library Public Catalog File Maintenance* (Long Beach, Calif.: CSUC, 15 March 1982).

3. Laurie R. Mielke, "Sermon on the amount: Costing out children's services," *Public Libraries* 30(5) (September/October 1991): 279–282.

4. Robert M. Hayes and Joseph Becker, *Handbook of Data Processing for Libraries*, 2d ed. (New York: John Wiley & Sons, 1972), chapter 4.

5. Rashelle S. Karp, "Volunteers in libraries: An update," in Gerard B. McCabe and Bernard Kreissman, eds., *Advances in Library Administration and Organization*, Volume 11 (Greenwich, Conn.: JAI Press, 1993), pp. 103ff; Stephen Duncombe, "Volunteers in city government: Disadvantages, and uses," *National Civic Review* 74(9) (1985): 356–364; Stephen Duncombe, "Volunteers in city government: Getting more than your money's worth," *National Civic Review* 75(5) (1986): 291–301; James M. Ferris, "Coprovision: Citizen time and money donations in public service provision," *Public Administration Review* 44(4) (1984): 324–333; Benjamin Gidron, "Volunteer workers: A labour economy perspective," *Labour and Society* 5(4) (1980): 355–365.

6. Charles P. Bourne and Madeleine Kasson, *Preliminary Report; Pre/Post Implementation Time and Methods Study of Library Public Catalog File Maintenance*.

7. Robert M. Hayes and Joseph Becker, *Handbook of Data Processing*.

8. *LCM—The Library Costing Model* (Los Angeles: Becker & Hayes, Inc.), 1993.

9. *Public Libraries in 50 States and the District of Columbia: 1990 (E.D. Tabs and data file)*. This ASCII file contains the database documentation including Methodology; User Guidelines for Processing Federal-State Cooperative System (FSCS) Public Libraries Data, 1990; Record Layout for 1990 Public Library Data File; Data Element Specifications for 1990.

FSCS is a cooperative system through which states submit individual public library data to NCES on a voluntary basis. At the state level, FSCS is administered by State Data Coordinators, appointed by the Chief Officer of each state library agency. The State Data Coordinator collects the requested data from all local public libraries and submits these data to NCES. In the 1991 submission year, all 50 states and the District of Columbia submitted data.

The respondents for this voluntary census were the 8,978 public libraries identified in the 50 states and the District of Columbia, by state library agencies. Data were not systematically collected from public libraries on Indian reservations. Data were not collected from military libraries that provide public library services.

One methodological issue in using these data is the time period covered by the data. The FSCS definition for reporting period is the latest twelve months for which data are available for each public library. This definition allows for several different reporting periods within a state and among states. There were nine different reporting periods used by states for these 1990 data. Collectively, these spanned a two-year time period (January 1, 1989–December 31, 1990).

Additional information on public library statistics can be obtained from Carrol Kindel or Adrienne Chute, Postsecondary Education Statistics Division, National Center for Education Statistics, 555 New Jersey Avenue NW, Washington, DC 20208-5652; telephone (202) 219-1371 or (202) 219-1772.

10

The Structure of Community Information Economies

INTRODUCTION

Previous chapters have stressed the importance of monitoring the community and society in which the public library is located. The public library currently occupies a primary, if poorly understood, role as an information distributor. In 1980, Malcolm Getz noted that the instability of public library financing was largely due to widespread ignorance about the social value of the services it provides. Given the increasing volatility of the information economy and the vagaries of political support, the library's social position as information distributor could be diminished. One of the imperatives of strategic public library management is that the library's economic role be both clarified and strengthened.[1]

This chapter presents a simplified model for describing the structure of community information economies as a tool for situating the public library in its strategic place in the community's information economy. As background, this introduction briefly summarizes the large-scale structure of information economies. Details of the model are then presented. The model is illustrated with application to the United States as a whole and then with one community (Los Angeles SMSA). Use of the model is discussed, considering issues of importance in planning, for the community, in general business, and in information industry business.

It is of special significance to public library strategic management as a tool

Figure 10.1
Three-Sector Structure of the Economy, 1860–1990

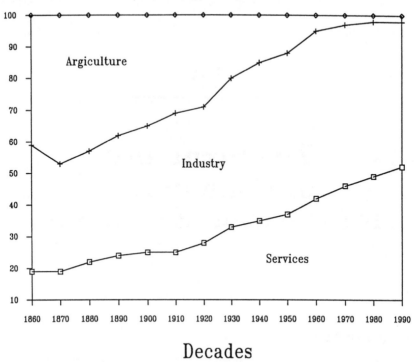

Decades

for assessing the library's position in serving those constituencies as well as assuring that the public in general is well served as the economic structures change.

THE CONTEXT

In his landmark study *The Information Economy of the United States*, Marc Porat replaced the traditional three sectors of the national economy—agriculture, industry, and services—with four sectors, adding an information sector to them (see Figures 10.1 and 10.2).[2]Based on the latter structure, he presented a distribution of the national work force in three major categories: (1) Primary Information Sector workers, (2) Secondary Information Sector workers, and (3) Non-information workers.

The first, the Primary Information sector, included all persons working in organizations whose primary product or service was essentially information-oriented. Illustrative examples of such organizations and activities are listed in Figure 10.3.

The second, the Secondary Sector, included those persons working in all other

Figure 10.2
Four-Sector Structure of the Economy, 1860–1990

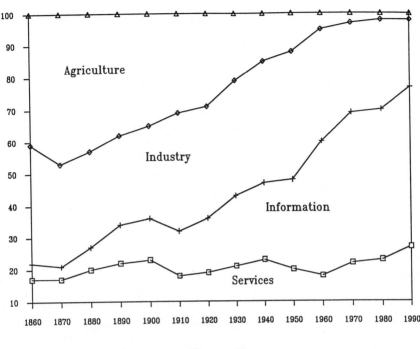

Decades

Figure 10.3
Typology of Industries

TYPOLOGY OF INDUSTRIES
IN THE
PRIMARY INFORMATION SECTOR

Knowledge Production & Invention
Information Distribution & Communication
Risk Management (Insurance, in particular)
Search & Coordination (Brokerage, in particular)
Information Processing & Transaction Handling
Computer & Telecommunications Hardware & Software
A variety of Governmental Activities
Information Support Facilities

Adapted from Porat, THE INFORMATION ECONOMY

organizations but whose activities were also essentially information-oriented. In these two sectors, the functions performed by information workers are essentially the same (see Figure 10.4).

Figure 10.4
Typology of Information Workers

TYPOLOGY OF INFORMATION WORKERS	
o INFORMATION PROCESSORS	Administrators & Managers Process Controllers Computing Center Staff
o INFORMATION PRODUCERS	Scientists & Engineers Information Gatherers Authors
o INFORMATION DISTRIBUTORS	Educators Market Coordinators Consultants Librarians
o TRANSACTION HANDLERS	Postal Workers Communications Workers Clerical & Accounting Staff Banking Staff

Figure 10.5
Distribution of the National Workforce

	NON-INFORMATION FUNCTIONS	INFORMATION FUNCTIONS
NON-INFORMATION INDUSTRIES	Non-Information Workers ———— 50%	Secondary Sector Information Workers ———— 25%
INFORMATION INDUSTRIES	Primary Sector Information Workers ———— 25%	

The Porat study has shown that over 50 percent of the nation's work force today is engaged in information-related activities, almost equally divided between the primary and secondary information sectors (see Figure 10.5).

Structure of Information Industries

Within each subsector, information products and services can be roughly, but usefully, classified into five components (see Figure 10.6) with obvious parallels across the subsectors:

• Information Production
• Information Distribution
• Transaction Management
• Information Hardware and Software
• Supporting Facilities and Services

Figure 10.6
Components of the Information Economy

	PRIMARY SECTOR	SECONDARY SECTOR
INFORMATION PRODUCTION	Research & Development Education Authors	Internal R&D Training Technical Writers
INFORMATION DISTRIBUTION	Publishing Libraries Television, Movies	Internal Publication Special Libraries Advertising
INFORMATION TRANSACTION HANDLING	Telecommunication Banking Brokerage	Internal Telecom Accounting Financial Management
INFORMATION HARDWARE & SOFTWARE	Computers Telecom Equipment Maintenance	Data Processing Staff Telecom Staff Maintenance
SUPPORTING FACILITIES	Buildings Supplies Maintenance	Buildings Supplies Maintenance

The boundary between the two sectors
is uncertain and changes over time.

Figure 10.7
Percentages of Services Out-Sourced

PERCENTAGE OF SERVICES OUT-SOURCED			
Function	1973	1978	1983
Accountance	35.4	34.5	34.0
Research & Development	10.7	11.2	15.2
Computer & Data Processing	12.0	19.1	20.2
Software Development	10.7	12.7	34.2
Staff Training	22.0	26.5	31.6
Recruitment	24.9	31.5	33.9
Management Services	7.2	11.1	14.7
Photocopying	15.5	13.9	14.3
Drafting Services	16.0	18.5	21.2
Market Research	11.0	14.0	18.3
Advertising	37.1	42.1	47.5
Public Relations	5.8	9.1	12.2

The parallels across the subsectors highlight the fact that management has the choice between committing resources to them in-house or contracting for them from the primary information sector. For valid management reasons, though, there does appear to be a steady trend toward drawing on the primary information sector, especially in areas such as software development and training (as illustrated in Figure 10.7 comparing, over time, the percentages of various activities that are "out-sourced").[3] To illustrate, industrial training is one of the areas of largest growth in the U.S. economy.

Libraries as a Component

Libraries are an identified part of the information economy. But clearly, when we talk of 50 percent of the nation's work force, we are dealing with a large-scale phenomenon, based on broad definition of information work, within which libraries and librarians are almost invisible. General studies of manpower distributions have, as a result, not given a clear picture of more specific elements at a level that would permit meaningful examination of libraries as a component of large-scale information economies. It is largely for this reason that the model being presented here was created.

Row and Column Totals

It is relatively easy to obtain data by which to measure the distribution of the work force by category of organization (from national input/output data) or by category of function (from labor statistics) (see Figures 10.8 and 10.9). Those represent the row and column totals, respectively, for the matrix of manpower distribution.

The problem of concern in this chapter is the estimation of the distribution of the labor force within this matrix—the "fine structure" of the information economy.

THE MODEL

The model presented is intended to be a descriptive basis for assessing that fine structure, not a predictive one, even though it will be presented numerically. So the numbers used to represent the relevant parameters are deliberately at a low level of precision—just one or two decimal digits. Furthermore, the number of parameters is limited. Figure 10.10 presents five categories, the parameters associated with each, and values used to represent each. For two categories—management and levels of information use—the parameter is the relevant proportion of total employment in an industry category.

The value for "management" is taken uniformly, over all categories of organization, at 10 percent, based on the reported data for employment in the United States. The values for "levels of use" (information and noninformation) are derived from the input/output accounts for the United States and reflect the relative levels for purchase of products and services by different categories of organization.

The values for the ratio "In-house/Out-source" are taken at 3/1 for all functions except those specific to each type of industry. This reflects data, as illustrated above, on that ratio for different specific functions. However, for information industries, there is evidence of a strong "diagonal dominance," with transaction industries purchasing heavily from transaction industries, information

Figure 10.8
Categories of Organizations

CATEGORIES OF ORGANIZATIONS	EXAMPLES
Low Technology	Agriculture Extractive Personal Services Transportation Manufacturing
High Technology	Chemistry Pharmaceuticals Electronics
Information Transaction	Communications Banking Brokerage
Information Hardware	Computers Telecomm Hardware
Information Production & Distribution	Education Research & Development Publishing Libraries Entertainment

Figure 10.9
Row and Column Totals

		Category of Function				
Category of Organization	Non Information Functions	Information Functions				Total by Organization
		Management	Support	Hardware	Substance	
Non-Information						
Low Tech High Tech						57.90 19.30
Information		? ? ? ? ? ? ? ?				

Facilities
  Transactions
  Hardware
  Distribution
						2.40
						5.30
						3.30
						11.80

Function Total	57.95	10.00	9.58	7.33	15.17	100.00

hardware purchasing heavily from hardware, and distribution purchasing heavily from distribution. For those diagonal elements, therefore, the ratio is taken at 1/1. For non-information industries, there is a similar diagonal dominance, taken at 1.33/1.

Figure 10.10
Parameters of the Model and Associated Values

CATEGORIES	PARAMETERS	VALUES
Management		0.10
Non-Information Use Levels	High level of use Medium level of use Low level of use	0.53 0.35 0.20
Information Use Levels	Minor level of use Low level of use Moderate level of use High level of use Very high level of use	0.01 0.03 0.06 0.20 0.40
In-house/Out-source	Off diagonal terms Non-Information Diagonal terms Information Diagonal terms	3.00 1.33 1.00
Levels of Development	California United States Other industrialized nations Non-industrialized nations Peasant economy nations	1.10 1.00 .75 .25 .10

The category "Levels of Development" involves a single parameter, but the table shows five representative values for economies at different stages in transition to "information economies."

Resulting Distributions

The values for these parameters are distributed as shown in Figures 10.11 and 10.12. In each of these two matrices, the diagonal elements have been emphasized to highlight the difference between them and the other elements.

Percentage Distribution of Work Force

The estimated fine structure for distribution of the work force is then derived by multiplying the values in corresponding cells of these two matrices with the respective row totals. The result is shown in Figure 10.13.

Despite the limited number of parameters and the low precision in the related values, the row and column totals are remarkably close to those from the original data:

Row Totals	Original Model	57.90 58.24	19.30 19.60	2.40 2.41	3.30 4.91	5.30 3.42	11.80 12.22
Column Totals	Original Model	57.95 57.57	10.00 10.00	9.58 9.58	7.33 8.48	15.17 15.16	100.00 100.80

Total Work Force

Given the absolute value for the total work force for the United States (taken at 120 million, for example), the distribution of persons can then easily be derived (see Figure 10.14).

USE OF THE MODEL

Librarians as Components of the Information Economy

Librarians are by definition part of the work force of the "substance" function and, especially, within the "information distribution" industries. In the United States in 1989, according to Bureau of Labor Statistics data, there were about 212,000 of them including both professional and nonprofessional staff of libraries and library-like agencies. They thus were about 1.3 percent of the work force for substantive information staffing.

The librarians are heavily concentrated within distribution industries, though, especially in educational institutions. For example, the major university libraries (those that are members of the Association of Research Libraries) in 1989 employed about 35,000 persons in libraries (25 percent being professionals); higher education as a whole employed about 90,000. Public libraries employed another 90,000. That leaves about 32,000 for the rest of industry, with about half being professionals (see Figure 10.15).

The distribution of professional librarians among the several classes of industry is derived from statistics for the Special Libraries Association in the United States. The important point is the mismatch between those numbers and the work force engaged in substantive information work in the low-technology industries. The implication is that there is a substantial need to upgrade the level of library support in those industries. Most particularly, the amount of use made of "published information" (the province of the librarian) is dramatically less in those industries than it is in the high technologies.

Community Policy Planning

To this point, the model has been derived as a representation of the information economy of the United States. If that were the end of it, there would be, at most, descriptive value. The intent in developing the model is to provide a basis for assessment of other contexts, especially those in communities in transition through the stages into the information age.

To that end, one more parameter is needed—one that represents the stage or level in that development. The underlying assumption is that the level of development is exhibited in the extent to which various kinds of information re-

Figure 10.11
Simplified Matrix of Input/Output Ratios

Category of Organization	Non Information Functions	Information Functions			
		Management	Support	Hardware	Substance
Non-Information					
Low Tech	0.53	0.10	0.03	0.01	0.03
High Tech	0.35	0.10	0.03	0.06	0.06
Information					
Facilities	0.53	0.10	0.03	0.01	0.03
Transactions	0.20	0.10	(0.20)	0.06	0.06
Hardware	0.35	0.10	0.03	(0.20)	0.06
Distribution	0.20	0.10	0.03	0.06	(0.40)

sources are used within the economy. That parameter (shown by "X") enters into the model as a multiplier on the percentage values shown above (see Figure 10.16).

Illustration with Data for Los Angeles SMSA

The following data (Figure 10.17) are from the 1983 and 1993 Bureau of Labor Statistics, comparing data for United States, California, and Los Angeles-Long Beach SMSA.[4]

Application of the model presented in this chapter to these data produces the following matrices (Figure 10.18) comparing the absolute distribution of the work force (in millions of workers) in noninformation work and substantive information work.

As this comparison shows, there would have been a modest increase by about 100,000 persons in low-technology industry, but note that they are nearly all in information work (i.e., manual labor essentially stayed constant). The bulk of the added jobs—over 200,000 of them—are in high-technology industries—in management, computers, and engineering. But about 130,000 of them are in information distribution services—publishing, information broker-age, and libraries. Functionally, the new positions are in management, com-puters, and substantive information work (the latter being the areas of largest concentration).

The substantive information workers include librarians. The model says that the number of professional librarian staff positions would have increased by 700 and total library staff, professional and nonprofessional, by 2,000. As a check on the extent to which the model fits reality, consider the following:

Figure 10.12
Simplified Matrix of In-house/Out-source Ratios

Category of Organization	Non Information Functions	Information Functions			
		Management	Support	Hardware	Substance
Non-Information					
Low Tech	1.33		3.00	3.00	3.00
High Tech	1.33		3.00	3.00	3.00
Information					
Facilities	1.33		3.00	3.00	3.00
Transactions	1.33		(1.00)	3.00	3.00
Hardware	1.33		3.00	(1.00)	3.00
Distribution	1.33		3.00	3.00	(1.00)

	1984	1994
Membership in ALA from California:	3,946	4,773
Membership in SLA from California:	1,000	1,200
Other not included among those:	2,000	2,500

The Los Angeles SMSA is generally about 30 percent of California, so applying that to the California figures, we get:

	1984	1994
Estimated professionals from Los Angeles:	2,084	2,540
The model estimates professional staffing levels as:	1,983	2,705

On the surface, the model would appear to be consistent with reported data, but the sequence of assumptions for calculation of the estimated actuals is itself rather uncertain.

The structural problem, of course, is that the persons who previously filled the manual labor jobs in low-technology work generally do not have the skills and preparation needed to fill the positions created in information work, so many of them are unemployed or at best employed in lower-paying, personal service jobs (such as fast-food service). Unemployment in Los Angeles in 1994 totaled about 460,000, which included, aside from the structural problem identified here, the residual effect of the recession and the portion of the population that at any time is unemployed for a variety of reasons. The point is that the structural problem complicates and compounds the more typical causes for unemployment.

Figure 10.13
Estimated Fine Structure for Workforce Distribution

Category of Organization	Category of Function					Total by Organization
	Non Information Functions	Information Functions				
		Management	Support	Hardware	Substance	
Non-Information						
Low Tech	40.81	5.79	5.21	1.22	5.21	58.24
High Tech	8.98	1.93	1.74	3.47	3.47	19.60
Information						
Facilities	1.69	0.24	0.22	0.05	0.22	2.41
Transactions	1.54	0.33	1.06	0.95	0.95	4.91
Hardware	1.41	0.53	0.30	0.66	0.59	3.42
Distribution	3.14	1.18	1.06	2.12	4.72	12.22
Function Total	57.57	10.00	9.58	8.47	15.16	100.80

Figure 10.14
Total Workforce Distribution

Category of Organization	Category of Function					Total by Organization
	Non Information Functions	Information Functions				
		Management	Support	Hardware	Substance	
Non-Information						
Low Tech	48.98	6.95	6.25	1.46	6.25	69.89
High Tech	10.78	2.32	2.08	4.17	4.17	23.52
Information						
Facilities	2.03	0.29	0.26	0.06	0.26	2.90
Transactions	1.69	0.64	1.27	1.14	1.14	5.89
Hardware	1.84	0.40	0.36	0.79	0.71	4.10
Distribution	3.77	1.42	1.27	2.55	5.66	14.67
Function Total	69.09	12.00	9.58	8.48	15.16	120.97

General Economic Policies

This chapter will now conclude with a brief commentary on the implications for community policy and business planning in an information-based, market-oriented economy. Underlying them is the nature of general economic policies. As shown in Figure 10.19, they include a number of politically explosive decisions, a number of sociologically disruptive transitions, and a number of capital-intensive requirements. Can these be accommodated and reconciled? While

Figure 10.15
Comparative Distribution of Librarians

INDUSTRY GROUP	Substance Functions	Library Staff	Ratio	Professional Librarians	Ratio
Non-Information					
Low Tech	6.25 M	6 K	0.10%	3.0 K	0.05%
High Tech	4.17 M	8 K	0.20%	4.0 K	0.10%
Information					
Facilities	0.26 M	0 K	0.10%	0.1 K	0.05%
Transactions	1.14 M	2 K	0.20%	1.0 K	0.10%
Hardware	0.71 M	1 K	0.20%	0.7 K	0.10%
Distribution	5.66 M	195 K	3.40%	50.0 K	0.85%
Function Total	18.19 M	212 K	1.16%	57.6 K	0.32%

Figure 10.16
Effect of Level of Development of Information Economy

	Category of Function				
Category of Organization	Non Information Functions	Information Functions			
		Management	Support	Hardware	Substance
Non-Information					
Low Tech	1	1	"X"	"X"	"X"
High Tech	1	1	"X"	"X"	"X"
Information					
Facilities	1	1	"X"	"X"	"X"
Transactions	1	1	1	"X"	"X"
Hardware	1	1	"X"	1	"X"
Distribution	1	1	"X"	"X"	1

we cannot here answer that question, we can say that they are all essential if an information-based, market-oriented economy is to be achieved in a community.

Encouragement to Use of Information

Assuming that the basic, general economic policy decisions have been made, there are less controversial but still crucial elements of community policy. The first is to provide encouragement and incentives for the development of a local information economy. A most crucial problem with information is the fact that there is differential use. Those who know the value of information, those who know how to use it are the ones who do so. But all statistics show that they are 10 to 20 percent of those who should be using information.

Figure 10.17
Statistics for U.S., California, and L.A. SMSA—1983 and 1993

	May 1983			May 1993		
	U.S.	Calif	L.A. SMSA	U.S.	Calif	L.A. SMSA
Population	237000	26000	8100	255062	30867	8900
Population above 16	184000	19000	6200	195672	23217	6764
Workforce	104912	11468	4080	121298	13699	4321
Unemployed	11328	1330	369	8925	1476	471
Agriculture	3371	400	150	3060	250	80
Non-Agri Employment	90213	9739	3561	109313	11973	3770
Mining	990	48	14	603	33	8
Construction	3808	338	93	4588	442	100
Manufacturing	19385	1860	847	18023	1818	686
Transport, Utilities	4955	531	194	5768	597	199
Trade	20512	2244	808	25371	2763	840
Finance	5424	646	239	6697	781	248
Services	19418	2316	890	29551	3440	1150
Government	15721	1757	477	18712	2100	538
Employed Workforce/Popu	0.39	0.39	0.46	0.44	0.40	0.43
Percent Agri	0.04	0.04	0.04	0.03	0.02	0.02
Percent Industry	0.26	0.22	0.26	0.20	0.19	0.21
Percent Services	0.76	0.78	0.73	0.81	0.83	0.80

Therefore, community information policy should be concerned with how to encourage managers and staff at all levels to use the information they need for maximally effective operations. That's not easy. There are barriers, both psychological and physical, to the use of information. Managers in fact would frequently prefer not to have information, especially if it may go counter to the decisions they want to make; it is sometimes difficult to obtain the information one needs when one needs it; it is difficult to weigh the validity and import of information when it is provided.

Despite all of these difficulties, however, the values to be gained for the total corporate success are so great that every effort should be spent to ensure that the barriers are removed, that managers are psychologically prepared to use information, and that the information resources are managed in such a way that the full range of needed information is available when it is needed:[5]

1. Better work force, better trained, and more capable of dealing with problems;

2. Better product development, based on more knowledge about the needs of the consumer;

3. Better engineering, based on availability and use of scientific and technical information;

4. Better marketing, including choices among markets and approaches to them;

5. Better economic data, leading to improved investment decisions and allocations of resources;

6. Better internal management, based on the use of information and the associated technologies for improved communication and decision making.

Figure 10.18
Absolute Distribution of Workforce (in Millions of Workers)

```
1983 — Absolute Distribution of Workforce (in Millions of Workers)

                    8.1 Population (in Millions)
         0.4 Percent Labor Force          1 Level of Development
```

Type	Non-Info Staff	Manageme Staff	Support Staff	Hardware Staff	Substant Staff	Total
Lo Tech	1.30	0.19	0.17	0.04	0.17	1.86
Hi Tech	0.29	0.06	0.06	0.11	0.11	0.64
Facilities	0.05	0.01	0.01	0.00	0.01	0.08
Transaction	0.05	0.02	0.03	0.03	0.03	0.16
Hardware	0.05	0.01	0.01	0.02	0.02	0.11
Distribution	0.09	0.04	0.04	0.07	0.16	0.40
Total	1.83	0.32	0.31	0.28	0.50	3.24

```
         Estimated Number of Library Staff              4958
         Estimated Number of Professional Librarians    1983


1993 — Absolute Distribution of Workforce (in Millions of Workers)

                    8.9 Population (in Millions)
         0.43 Percent Labor Force          1.14 Level of Development
```

Type	Non-Info Staff	Manageme Staff	Support Staff	Hardware Staff	Substant Staff	Total
Lo Tech	1.32	0.20	0.20	0.05	0.20	1.97
Hi Tech	0.33	0.09	0.09	0.18	0.18	0.86
Facilities	0.07	0.01	0.01	0.00	0.01	0.11
Transaction	0.06	0.02	0.04	0.04	0.04	0.21
Hardware	0.06	0.01	0.02	0.03	0.03	0.15
Distribution	0.10	0.05	0.05	0.11	0.21	0.53
Total	1.95	0.38	0.41	0.41	0.68	3.83

```
         Estimated Number of Library Staff              6763
         Estimated Number of Professional Librarians    2705
```

Incentive for Development of Information Industries

Balancing these aspects, of course, are significant negative factors that can prevent companies from making the necessary internal investments in information resources but that, as a result, provide the opportunities for information entrepreneurs to "fill the gaps." Since there will be great risks for them in doing so, it is essential that there be incentives to reward those risks.

1. *Evident costs.* Most information activities involve very evident costs, in manpower, in equipment, and in purchases.

2. *Uncertain return.* And they are also characterized by very uncertain returns. Rarely are the positive results of any of the "benefits" listed above clearly attributable to the availability of the information on which they were based. In many cases, the decisions could have been made without the information; in some cases, they may

Figure 10.19
Community Policy Implications

```
General Economic Policies
  Encourage Entrepreneurship
  Shift from Low Technology to High Technology
  Shift from Production of Physical Goods to Information
Development of the "Information Economy"
  Encouragement to Effective Use of Information in Business
  Incentives for Development of Information Industries
  Information Skills Development
Management of Information Enterprises
  Technical Information Skills
  Support Staff
```

even be made counter to the information.

3. *Long-term return.* And even when the value is evident, it is likely that the return is only over the long term, while the expenditure is made in the immediate term. The result is that most information investment must be amortized over a long period of time.

4. *Not directly productive.* Furthermore, only in rare situations (and most of those in the "information industries" themselves) is information directly productive. Its value lies in the better uses of other resources, not in the direct contribution to production. (Although increasing use of computer-based technologies is changing this situation and increasing the direct contribution to production attributable to "information," in the form of programs and data, for most purposes today the role of information is supportive at most.)

5. *Overhead expense.* As a result, in virtually every accounting practice, information is treated as an "overhead" expense and therefore subject to all of the cost-cutting attitudes associated with overhead expenses.

Information Skills Development

Throughout this chapter—indeed, the entire book—there has been a continuing theme of needed skills for the information professional—the librarian, the information scientist, the information manager—in effecting this change, in increasing the awareness of information and of its value, which is crucial. There must be information professionals with qualifications adequate to support management and to justify their investment in information resources. Support to this kind of educational investment clearly should be a national priority as well as a community commitment.

CONCLUSION

The objective in presenting this model was to provide a simple structure within which to experiment with the effects of alternative strategies in the development of community economies. Among the most crucial requirements is an adequate work force of "information professionals," among which librarians have been used as an illustrative example. The model permits one easily to assess areas which lack adequate staff and to formulate policies for filling the needs.

The model also provides a basis on which business entrepreneurs, as well as public policy makers, can assess the areas of business opportunities as the information economy develops. It permits identification of growth and decline as the economy and size of the population change.

As presented, the model is deliberately simplified, with a limited number of parameters deliberately presented at a low level of precision, but the values generated match the actual data closely enough to warrant its use as a tool for identification of areas in which greater accuracy and reliability are needed.

NOTES

1. Malcolm Getz, *Public Libraries: An Economic View* (Baltimore: Johns Hopkins University Press, 1980), p. 172.

2. Marc Uri Porat, *The Information Economy: Definition and Measurement* (Washington, D.C.: U.S. Department of Commerce, Office of Telecommunications, 1977).

3. Donald Siegel and Zvi Griliches, *Purchased Services, Outsourcing, Computers, and Productivity in Manufacturing* (Cambridge, Mass.: National Bureau of Economic Research, Inc., 1991).

4. *Employment and Earnings* (Washington, D.C.: U.S. Department of Labor, Bureau of Labor Statistics, May 1983, May 1993).

5. Toni Carbo Bearman, Polly Guynup, and Sandra N. Milevski, "Information and productivity," *Journal of the American Society for Information Science* 36(6) (1985): 369–375; Daniel Bell, "The Social Framework of the Information Society," in *The Computer Age: A Twenty-Year Review*, ed. Michael L. Dertouzos and Joel Moses (Cambridge, Mass.: The MIT Press, 1979), pp. 163–211; Harold Borko, "Information and knowledge worker productivity," *Information Processing & Management* 19(4) (1983): 203–212; Robert M. Hayes, ed., *Libraries and the Information Economy of California: A Conference Sponsored by the California State Library* (Los Angeles: GSLIS/UCLA, 1985); Robert M. Hayes and Timothy Erickson, "Added value as a function of purchases of information services," *The Information Society* 1(4) (December 1982): 307–338; Forest Woody Horton, Jr., "Rethinking the role of information," *Government Computer News* 2(4) (1982): 2, 24; Michael Rubin, *The Information Economy* (Denver: Libraries Unlimited, 1983).

Bibliography

Aaker, David A. *Developing Business Strategies.* 2d ed. New York: John Wiley, 1988.

Ackoff, Russell. *The Design of Social Research.* Chicago: University of Chicago Press, 1953.

Advisory Committee to the Department of Housing and Urban Development. *Revenue Sharing and the Planning Process: Shifting the Locus of Responsibility for Domestic Problem Solving.* Washington, D.C.: National Academy of Sciences, 1974.

Aguilar, William. "The Application of Relative Use and Interlibrary Demand in Collection Development." *Collection Management* 8(1) (1986): 15–24.

"ALA Files Appeal for Full Disclosure" (FBI's Library Awareness Program). *Wilson Library Bulletin* 64(6) (February 1990): 11–13.

Allen, Kenneth B. *Minutes of the Ninety-ninth Annual Meeting, the Association of Research Libraries.* Washington, D.C.: ARL, 1982.

Allen, Leslie H., ed. *Bryan and Darrow at Dayton; the Record and Documents of the "Bible-evolution Trial."* New York: A. Lee & Company, 1925.

American Enterprise Institute for Public Policy Research. *The Administration's Plan to Reauthorize Revenue Sharing, 1980, 96th Congress, 2nd session.* Washington, D.C.: American Enterprise Institute for Public Policy Research, 1980.

American Library Association. *Guidelines for Collection Development.* Chicago: American Library Association, 1979.

Ammons, David. "Reputational Leaders in Local Government Productivity and Innovation." *Public Productivity and Management Review* 15(1) (Fall 1991): 19–43.

Anderson, A. J., Martha M. Malosky, and Ellen L. Miller. "The FBI Wants You—to Spy." *Library Journal* 114(11) (15 June 1989): 37–40.

Andrews, R. N. L., ed. *Land in America: Commodity or Natural Resource?* Lexington, Mass.: Lexington Books, 1979.

"Angry Virginia Beach Mom Wants Her Kid's Borrowing Restricted." *American Libraries* (January 1994): 9.

Annual Report of the Office of Revenue Sharing. Washington, D.C.: GPO, 1974.

"ARL and RLG to Study ILL Costs." *Library Hotline* 21(17) (17 April 1992): 102.

"ARL, Cause, Educom Form New Information Resources Coalition." *Manage IT* 1(2) (April 1990): 1–2.

ARL/RLG Interlibrary Loan Cost Study: Worksheet. Washington, D.C.: ARL, 1992.

Armor, David J. *Sociology and School Busing Policy.* Santa Monica, Calif.: Rand Corporation, 1976.

Arms, Caroline. "Libraries and Electronic Information: The technological Context." Part two. *Educom Review* 24(3) (Fall 1989): 34–43.

Aronson, J. Richard. "Municipal Indicators," In *Crisis and Constraint in Municipal Finance*, ed. James H. Carr. New Brunswick, N.J.: Center for Urban Policy Research, 1984, pp. 3–41.

Ault, Ulrika Ekman. "The FBI's Library Awareness Program: Is Big Brother Reading Over Your Shoulder?" *New York University Law Review* 65(6) (December 1990): 1532–1565.

Automation and the Middle Manager: What Has Happened and What the Future Holds. New York: American Foundation on Automation and Employment, 1966.

Avram, Henriette D. "Copyright in the Electronic Environment." *Educom Review* 24(3) (Fall 1989): 31–33.

Axford, H. W. "Collection Management: A New Dimension." *Journal of Community Librarianship* 6 (1981): 324–329.

Baden, J. "Agricultural Land Preservation: Threshing the Wheat from the Chaff." *Institute on Planning, Zoning, and Eminent Domain.* New York: Matthew Bender, 1983.

————, ed. *The Vanishing Farmland Crisis: Critical Views of the Movement to Preserve Agricultural Land.* Lawrence: Kansas University Press, 1984.

Baecker, Ronald, and William Buxton. *Readings in Human-Computer Interaction: A Multidisciplinary Approach.* Los Altos, Calif.: Morgan Kaufmann, 1987.

Baker, Sharon L. *The Responsive Public Library Collection: How to Develop and Market It.* Englewood, Colo.: Libraries Unlimited, 1993.

Baltimore County Public Library's Blue Ribbon Committee. *Give 'Em What They Want! Managing the Public's Library.* Chicago: American Library Association, 1992.

Bamford, James. *The Puzzle Palace: A Report on America's Most Secret Agency.* Boston: Houghton-Mifflin, 1982.

Banfield, Edward C. *The Unheavenly City Revisited.* Boston: Little, Brown, 1974.

Barnekov, Timothy, Robin Boyle, and Daniel Rich. *Privatism and Urban Policy in Britain and the United States.* New York: Oxford University Press, 1989.

Baughman, James C. *Policy Making for Public Library Trustees.* Englewood, Colo.: Libraries Unlimited, 1993.

Bearman, Toni Carbo, Polly Guynup, and Sandra N. Milevski. "Information and Productivity." *Journal of the American Society for Information Science* 36(6) (1985): 369–375.

Beck, Robert N. "Issues of Imaging Science for Future Consideration." *Proceedings of the National Academy of Sciences of the United States* 90(21) (1 November 1993): 9803–9808.

Bell, Daniel. "The Social Framework of the Information Society." In *The Computer*

Age: A Twenty-Year Review. ed. Michael L. Dertouzos and Joel Moses. Cambridge, Mass.: The MIT Press, 1979, pp. 163–211.

Bellah, Robert et al. *Habits of the Heart: Individualism and Commitment in American Life*. Berkeley, Calif.: University of California Press, 1985.

———. *The Good Society*. New York: Knopf, 1992.

Benne, Mae. *Principles of Children's Services in Public Libraries*. Chicago: American Library Association, 1991.

Berger, Mike. "The Patron Meets the Melvyl Catalog: A Short History of the Melvyl Patron Interface." *DLA Bulletin* 12(10) (Spring 1992): 6–7, 24–26.

Berk, Emily, and Joseph Devlin, eds. *Hypertext/Hypermedia Handbook*. New York: Intertext Publications, McGraw-Hill, c1991.

Berman, Paul, ed. *Debating P.C.: The Controversy Over Political Correctness on College Campuses*. New York: Laurel, published by Dell, 1992.

"Beyond the Williamson Act: Alternatives for More Effective Preservation of Agricultural Land in California." *Pacific Law Journal* 15 (1984): 1151–1180.

Biggs, Mary, and Glenna Kramer. "We Have Been There Too: Library Board Essentials for Effectiveness." *Wilson Library Bulletin* 68(9) (May 1994): 32–35.

Bookstein, Abraham. "Questionnaire research in a Library Setting." *Journal of Public Librarianship* 1(1) (1985): 24–28.

Borgman, Christine L., Andrea L. Gallagher, Sandra G. Hirsh, and Virginia A. Walter. "Children's Searching Behavior on Browsing and Keyword Online Catalogs: The Science Library Catalog Project." *Journal of the American Society for Information Science*, in press.

Borko, Harold. "Information and Knowledge Worker Productivity." *Information Processing & Management* 19(4) (1993): 203–212.

Borman, Stu. "AAAS to Launch On-line Peer-reviewed Journal." (American Association for the Advancement of Science: The Online Journal of Current Clinical Trials) *Chemical & Engineering News* 69(39) (30 September 1991): 8.

Boulton, William R. *Business Policy: The Art of Strategic Management*. New York: Macmillan, 1984.

Bourne, Charles P., and Madeleine Kasson. *Preliminary Report on the Review and Development of Standard Cost Data for Selected Library Technical Processing Functions*. Palo Alto, Calif.: Information General Corp., 1969.

Bozeman, Barry, and Jeffrey D. Straussman. *Public Management Strategies: Guidelines for Managerial Effectiveness*. San Francisco: Jossey-Bass, 1990.

Bradbury, D. A. "Agricultural Law: Suburban Sprawl and the Right to Farm." *Washburn Law Journal* 22 (1983): 448–468.

Break, George F. *Financing Government in a Federal System*. Washington, D.C.: Brookings Institution, c1980. (Discusses Tiebout model, pp. 203ff.)

———. *Intergovernmental Fiscal Relations in the United States*. Washington, D.C.: Brookings Institution, 1967.

Brittle Books: Reports of the Committee on Preservation and Access. Washington, D.C.: Council on Library Resources, 1986.

Broadus, Robert. "Use Studies of Library Collections." *Library Resources and Technical Services* 24(4) (1980): 317–324.

Brown, Rowland C. W. "Brushstrokes in Flight: A Strategic Overview of Trends in Technology in Higher Education." In *The Electronic Campus—An Information*

Strategy, ed. Lynne J. Brindley. Proceedings of the Conference in Banbury, England, 28–30 October 1988.

Browning, F. *The Vanishing Land: The Corporate Theft of America*. New York: Harper & Row, 1975.

Brudney, Jeffrey L. *Fostering Volunteer Programs in the Public Sector: Planning, Initiating, and Managing Voluntary Activities*. San Francisco: Jossey-Bass, 1990.

Bulkeley, William M. "Cipher Probe: Popularity Overseas of Encryption Code Has the U.S. Worried; Grand Jury Wonders if Creator 'Exported' the Program Through the Internet; 'Genie' is Out of the Bottle." *Wall Street Journal*, 28 April 1994, p. A1.

Buncher, Judith F., ed. *The School Busing Controversy, 1970–75*. New York: Facts on File, 1975.

Bunge, Charles A. "Responsive Reference Service: Breaking Down the Age Barriers." *School Library Journal* (March 1994): 142–145.

Burns, Robert W., Jr. "Library Use as a Performance Measure: Its Background and Rationale." *Journal of Community Librarianship* 4(1) (1978): 4–11.

Busey, Paula, and Tom Doerr. "Kid's Catalog: An Information Retrieval System for Children." *Journal of Youth Services in Libraries* 7(1) (Fall 1993): 77–84.

Butler, Meredith, and Bonnie Gratch. "Planning a User Study: The Process Defined." *College and Research Libraries* 43(4) (1982): 320–330.

Byerly, Greg. *Pornography, the Conflict over Sexually Explicit Materials in the United States: An Annotated Bibliography*. New York: Garland, 1980.

California Legislature. Senate Committee on Local Government. *Your Guide to Open Meetings: The Ralph M. Brown Act*. Sacramento: Joint Publications, 1989.

Cameron, Alexander, Betsy Cornwell, and Joanne Tate. "Public Library Boards: A Creative Balance." *CLJ* 49(2) (April 1992): 135–139.

Card, Moran, Allen Newell, and Thomas P. Moran. *The Psychology of Human-Computer Interaction*. Hillsdale, N.J.: Lawrence Erlbaum Associates, 1983.

Carlson, David B. et al. *Adrift in a Sea of Change: California's Public Libraries Struggle to Meet the Information Needs of Multicultural Communities*. Center for Policy Development, 1990.

Carnevale, Anthony P. et al. *New Developments in Worker Training: A Legacy for the 1990s*. Madison, Wis.: Industrial Relations Research Association, 1990.

Carroll, Bonnie, and Donald W. King. "Value of Information." *Drexel Library Quarterly* 21 (Summer 1985): 39–60.

Carroll, John M. *Interfacing Thought: Cognitive Aspects of Human-Computer Interaction*. Cambridge, Mass.: Bradford/MIT Press, 1987.

"CD-ROM Database Sales Should Hit about 2.2 Mil by 1996 vs. 1.4 Mil in 1991." *Computing World* (March 1992): 9.

Certo, Samuel C., and J. Paul Peter. *Strategic Management*. New York: Random House, 1988.

Challenged Materials: An Interpretation of the Library Bill of Rights. Chicago: American Library Association. Adopted 14 July 1971, amended 1 July 1981 and 10 January 1990.

Checkland, Peter. *Systems Thinking, Systems Practice*. Chichester, England: John Wiley & Sons, 1981.

Chen, Ching-Chih, and Peter Hernon. *Information-Seeking: Assessing and Anticipating User Needs*. New York: Neal-Schuman, 1982.

Childers, Thomas, and Nancy A. Van House. *What's Good? Describing Your Public Library's Effectiveness*. Chicago: American Library Association, 1993.

Choi, Jung Min, and John W. Murphy. *The Politics and Philosophy of Political Correctness*. Westport, Conn.: Praeger, 1992.

Christensen, John O. *Intellectual Freedom and Libraries: A Selective Bibliography*. Monticello, Ill.: Vance Bibliographies, 1991.

———. *Legal Issues in Public and School Libraries: Some Recent References*. Monticello, Ill.: Vance Bibliographies, 1990.

———. *Obscenity, Pornography, and Libraries: A Selective Bibliography*. Monticello, Ill.: Vance Bibliographies, 1991.

Christiansen, Dorothy E., Roger C. Davis, and Jutta Reed-Scott. "Guidelines to Collection Evaluation through Use and User Studies." *Library Resources and Technical Services* 27(4) (October/December): 432–440.

Church, Steven S. "User Criteria for Evaluation of Library Services." *Journal of Library Administration* 2(1) (1981): 35–46.

Chute, Alan G. et al. "Distance Education Futures: Information Needs and Technology Options." *Performance and Instruction* 30 (November/December 1991): 1–6.

Cirino, Paul John. *The Business of Running a Library: A Handbook for Public Library Directors*. Jefferson, N.C.: McFarland, 1991.

Cisco, Susan L. "Document Imaging Finding Niche in Petroleum Industry." *Oil and Gas Journal* 90(45) (9 November 1992): 85–90.

Citizens' Task Force on Alternative Financing. *Recommendations for Financing the Pasadena Public Library System*. Pasadena, Calif.: Pasadena Public Library Commission, 2 February 1993.

City Fiscal Conditions. Washington, D.C.: National League of Cities, 1986.

Clapp, Verner W., and Robert T. Jordan. "Quantitative Criteria for Adequacy of Community Library Collections." *College and Research Libraries* 50 (March 1989): 153–163.

Cleland, David I. *Matrix Management Systems Handbook*. New York: Van Nostrand Reinhold Co., 1984.

Cline, Nancy. "Information Resources and the National Network." *Educom Review* 25(2) (Summer 1990): 30–34.

Clinton, Bill, and Al Gore. *Putting People First: How We Can All Change America*. New York: Times Books, 1992.

Cloonan, Michele V. "The Censorship of *The Adventures of Huckleberry Finn*: An Investigation." *Top of the News* 41(2) (Winter 1984).

Code of Federal Regulations, 2 April 1982 (pp. 116–178). Executive Order 12356, National Security Information.

Code of Federal Regulations, revised as of 1 July 1993, volume 32 (National Defense).

Colin, K., George N. Lindsey, and Daniel Callahan. "Toward Usable User Studies." *Journal of the American Society for Information Science* 31 (1980): 347–356.

Collison, Michele. "Biologist's Theory of Creation Gets Him into Hot Water at San Francisco State U." *Chronicle of Higher Education* 40(20) (19 January 1994), p. A20.

Committee on Science and Creationism, National Academy of Sciences. *Science and*

Creationism: A View from the National Academy of Sciences. Washington, D.C.: National Academy Press, 1984.

Conatser, Kelly R. "In or Out?—A simple 1-2-3 Model Reveals Whether Outsourcing Is for You." *Lotus* 8(8) (August 1992): 36–40.

Connors, J. L., and T. A. Romberg. "Middle Management and Quality Control." *Human Organization* 50(1) (Spring 1991): 61–65.

Cortez, Edwin M., and Tom Smorch. *Planning Second Generation Automated Library Systems.* Westport, Conn.: Greenwood Press, 1993, pp. 70–71.

"Court Enlarges Protection for Book Reviews." *News Media & the Law* 18(2) (Spring 1994): 3–4.

Crispin, Joanne L., ed. *The Americans with Disabilities Act: Its Impact on Libraries.* Chicago: American Library Association, 1993.

"Critics of 'The Speaker' Scored for Censorship." *Library Journal* 104(3) (1 February 1979): 335.

Cuciti, Peggy L. *City Need and the Responsiveness of Federal Grants Programs.* Report for the Subcommittee on the City of the Committee on Banking, Finance and Urban Affairs, House of Representatives, 95th Cong., 2nd sess. Washington, D.C.: GPO, 1978.

Cushman, J., and R. M. Hayes. *Analysis of Usage of the Central Library of the Los Angeles Public Library.* Los Angeles: Institute of Library Research, 1968.

D'Elia, G. *The Role of the Public Library in Society.* Evanston, Ill.: Urban Libraries Council, 1993.

D'Elia, George, Eleanor Jo Rodger, and Carole Williams. "Involving Patrons in the Role-Setting Process." *Public Libraries* 30(6) (November/December 1991).

"D. C. Circuit Says Opinion Can Be Libelous." *National Law Journal* 16(27) (7 March 1994): 6.

Dandeker, Christopher. "Surveillance in the Stacks: The FBI's Library Awareness Program." *Annals of the American Academy of Political and Social Science* 521 (May 1992): 202–204.

"Database Vendors Revenues Projection." *Information* (part 1) (October 1989): 6.

De Camp, L. Sprague. *The Great Monkey Trial.* Garden City, N.Y.: Doubleday, 1968.

De la Pena McCook, Kathleen, and Paula Geist. "Hispanic Library Services in South Florida." *Public Libraries* 34(1) (February 1995): 34–37.

Dealing with the Deficit Now: A Policy Statement. Washington, D.C.: Board of Trustees of the National Planning Association, 1993.

DeCandido, Graceanne A. "FBI Presents 'Library Awareness' to NCLIS at Closed Meeting." *Library Journal* 113(7) (15 April 1988): 16.

———. "FBI Investigated Librarians Who Opposed Library Awareness Program." *Library Journal* 114(20) (December 1989): 19.

———. "Virtual Library Promulgated by Library/Education Coalition." *Library Journal* 115(7) (15 April 1990): 14.

Defense Conversion: Redirecting R&D. Washington, D.C.: Office of Technology Assessment, Congress of the U.S., 1993.

DelFattore, Joan. *Why Johnnie Shouldn't Read: Textbook Censorship in America.* New Haven: Yale University Press, 1992.

Delonas, Nicholas. "The Time Series Machine." *Lotus* (November 1991).

DeMont, Roger, Larry Hillman, and Gerald Mansergh, eds. *Busing, Taxes, and Desegregation.* Detroit: Metropolitan Detroit Bureau of School Studies, 1973.

Dervin, Brenda, and Michael Nilan. "Information Needs and Uses." *Annual Review of Information Science and Technology* 21 (1986): 3–33.

Directory of Adaptive Technologies to Aid Library Patrons and Staff with Disabilities. Chicago: American Library Association, 1994.

Diversity in Collection Development: An Interpretation of the Library Bill of Rights. Chicago: American Library Association. Adopted 14 July 1982, amended 10 January 1990.

"Don't Worry, Be Happy: Why Clipper is Good for You." *Wired* (June 1994): 132.

Dougherty, Richard M. "An Ideal Win-Win Situation: The National Electronic Highway." *American Libraries* (February 1991): 182.

Dougherty, Richard M., and Fred J. Heinritz. *Scientific Management of Library Operations.* Metuchen, N.J.: Scarecrow Press, 1982.

Dowd, Frances Smardo. *Latchkey Children in the Library and Community: Issues, Strategies, and Programs.* Phoenix, Ariz.: Oryx, 1991.

Dowd, Sheila T. "The Formulation of a Collection Development Policy Statement." *Collection Development in Libraries: A Treatise.* Greenwich, Conn.: JAI Press, 1980, pp. 67–87.

Downing, Paul B. "User Charges and Service Fees." In *Crisis and Constraint in Municipal Finance,* ed. James H. Carr. New Brunswick, N.J.: Center for Urban Policy Research, 1984, pp. 83–92.

Draper, Stephen, and Donald Norman. *User Centered System Design.* Hillsdale, N.J.: Lawrence Erlbaum Associates, 1986.

Drucker, Peter F. *Innovation and Entrepreneurship: Practice and Principles.* New York: HarperCollins, 1985.

Duncombe, Stephen. "Volunteers in City Government: Disadvantages, and Uses." *National Civic Review* 74(9) (1985): 356–364.

———. "Volunteers in City Government: Getting More Than Your Money's Worth." *National Civic Review* 75(5) (1986): 291–301.

Durrance, Joan C. "Information Needs: Old Song, New Tune." In *Rethinking the Library in the Information Age,* ed. A. Mathews. Washington, D.C.: U.S. Department of Education, 1989, pp. 159–177.

Ehrich, Roger W., and Robert C. Williges. *Human-Computer Dialogue Design.* New York: Elsevier Science, 1986.

Employment and Earnings. Washington, D.C.: U.S. Department of Labor, Bureau of Labor Statistics, May 1983.

Everett, David. "Full-text Online Databases and Document Delivery in an Academic Library." *Online* 17(2) (March 1993): 22.

"Eye on Censorship: Growing Challenges to Libraries Target Materials on Sexuality." *American Libraries* (November 1993): 902–903.

Faigel, Martin. "Methods and Issues in Collection Evaluation Today." *Library Acquisitions: Practice and Theory* 9(1) (1985): 21–35.

Falwell, Jerry. "The Religious Right Must Guard American Values." In *Opposing Viewpoint Pamphlets,* ed. David L. Bender. St. Paul, Minn.: Greenhaven Press, 1985.

"FBI to Consider Release of 'Awareness Program' Material." *American Libraries* (June 1989): 481.

Ferris, James M. "Coprovision: Citizen Time and Money Donations in Public Service Provision." *Public Administration Review* 44(4) (1984): 324–333.

Fields, Howard. "In Surprise, Court Reverses Itself on Moldea Ruling." *Publishers Weekly* 241(19) (9 May 1994): 11–13.

————. "Librarians Challenge FBI on Extent of Its Investigation (Reporting of 'Foreign-Looking' Users of Certain Library Materials)." *Publishers Weekly* 234(2) (8 July 1988): 11.

————. "People for American Way Fund Suit Against FBI Library Informant Plan." *Publishers Weekly* 233(24) (17 June 1988): 16.

Fisk, Donald et al. "Private Provision of Public Services: An Overview." In *Crisis and Constraint in Municipal Finance*, ed. James H. Carr. New Brunswick, N.J.: Center for Urban Policy Research, 1984, pp. 233–242.

Flanders, Bruce. "A Delicate Balance: Keeping Children Out of the Gutters Along the Information Highway." *School Library Journal* (October 1994): 32–35.

————. "Spectacular Systems!" *American Libraries* (October 1989): 915–922.

Foerstel, Herbert N. *Banned in the U.S.A.: A Reference Guide to Book Censorship in Schools and Public Libraries*. Westport, Conn.: Greenwood Press, 1994.

Foos, Donald D., and Nancy C. Pack. *How Libraries Must Comply with the Americans With Disabilities Act*. Phoenix, Ariz.: Oryx, 1992.

Forrester, Jay. *Urban Dynamics*. Cambridge, Mass.: MIT Press, 1969.

Fortune 127(6), 22 March 1993, pp. 62–64ff.

Freedman, Alfred M. *Aspects of the Community Mental Health Centers Act*. Bethesda, Md.: National Institute of Mental Health, 1966.

Fulop, L. "Middle Managers—Victims or Vanguards of the Entrepreneurial Movement." *Journal of Management Studies* 28(1): 25–54.

"Funhouse Mirror." (FBI Library—patron surveillance, editorial). *Progressive* 54(1) (January 1990): 10.

Galvin, Thomas J. "Research library performance in the delivery of electronic information." *OCLC Newsletter* (March/April 1992): 20–21.

Gaughan, Tom. "Taking the Pulse of Library Education." *American Libraries* (January 1992): 24–25, 120.

Gersh, Debra. "Moldea Appeals Dismissal of $10 Million Libel Suit" (*Moldea v. New York Times Co.*). *Editor & Publisher* 126(28) (10 July 1993): 16.

Gertzog, Alice, and Edwin Beckerman. *Administration of the Public Library*. Metuchen, N.J.: Scarecrow Press, 1994.

Gest, Emily. "The Jobs of the Past, the Jobs of the Future." *Los Angeles Times Magazine*, 20 August 1995, pp. 26–27.

Getz, Malcolm. *Public Libraries: An Economic View*. Baltimore, Md.: John Hopkins University Press, 1980.

Gidron, Benjamin. "Volunteer Workers: A Labour Economy Perspective." *Labour and Society* 5(4) (1980): 355–365.

Gilb, Tom, and Gerald M. Weinberg. *Humanized Input: Techniques for Reliable Keyboard Input*. Wellesley Hills, Mass.: QED Information Sciences, Inc., 1977.

Glanz, Jeffrey. *Bureaucracy and Professionalism: The Evolution of Public School Supervision*. Rutherford, N.J.: Fairleigh Dickinson University Press, 1991.

Glitz, Beryl. "The California Multitype Library Network: An Update." *Pacific Southwest Regional Medical Library Service* (January/February 1991): 1, 4.

Gluck, Myke. *HyperCard, Hypertext, and Hypermedia for Libraries and Media Centers*. Englewood, Colo.: Libraries Unlimited, 1989.

Glueck, William F., and Lawrence R. Jauch. *Business Policy and Strategic Management*. New York: McGraw-Hill, 1984.

Godet, Michel. *Scenarios and Strategic Management*. London: Butterworths, 1987.

Gore, Albert. "Remarks on the NREN." *Educom Review* 25(2) (Summer 1990): 12–16.
"Grand Jury Ponders Is Creator 'Exported' through the Internet," "Genie is out of the
Bottle," *Wall Street Journal*, 28 April 1994, p. A1.
Grebstein, Sheldon Norman, ed. *Monkey Trial; The State of Tennessee vs. John Thomas
Scopes.* Boston: Houghton Mifflin, 1960.
Greenbaum, Thomas L. *The Practical Handbook and Guide to Focus Group Research.*
Lexington, Mass.: D.C. Heath, 1988.
Greer, Roger C., and Martha L. Hale. "The Community Analysis Process." In *Public
Librarianship: A Reader*, ed. Jane Robbins-Carter. Littleton, Colo.: Libraries Un-
limited, 1982, pp. 358–366.
Griffiths, Jose-Marie, and Donald W. King. *Intellectual Property Rights in an Age of
Electronics and Information.* Washington, D.C.: Office of Technology Assess-
ment, U.S. Congress, 1986.
———. *New Directions in Library and Information Science Education.* White Plains,
N.Y.: Published by Knowledge Industry Publications for the American Society
for Information Science, 1986.
Guide to Evaluation of Library Collections. Chicago: American Library Association,
1989.
Guide to Using Graph-Text, a Document Retrieval System for Scientific Journals. Pre-
liminary Edition. Dublin, Ohio: OCLC, August 1986.
"GUIDON Improves Internet Access to Electronic Journal" (Online Journal of Current
Clinical Trials). *Online* 17(3) (May 1993): 83.
Haas, Warren J. "Library Schools in Research Universities." *35th Annual Report 1991.*
Washington, D.C.: Council on Library Resources, 1992, pp. 27–33.
Hall, Richard B. "The Vote is In: Undeniably Operational." *Library Journal* 120(11)
(15 June 1995): 40–45.
Hanson, Christopher. "Playing 'Chicken' with the First Amendment" (the likely impact
of *Moldea v. The New York Times Co.*, on opinion writing). *Columbia Journalism
Review* 33(1) (May/June 1994): 21–23.
Harmon, Amy. "Cyberprivacy and the 'Clipper'." *Los Angeles Times*, 8 June 1994, p.
D1.
Harris, C. L. "Columbia University Library's Staff Development Seminar." *Journal of
Academic Librarianship* 17(2) (3 May 1991): 71–73.
Harris, Colin. "Surveying the User and User Studies." *Information and Library Manager*
5(3) (1985): 9–14.
Hax, Arnoldo C., and Nicholas S. Majluf. *Strategic Management: An Integrative Per-
spective.* Englewood Cliffs, N.J.: Prentice-Hall, 1984.
Hayden, Dolores. *Redesigning the American Dream: The Future of Housing, Work and
Family Life.* New York: W. W. Norton, 1984.
Hayes, Robert M. "@RISK." *Information Today* 9(8) (September 1992).
———. "A Commentary on the NCLIS Public Sector/Private Sector Task Force and Its
Report." *Minutes of the Ninety-Ninth Annual Meeting, The Association of Re-
search Libraries.* Washington, D.C.: ARL, 1982, pp. 12–41.
———. "Distributed Library Networks: Programs and Problems." *The Responsibility of
the University Library Collection in Meeting the Needs of Its Campus and Local
Community.* La Jolla, Calif.: Friends of the UCSD Library, 1976.
———. *Evaluation of the Los Angeles Public Library: A Survey of the Users and of the
General Public.* Los Angeles: GSLIS/UCLA, 1978.

————. "InfoMapper." *Information Today* 9(8) (September 1992).

————. "Long-range Strategic Planning for Information Resources in the Research University." In *Advances in Library Administration and Organization*, ed. Gerard B. McCabe and Bernard Kreissman. New York: JAI Press, 1992.

————. "The Management of Library Resources: The Balance between Capital and Staff in Providing Services." *Library Research* 1(2) (Summer 1979): 119–142.

————. *Strategic Management for Academic Libraries*. Westport, Conn.: Greenwood Press, 1993.

————. *Universities, Information Technology, and Academic Libraries: The Next Twenty Years. The Report of the CLR Sponsored Frontiers Conference, Lake Arrowhead, December 1981*. Norwood, N.J.: Ablex Press, 1986.

Hayes, Robert M., ed. *Libraries and the Information Economy of California*. Los Angeles: GSLIS/UCLA, 1985. A Conference Sponsored by the California State Library.

Hayes, Robert M., and Susan Palmer. "The Effects of Distance upon Use of Libraries: Case Studies Based on a Survey of Users of the Los Angeles Public Library Central Library and Branches." *Library and Information Science Research* 5(1) (Spring 1983): 67–100.

Hayes, Robert M. et al. "An Application of the Cobb-Douglas Model to the Association of Research Libraries." *Library and Information Science Research* 5(3) (Fall 1983): 291–326.

Hayes, Robert M., and Joseph Becker. *Handbook of Data Processing for Libraries*. 2d ed. New York: John Wiley & Sons, 1972, chapter 4.

Hayes, Robert M., and Timothy Erickson. "Added Value as a Function of Purchases of Information Services." *The Information Society* 1(4) (December 1982): 307–338.

Haywood, Trevor. *Changing Faculty Environments*. Birmingham: Birmingham Polytechnic, 1991.

Head, John W., and Gerard McCabe, eds. *Insider's Guide to Library Automation*. Westport, Conn.: Greenwood Press, 1993.

Heim, Kathleen M., and Danny P. Wallace, eds. *Adult Services: An Enduring Focus for Public Libraries*. Chicago: American Library Association, 1990.

Helmer, Olaf. *Looking Forward: A Guide to Futures Research*. Beverly Hills, Calif.: Sage Publications, 1983.

————. *The Delphi Method for Systematizing Judgements about the Future*. Los Angeles: UCLA Institute of Government and Public Affairs, 1966.

Hentoff, Nat. *Free Speech for Me but Not for Thee: How the American Left and Right Relentlessly Censor Each Other*. New York: HarperCollins Publishers, 1992.

————. "The Senate's Cybercensors" (Communications Decency Act, part of telecommunications bill). *Washington Post*, 1 July 1995.

Herman, James et al. "Shaping the 1990s: A New Way of Looking at the Future Helps Industry Participants Develop Their Visions of the Next Five Years." *Computerworld*, 27 November 1989, pp. 77–85.

Hildebrand, Carol. "IRS to Overhaul System in Bid to Reduce Its Reliance on Paper." *Computerworld*, 17 June 1991, p. 8.

Hildebrand, Janet. "Is Privacy Reserved for Adults? Children's Rights in the Public Library." *School Library Journal* 37(1) (January 1991): 21–25.

Hite, J. C. *Room and Situation: The Political Economy of Land-Use Policy*. Chicago: Nelson-Hall, 1979.

Hockey, Susan. "The Role of Electronic Information in Higher Education: The Faculty Perspective." *OCLC Academic Libraries Directors' Conference.* 1992.

Hoffman, Thomas. "Imaging Cures Hospital's Paper Woes: Memorial Sloan-Kettering Saving More Than $140K/Year with a Healthy Dose of Document Imaging." *Computerworld* 26(26) (29 June 1992): 74.

Homeschoolers and the Public Library: A Resource Guide for Libraries Serving Homeschoolers. Chicago: Public Library Association, 1995.

Horn, Robert E. *Mapping Hypertext: The Analysis, Organization, and Display of Knowledge for the Next Generation of On-line Text and Graphics.* Lexington, Mass.: Lexington Institute, c1989.

Horton, Forest Woody, Jr. "Rethinking the Role of Information." *Government Computer News* 2(4) (1982): 2, 24.

House Science, Space and Technology Committee. Subcommittee on Technology, Environment, and Aviation. *Hearings,* 3 May 1994.

Howell, James M., and Charles F. Stamm. *Urban Fiscal Stress: A Comparative Analysis of 66 U.S. Cities.* Lexington, Mass.: Lexington Books, 1979. (Prior publication by the First National Bank of Boston and Touche Ross & Co.)

Huray, Paul G., and David B. Nelson. "The Federal High-performance Computing Program." *Educom Review* 25(2) (Summer 1990): 17–24.

Hyatt, Shirley. "New Era Communications Gives Libraries New Options." *OCLC Newsletter* (May/June 1992): 15–19.

Hyde, Albert C. "The Proverbs of Total Quality Management: Recharting the Path to Quality Improvement in the Public Sector." *Public Productivity and Management Review* 16(1) (Fall 1992): 25–38.

Ihrig, Alice B. *Decision Making for Public Libraries.* Hamden, Conn.: Library Professional Publications, 1989.

Iles, Doug. "CD-ROM Enters Mainstream IS." *Computerworld,* 5 June 1989, pp. 75–80.

Intellectual Freedom Manual. Compiled by the Office for Intellectual Freedom of the American Library Association. 4th ed. Chicago: American Library Association, 1992.

Intellectual Property Rights and Fair Use: Strengthening Scholarly Communication in the 1990s. Proceedings of the 9th Annual Conference of Research Library Directors. Dublin, Ohio: OCLC, 1991.

Interlibrary Loan Discussion Panel: Final Report. Dublin, Ohio: OCLC, October 1990.

Irvine, Ann. "Is Centralized Collection Development Better? The Results of a Survey." *Public Libraries* 34(4) (July/August 1995): 216–218.

Jewett, Charles Coffin. *On the Construction of Catalogues of Libraries, and Their Publication by Means of Separate, Stereotyped Titles.* 2d ed. Washington, D.C.: Smithsonian Institution, 1853.

Johnson, Debra Wilcox. "Focus Groups." In *Tell It! Evaluation Sourcebook and Training Manual,* ed. Douglas Zweizig et al. Madison: School of Library and Information Studies, University of Wisconsin–Madison, 1994, pp. 161–170.

Jones, Clara S. "Reflections on 'The Speaker'." *Wilson Library Bulletin* 52(1) (September 1977): 51–55.

Josey, E. J. "Building Coalitions to Support Library and Information Services." In *Politics and the Support of Libraries,* ed. E. J. Josey and Kenneth E. Shearer. New York: Neal-Schuman, 1990, pp. 241–250.

Jul, Erik. "Ben Schneiderman Speaks on User Interface Design." *OCLC Newsletter* (May/June 1992): 10–11.

———. "Graph-text Project Provides Basis for Online Journal." *OCLC Update* (October 1991).

———. "Project to Analyze Internet Information Is Underway." *OCLC Newsletter* (March/April 1992): 13–15.

Justis, Robert T. et al. *Strategic Management and Policy.* Englewood Cliffs, N.J.: Prentice-Hall, 1985.

Kahn, David. *The Codebreakers.* New York: Macmillan, 1967.

Kahn, Philippe. "Forces Shaping Academic Software Development." *Educom Review* 24(4) (Winter 1989): 24–25.

Kanter, Herschel, and Richard H. Van Atta. *Integrating Defense into the Civilian Technology and Industrial Base: Supporting Material for Adjusting to the Drawdown: Report of the Defense Conversion Commission.* Washington, D.C.: Department of Defense, 1993.

Karp, Rashelle S. "Volunteers in Libraries: In An Update." *Advances in Library Administration and Organization,* volume 11, ed. Gerard B. McCabe and Bernard Kreissman. Greenwich, Conn.: JAI Press, 1993, 103ff.

Kaske, N. K. "Evaluation of Current Collection Utilization Methodologies and Findings." *Collection Management* 3(2–3) (1979): 197–199.

Kehoe, Brendan P. *Zen and the Art of the Internet.* Chester, Penn.: Widener University, January 1992.

Kelly, Lauren. "Budgeting in Nonprofit Organizations." *Drexel Library Quarterly* 21(3) (Summer 1985): 3–18.

Kemp, Roger L. "The Creative Management of Library Services." *Public Libraries* 34(4) (July/August 1995): 212–215.

Kennedy, John F. "The Candidates and the Arts." *Saturday Review of Literature,* 29 October 1960, p. 44.

Kent, Allen, and Thomas J. Galvin. *The Structure and Governance of Library Networks.* New York: Marcel Dekker, 1979.

Keyhani, Andrea. "The Online Journal of Current Clinical Trials: An Innovation in Electronic Publishing." *Database* 16(1) (February 1993): 14.

Kibbey, Mark, and Nancy H. Evans. "The Network Is the Library." *Educom Review* 24(3) (Fall 1989): 15–20.

Kidston, James S. "The Validity of Questionnaire Responses." *Library Quarterly* 55(2) (1985): 133–150.

Kies, Cosette. *Marketing and Public Relations for Libraries.* Metuchen, N.J.: Scarecrow Press, 1987.

Kiesler, S. B., and L. S. Sproull, eds. *Computing and Change on Campus.* New York: Cambridge University Press, 1987.

Kirby, Andrew, ed. *The Pentagon and the Cities.* Volume 40, Urban Affairs Annual Reviews. Newbury Park, Calif.: Sage Publications, 1992.

Knee, Michael. *Hypertext/Hypermedia: An Annotated Bibliography.* Westport, Conn.: Greenwood Press, 1990.

Knight, Kenneth, ed. *Matrix Management.* New York: PBI, 1977.

Koontz, Christine M. "Retail Location Theory: Can It Help Solve the Public Library Location Dilemma." In *Research Issues in Public Librarianship,* ed. Joy M. Greiner. Westport, Conn.: Greenwood Press, 1994.

Koteen, Jack. *Strategic Management in Public and Nonprofit Organizations*. New York: Praeger, 1989.

Krueger, Richard A. *Focus Groups*. Newbury Park, Calif.: Sage, 1988.

Ladd, Helen F., and John Yinger. *America's Ailing Cities: Fiscal Health and the Design of Urban Policy*. Baltimore: Johns Hopkins University Press, 1989.

Ladenson, Alex, ed. *American Library Laws*. Chicago: American Library Association, 1983.

Lancaster, F. W. "Whither Libraries? or, Wither Libraries." *College and Research Libraries* 39(5) (September 1978).

Lancaster, F. Wilfrid. *The Measurement and Evaluation of Library Services*. Washington, D.C.: Information Resources Press, 1977.

————. "Evaluating Collections by Their Use." *Collection Management* 4(1–2) (1982): 15–43.

LCM—The Library Costing Model. Los Angeles, Calif.: Becker & Hayes, Inc., 1993.

Leeds, Jeff. "Cyberspace Copyright Proposal Draws Praise." *Los Angeles Times*, 8 July 1994, p. D1.

Leerburger, Benedict A. *Promoting and Marketing the Library*, rev. ed. Boston: Hall, 1989.

Lehman, Bruce A. *Intellectual Property and the National Information Infrastructure*. The Report of the Working Group on Intellectual Property Rights. Washington, D.C., September 1995.

Lesser, Barry. *The Glenerin Report: Access: Information Distribution, Efficiency, and Protection*. A Report on a Conference held at the Glenerin Inn, Mississauga, Ontario, May 13–15, 1987. Halifax, N.S.: Institute for Research on Public Policy, 1988?

Levy, Steven. "No Place for Kids? A Parents' Guide to Sex on the Net." *Newsweek* 126(1), 3 July 1995, pp. 47–50.

————. "The Cyberpunks vs. Uncle Sam." *New York Times Magazine*, 12 June 1994, pp. 44–51, 60, 70.

Lewis, Carol W., and Anthony Logalbo. "Cutback Principles and Practices." In *Crisis and Constraint in Municipal Finance*, ed. James H. Carr. New Brunswick, N.J.: Center for Urban Policy Research, 1984, pp. 83–92.

Lewis, D. W. "8 Truths for Middle Managers in Lean Times." *Library Journal* 116(14) (1 September 1991): 315–316.

Lewis, Peter H. "Of Privacy and Security: The Clipper Chip Debate." *New York Times*, 24 April 1994, p. F5.

————. "Doubts Are Raised on Actual Number of Internet's Users." *New York Times*, 10 August 1994, p. 1.

Libraries & Technology: A Strategic Plan for the Use of Advanced Technologies for Library Resource Sharing in New York State. Albany: N.Y. State Library, 1987.

"Library of the Future? in Calif." *American Libraries* 26(7) (July/August 1995): 634–636.

"Library Seeks to Host New Magnet School." *Los Angeles Times*, 26 March 1994.

Lopez, Manuel D. "The Lopez or Citation Technique of In-depth Collection Evaluation Explicated." *College and Research Libraries* 44(3) (1983): 251–255.

Los Angeles Times, 24 May 1994.

"Lotus Plans to Appeal Case Against Borland to Supreme Court." *Wall Street Journal*, 24 March 1995.

Lowry, Charles B. "Resource Sharing or Cost Shifting?—The Unequal Burden of Cooperative Cataloging and ILL in Network." *College and Research Libraries* (January 1990): 11–19.

Lukenbill, W. Bernard. *AIDS and HIV Programs and Services for Libraries.* Englewood, Colo.: Libraries Unlimited, 1994.

Lynch, Clifford A. "Library Automation and the National Network." *Educom Review* 24(3) (Fall 1989): 21–26.

———."Telecommunications and Libraries." *DLA Bulletin* 6(1) (Fall 1986): 1, 3.

Lynn, Barry W. "Vista's School Board: Model for Disaster." *Church & State* 46(8) (September 1993): 23.

Macmillan, Ian C. "Competitive Strategies for Not-for-Profit Agencies." In *Advances in Strategic Management,* vol. 1, ed. Robert Lamb. Greenwich, Conn.: JAI Press, 1983, pp. 61–82.

Magid, Lawrence J. "Porn Ban Risks On-line Censorship" (proposed Senate Bill S-314). *Los Angeles Times,* 15 March 1995.

Makowski, Silk. "Serious about Series: Selection Criteria for a Neglected Genre." *VOYA* (February 1994): 349–351.

Makridakis, Spyros, and Steven C. Wheelwright. *The Handbook of Forecasting.* New York: Wiley, 1987.

———. *Forecasting Methods for Management,* 5th ed. N.p., 1989.

Marchant, Maurice P. "The Closing of the Library School at Brigham Young University." *American Libraries* (January 1992): 32–36.

"Market Share of CD-ROM Information Products Tabulated by Type of Product for 1988 and 1990. *Computerworld,* 30 January 1989, p. 77.

Markoff, John. "An Administration Reversal on Wiretapping Technology." *New York Times,* 21 July 1994, p. C1.

Marks, Alexandra. "The Telecom Revolution: At What Price?" (analysis of the proposed Telecommunications Act of 1995). *Christian Science Monitor,* 7 August 1995, p. 1.

Martin, Lowell. "User Studies and Library Planning." *Library Trends* 24 (January 1976): 483–495.

Martyn, John et al. *Information UK 2000.* London: British Library Research, Bowker-Saur, 1990.

Mason, Marilyn Gell. "Politics and the Public Library: A Management Guide." In *Politics and the Support of Libraries,* ed. E. J. Josey and Kenneth D. Shearer. New York: Neal-Schuman, 1990, pp. 112–123.

McClure, Charles R., and Carol A. Hert. "Specialization in Library/Information Science Education: Issues, Scenarios, and the Need for Action." *Proceedings of the Conference on Specialization in Library/Information Science Education.* Ann Arbor: SLIS, University of Michigan, 6–8 November 1991.

McClure, Charles R., John Carlo Bertot, and Douglas L. Zweizig. *Public Libraries and the Internet: Study Results, Policy Issues, and Recommendation.* Washington, D.C.: NCLIS, 1994.

McClure, Charles R. et al. *Planning and Role Setting for Public Libraries: A Manual of Options and Procedures.* Chicago: American Library Association, 1987.

McGeary, Michael G. H., and Laurence E. Lynn Jr., eds. *Urban Change and Poverty.* Washington, D.C.: National Academy Press, 1988, pp. 44–49.

McGill, Michael J. "Z39.50 Benefits for Designers and Users." *Educom Review* 24(3) (Fall 1989): 27–30.

McGuire, Stryker. "When Fundamentalists Run the Schools (Christian majority on Vista, California, school board)." *Newsweek* 122(19), 8 November 1993, p. 46.

Meadows, Jack A. "Higher Education and the Influence of Information Technology: Research." In *The Electronic Campus—An Information Strategy*, ed. Lynned Brindley. Proceedings of the Conference in Banbury, England, 28–30 October 1988.

Mellon, Constance A. *Naturalistic Inquiry for Library Science: Methods and Applications for Research, Evaluation, and Teaching*. Westport, Conn.: Greenwood, 1990.

Meltzer, J. *Metroplus to Metroplex: The Social and Spatial Planning of Cities*. Baltimore: Johns Hopkins University Press, 1984.

Merrill-Oldham, Jan et al. *Preservation Program Models: A Study Project and Report*. Washington, D.C.: ARL, 1991.

Metoyer-Duran, Cheryl. *Gatekeepers in Ethnolinguistic Communities*. Norwood, N.J.: Ablex, 1993.

Mielke, Laurie R. "Sermon on the Amount: Costing Out Children's Services." *Public Libraries* 30(5) (September/October 1991): 279–282.

Miles, Matthew B., and A. Michael Huberman. *Qualitative Data Analysis*. 2d ed. Thousand Oaks, Calif.: Sage, 1994.

Miller, David C. *Special Report: Publishers, Libraries, & CD-ROM*. Benicia, Calif.: DCM Associates, March 1987 (Prepared for Fred Meyer Charitable Trust).

———. *The New Optical Media in the Library and the Academy Tomorrow*. Benicia, Calif.: DCM Associates, August 1986 (Prepared for Fred Meyer Charitable Trust).

———. *The New Optical Media Mid-1986: A Status Report*. Benicia, Calif.: DCM Associates, August 1986 (Prepared for Fred Meyer Charitable Trust).

Milles, James. *Legal Problems Relating to Scarcity of Agricultural and Urban Housing Land: A Selective Bibliography, 1970–1987*. Monticello, Ill.: Vance Bibliographies, June 1988.

Mills, Mike. "House Approves Phone, Cable Bill; Act Would Open Market for Local Calls, End TV System Rate Curbs." *Washington Post*, 5 August 1995.

Millson-Martula, Christopher. "Use Studies and Serials Rationalization: A Review." *The Serials Librarian* 15(1–2) (1988): 121–136.

Molz, R. Kathleen. *Library Planning and Policy Making: The Legacy of the Public and Private Sectors*. Metuchen, N.J.: Scarecrow Press, 1990.

Monroe, Margaret Ellen, and Kathleen M. Heim. *Partners for Lifelong Learning: Public Libraries & Adult Education*. Washington, D.C.: Office of Library Programs, U.S. Dept. of Education, Office of Educational Research and Improvement, 1991.

Mooers, Calvin. *Zator Technical Bulletin 136*. December 1959.

Moran, Barbara B. "Construction of the Questionnaire in Survey Research." *Public Libraries* 24(2) (1985): 75–76.

Morse, Philip M. "Measures of Library Effectiveness." *Library Quarterly* 42(1) (January 1972): 15–30.

Mosier, Jane N., and Sidney L. Smith. *Guidelines for Designing User Interface Software*. N.p., August 1986.

MultiCultural Review: Dedicated to a Better Understanding of Ethnic, Racial, and Religious Diversity. Westport, Conn.: GP Subscription Publications, 1992.

Nathan, Richard P., and Charles Adam. "Understanding Central City Hardship." *Political Science Quarterly* 91 (Spring 1976): 47–62.

National Institute of Mental Health. *The Community Mental Health Centers Act (1963);*

A Commentary, Based on Title II of Public law 88–164, "Mental Retardation Facilities and Community Mental Health Centers Construction Act of 1964." Bethesda, Md.: Public Health Service, 1965.

Neff, Raymond K. "Merging Libraries and Computer Centers: Manifest Destiny or Manifestly Deranged?" *Educom Bulletin* 20(4) (Winter 1985): 8–12, 16.

Nelson, Jaleen. "Sledge Hammers and Scalpels: The FBI Digital Wiretap Bill and Its Effect on Freeflow of Information and Piracy." *UCLA Law Review* 1139 (1994): 1168.

Nelson, Theodor H. *Literary Machines: The Report on, and of, Project Xanadu Concerning Word Processing, Electronic Publishing, Hypertext, Thinkertoys, Tomorrow's Intellectual Revolution, and Certain Other Topics Including Knowledge, Education, Freedom.* San Antonio, Tex.: T. H. Nelson, 1987.

"New Online Journal to Speed Publication of Peer-reviewed Reports on Clinical Trials of Medical Treatments." *OCLC Update* (October 1991).

Nickerson, Raymond. *Using Computers: Human Factors in Information Systems.* Cambridge, Mass.: Bradford/MIT Press, 1986.

Nimmer, David. *The Berne Convention Implementation Act of 1988.* New York: Bender, 1989.

NITA Information Services Report. Washington, D.C.: Department of Commerce, August 1988.

Noble, William. *Bookbanning in America: Who Bans Books? And Why?* Middlebury, Vt.: P. S. Eriksson, 1990.

Numbers, Ronald. *The Creationists: The Evolution of Scientific Creationism.* New York: Knopf, 1992.

Nutter, Susan K. "Online Systems and the Management of Collections: Use and Implications." In *Advances in Library Automation and Networking*, vol. 1, ed. Joe A. Hewitt. Greenwich, Conn.: JAI Press, 1987, pp. 125–149.

Nyce, James M., and Paul Kahn. *From Memex to Hypertext: Vannevar Bush and the Mind's Machine.* Boston: Academic Press, 1991.

Obert, Beverly. "Collection Development Through Student Surveys and Collection Analysis." *Illinois Libraries* 70(1) (1988): 46–53.

OCLC Gateway Project. Dublin, Ohio: OCLC, Inc., 1992.

Olsen, Wallace C. *Toward an Integrated Information System.* Ithaca, N.Y.: Cornell University Press, 1986.

Osborne, David, and Ted Gaebler. *Reinventing Government: How the Entrepreneurial Spirit Is Transforming the Public Sector from Schoolhouse to Statehouse, City Hall to the Pentagon.* Reading, Mass.: Addison-Wesley, 1992.

Osburn, Charles B. "Non-use and User Studies in Collection Development." *Collection Management* 4(1–2) (1982): 45–53.

Outcasts on Main Street. Report of the Federal Task Force on Homelessness and Severe Mental Illness. Washington, D.C.: Dept. of Health and Human Services, February 1992.

Padilla, Amado M. *Public Library Services for Immigrant Populations in California: A Report to the State Librarian of California.* Sacramento: California State Library Foundation, 1991.

Paisley, William, and Matilda Butler. "The First Wave: CD-ROM Adoption in Offices and Libraries." *Microcomputers for Information Management* 4(2) (June 1987): 109–127.

Pammer, William J., Jr. *Managing Fiscal Strain in Major American Cities: Understanding Retrenchment in the Public Sector.* Westport, Conn.: Greenwood, 1990, pp. 16–23.

Patton, Michael Quinn. *How to Use Qualitative Methods in Evaluation.* Newbury Park, Calif.: Sage, 1987.

Payne, Judith. *Public Libraries Face California's Ethnic and Racial Diversity.* Santa Monica: Rand Corporation, 1988.

Pelzman, Frankie. "Washington Observer" (FBI's Library Awareness Program). *Wilson Library Bulletin* 64(5) (January 1990): 13–18.

Pincus, Fred L. "The Left Must Guard American Values." In *Opposing Viewpoint Pamphlets*, ed. David L. Bender. St. Paul, Minn.: Greenhaven Press, 1985.

Piternick, George. "ARL Statistics—Handle with Care." *College and Research Libraries* 38 (September 1977): 419–423.

Pitta, Julie. "Judge Overturns Copyright Ruling against Borland." *Los Angeles Times*, 10 March 1995.

PLA Policy Manual Committee. *PLA Handbook for Writers of Public Library Policies.* Chicago: Public Library Association, 1993.

Platenic, Suzanne. "Should I or Shouldn't I?" *Beyond Computing.* Premier Issue 1992, pp. 26–33.

Polly, Jean Armous, and Steve Cisler. "Should Public Libraries Connect?" *Library Journal* 119(6) (15 March 1994): 24–26.

Porat, Marc Uri. *The Information Economy: Definition and Measurement.* Washington, D.C.: U.S. Department of Commerce, Office of Telecommunications, May 1977.

Powell, Ronald R. *The Relationship of Library User Studies to Performance Measures: A Review of the Literature.* Chicago: University of Illinois Press, 1985.

Prentice, Ann. "Budgeting and Accounting: A Selected Bibliography." *Drexel Library Quarterly* 21(3) (Summer 1985): 106–112.

Pre/post Implementation Time and Methods Study of Library Public Catalog File Maintenance. Long Beach, Calif.: CSUC, 15 March 1982.

"Project JANUS at Columbia University." *Computing News* 5(4) (December 1993). A publication of Columbia University Academic Information Systems.

PROMT, Predicasts Overview of Markets and Technology. Cleveland, Ohio: Predicasts, Inc.

Public Sector/Private Sector Interaction in Providing Information Services: Report to the NCLIS from the Public Sector/Private Sector Task Force. Washington D.C.: NCLIS, 1982.

Publishers Weekly 241(29) (18 July 1994): 17.

Putnam, George Haven. *The Censorship of the Church of Rome.* New York: B. Blom, 1967.

Racial and Ethnic Diversity of America's Elderly Population. Washington, D.C.: U.S. Dept. of Commerce, Economics and Statistics Administration, Bureau of the Census; U.S. Dept. of Health and Human Services, National Institutes of Health, 1993.

Reaching People: A Manual on Public Education for Libraries Serving Blind and Physically Handicapped Individuals. Washington, D.C.: National Library Service for the Blind and Physically Handicapped, Library of Congress, 1992.

Renford, Beverly, and Andrew Ries. "Online Journal of Current Clinical Trials." *The Journal of the American Medical Association* 269(13) (7 April 1993): 1697.

Reports: On President Clinton's Economic and Deficit-reduction Plan, and Address to a Joint Session of Congress, February 17, 1993. Washington, D.C.: BNA, 1993.

"Restraints on Children's Access Controversy." *American Libraries* (July/August 1990): 628–629.

"Restructuring of Calif. Public Libraries Urged." *American Libraries* 26(7) (July/August 1995): 627–629.

Ricketson, Sam. *The Berne Convention for the Protection of Literary and Artistic Works: 1886–1986.* London: Centre for Commercial Law Studies, Queen Mary College, Kluwer, 1987.

Riordan, Teresa. "Writing Copyright Law for an Information Age." *New York Times*, 7 July 1994, p. C1.

Robbins, Jane B. "Interviewing." In *Tell It! Evaluation Sourcebook and Training Manual,* ed. Douglas Zweizig et al. Madison: School of Library and Information Studies, University of Wisconsin–Madison, 1994.

Roberts, Fred S. *Measurement Theory with Applications to Decision Making, Utility, and the Social Sciences.* Reading, Mass.: Addison-Wesley, 1979.

Roberts, Michael M. "The NREN and Commercial Services." *Educom Review* 24(4) (Winter 1989): 10–11.

Rochell, Carlton. *Wheeler and Goldhor's Practical Administration of Public Libraries.* New York: Harper & Row, 1981.

Rogers, Susan M. "Educational Applications of the NREN." *Educom Review* 25(2) (Summer 1990): 25–29.

Rosen, Sherwin. "Wage-based Indexes of Urban Quality of Life." In *Current Issues in Urban Economics,* ed. Peter Mieszkowski and Mahlon Straszheim. Baltimore: Johns Hopkins University Press, 1979, pp. 74–104.

Rubin, Lillian B. *Busing and Backlash; White against White in a California School District.* Berkeley: University of California Press, 1972.

Rubin, Michael. *The Information Economy.* Denver: Libraries Unlimited, 1983.

Russell, John. "If Knowledge Is Power and Only the Educated Are Free, We Are in Trouble." *Pasadena Weekly,* 22 January 1993, p. 1.

Saaty, Thomas L. *Mathematical Methods of Operations Research.* New York: McGraw-Hill, 1959.

———. *Thinking with Models: Mathematical Models in the Physical, Biological, and Social Sciences.* New York: Pergamon Press, 1981.

Sadowski, Michael J., and Randy Meyer. "New St. Louis Policy Raises Questions of Parental Control." *School Library Journal* (May 1994): 10–11.

Sager, Don. "Public Library Service to Homeschoolers." *Public Libraries* 34(4) (July/August 1995): 201–205.

"Sales of Electronic Databases to Grow 20% in 1989 vs. 1988." *New York Times,* 30 December 1988, p. 23.

Sarloe, Bart. "Achieving Client-centered Collection Development in Small and Medium-sized Community Libraries." *College & Research Libraries* 50 (May 1989): 344–353.

Schmidt, Warren H., and Jerome P. Finnigan. *The Race without a Finish Line: America's Quest for Total Quality.* San Francisco: Jossey-Bass, 1992.

Schneider, Mark. *The Competitive City: The Political Economy of Suburbia.* Pittsburgh: University of Pittsburgh Press, 1989.

Schneiderman, Ben. *Hypertext Hands-On! An Introduction to a New Way of Organizing and Accessing Information.* Reading, Mass.: Addison-Wesley, 1989.

———. *Designing the User Interface: Strategies for Effective Human-Computer Interaction.* Reading, Mass.: Addison-Wesley, 1986.

Schultz, Debra L. *To Reclaim a Legacy of Diversity: Analyzing the "Political Correctness" Debates in Higher Education.* A report prepared by the National Council for Research on Women. New York: The Council, 1993.

Schwartz, Bernard. *Swann's Way: The School Busing Case and the Supreme Court.* New York: Oxford University Press, 1986.

Seelmeyer, John. "The Anatomy of a Library School Shutdown." *American Libraries* (February 1985): 95–96, 113.

Seidman, I. E. *Interviewing as Qualitative Research: A Guide for Researchers in Education and the Social Sciences.* New York: Teachers College Press, 1991.

Sellen, Betty Carol, and Patricia A. Young. *Feminists, Pornography, and the Law.* Hamden, Conn.: Library Professional Publications, 1987.

Seo, Diane. "Students in Magnet School Go High-Tech." *Los Angeles Times,* September 19, 1994, p. B1.

Seyer, Philip C. *Understanding Hypertext: Concepts and Applications.* Blue Ridge Summit, Penn.: Windcrest, 1991.

Shank, Russell (Chair) et al. *Report of the ALA Special Committee on Library School Closings.* Chicago: American Library Association, June 1991.

Shankar, Ganga, and Gerald D. Skoog. "Emphasis Given Evolution and Creationism by Texas High School Biology Teachers." *Science Education* 77(2) (April 1993): 221–233.

Shaughnessy, Thomas W. "Benchmarking, Total Quality Management, and Libraries." *Library Administration and Management* 7 (Winter 1993): 7–12.

Sheerin, William E. "Absolutism on Access and Confidentiality; Principled or Irresponsible?" *American Libraries* (May 1991): 440–444.

Shiver, Jube, Jr. "Sweeping Reform of Communications Laws Clears Senate (bill allows greater competition within long-distance carrier, local phone and cable TV markets)." *Los Angeles Times,* 16 June 1995.

Shore, Steven N. "Scientific Creationism: The Social Agenda of a Pseudoscience." *Skeptical Inquirer* 17(1) (Fall 1992): 70–73.

Siegel, Donald, and Zvi Griliches. *Purchased Services, Outsourcing, Computers, and Productivity in Manufacturing.* Cambridge, Mass.: National Bureau of Economic Research, April 1991.

Smits, W. A. *United States Adherence to the Berne Convention: A Missed Opportunity for Moral Rights Protection?* Ph.D. dissertation, UCLA, 1989.

St. Lifer, Evan. "Public Libraries Meet Fiscal Reality Head On." *Library Journal* 120 (1) (January 1995): 44–47.

"State Budget Woes Threaten U. of South Fla. Library School." *American Libraries* (November 1991): 926.

Statistical Abstract of the United States. Washington, D.C.: U.S. Department of Commerce, Social and Economic Statistics Administration, Bureau of the Census, 1994.

Statistical Report '95: Public Library Data Service. Chicago: Public Library Association, 1995.

Steadman, Charles W. *The National Debt Conclusion: Establishing the Debt Repayment Plan.* Westport, Conn.: Praeger, 1993.

Stein, Jay M., ed. *Public Infrastructure Planning and Management.* Newbury Park, Calif.: Sage Publications, 1988.

Stewart, Linda, Katherin Chiang, and Bill Coons, eds. *Public Access CD-ROMs in Libraries*. Westport, Conn.: Meckler, 1990.

Strategic Vision for Professional Librarians. Strategic Vision Discussion Group, Steering Committee. December 1991.

"Surveillance Among the Library Stacks (FBI wants National Security Archive to report on suspicious foreign patrons)." *Science News* 133(24) (11 June 1988): 382.

Swan, John. "Surveillance in the Stacks: The FBI's Library Awareness Program." *Library Journal* 116(1) (January 1991): 162.

Swartz, Thomas R., and Frank J. Bonello, eds. *Urban Finance Under Siege*. Armonk, N.Y.: M. E. Sharpe, Inc., 1993.

Swiss, James E. "Adapting Total Quality Management (TQM) to Government." *Public Administration Review* 52 (July/August 1992): 356–361.

"Technology Assessment at OCLC." *OCLC Newsletter* 179 (May/June 1989).

"Technology is Dramatically Changing the Way Librarians Work." *Library Journal* 119(21) (1 November 1994): 49.

"The Debate Nobody Won." *Library Journal* 102(14) (1 August 1977): 1573–1580.

" 'The Speaker' Debate Goes On: Cheers & Jeers." *Library Journal* 103(15) (1 September 1978): 1550–1551.

Thomas, Cal. "Radical Left Censorship Undermines Education." In *Opposing Viewpoint Pamphlets*, ed. David L. Bender. St. Paul, Minn.: Greenhaven Press, 1985.

Thomas, Fannette H. *Children's Services in the American Public Library: A Selected Bibliography*. Westport, Conn.: Greenwood Press, 1990.

Thompson, James. *The End of Libraries*. London: Bingley Press, 1982.

Tiebout, Charles M. "A Pure Theory of Local Expenditures." *Journal of Political Economy* 64 (October 1956): 416–424.

Toffler, Alvin. *Power Shift*. New York: Bantam Books, 1990.

———"Toffler's Next Shock." *World Monitor* (November 1990): 34–44.

Tomeski, Edward A., and Harold Lazarus. *People-Oriented Computer Systems*. New York: Van Nostrand, 1975, chapters 1–4.

Tompkins, Jerry R., ed. *D-days at Dayton: Reflections on the Scopes Trial*. Baton Rouge: Louisiana State University Press, 1965.

Trezza, Alphonse F., ed. *Effective Access to Information: Today's Challenge, Tomorrow's Opportunity*. Boston: G. K. Hall, 1989.

Tukey, John W. *Exploratory Data Analysis*. Reading, Mass.: Addison-Wesley, 1977.

U.S. Congress. House Committee on the Judiciary. *Berne Convention Implementation Act of 1987*. Hearings before the Subcommittee: June 17, July 23, September 16 and 30, 1987; February 9 and 10, 1988. Washington, D.C.: GPO, 1988.

U.S. Congress. House Permanent Select Committee on Intelligence. *H.R. 4165, National Security Act of 1992*. Supt. of Docs., Congressional Sales Office, 1992.

U.S. Congress. Senate Committee on the Judiciary. *The Berne Convention*. Hearings before the Subcommittee: February 18 and March 3, 1988. Washington, D.C.: GPO, 1988.

U.S. Congress. Senate Committee on the Judiciary. *Moral Rights in Our Copyright Laws*. Hearings before the Subcommittee: June 20, September 20, and October 24, 1989. Washington, D.C.: GPO, 1990.

U.S. Environmental Protection Agency. Office of Research and Monitoring. *The Quality of Life Concept: A Potential New Tool for Decision-Making*. 1973.

U.S. House Committee on Education and Labor. Subcommittee on Postsecondary Education. *Hearing on the Reauthorization of the Library Services and Construction Act.* Washington, D.C.: GPO, 1989.

U.S. House Committee on Science, Space, and Technology. *Defense Conversion Initiatives: Progress and Plans.* Washington, D.C.: GPO, 1993.

U.S. House Committee on the Judiciary. Subcommittee on Courts, Civil Liberties, and the Administration of Justice. *Limitations on Court-ordered Busing—Neighborhood School Act.* Washington, D.C.: GPO, 1983.

U.S. House of Representatives. *National Information Infrastructure Act of 1993*—HR 1757. Washington, D.C.: GPO, 1993.

U.S. National Telecommunications and Information Administration. *The NTIA Infrastructure Report: Telecommunications in the Age of Information.* Washington, D.C.: U.S. Dept. of Commerce, NTIA, 1991.

U.S. Senate Committee on the Judiciary. Subcommittee on the Constitution. *The 14th Amendment and School Busing.* Washington, D.C.: GPO, 1983.

U.S. Senate Committee on Labor and Public Welfare. Subcommittee on Health. *Community Mental Health Centers Act; History of the Program and Current Problems and Issues.* Washington, D.C.: GPO, 1973.

User Surveys. SPEC Kit 148. Washington, D.C.: Association of Research Libraries, Office of Management Studies, Systems and Procedures Exchange Center, 1988.

User Surveys and Evaluation of Library Services. SPEC Kit 71. Washington, D.C.: Association of Research Libraries, Office of Management Studies, Systems Procedures and Exchange Center, 1981.

User Surveys in ARL Libraries. SPEC Kit 101. Washington, D.C.: Association of Research Libraries, Office of Management Studies, Systems Procedures and Exchange Center, 1984.

Van House, Nancy A., and Thomas A. Childers. *The Public Library Effectiveness Study: The Complete Report.* Chicago: American Library Association, 1993.

Van House, Nancy A. et al. *Output Measures for Public Libraries.* 2d ed. Chicago: American Library Association, 1987.

Vartabedian, Ralph. "Landmark Reform of Communications Laws OKd in House (the House of Representatives passes the Communications Act of 1995)." *Los Angeles Times,* 5 August 1995.

"Vista School Board Takes Up 'Creation Science' Issue Again" (Vista, California). *Church & State* 46(5) (May 1993): 19–20.

Voigt, Melvin. "Acquisition Rates in University Libraries." *College & Research Libraries* 36 (July 1975): 263–271.

Waldhart, Thomas J. "Resource Sharing by Public Libraries." *Public Libraries* 34(4) (July/August 1995): 220–223.

Walter, Virginia A. *Output Measures and More: Planning and Evaluating Public Library Services for Young Adults.* Chicago: American Library Association, 1995.

———. *Output Measures for Public Library Service to Children: A Manual of Standardized Procedures.* Chicago: American Library Association, 1995.

———. "Evaluating Library Services and Programs." In *Youth Services Librarians as Managers: A How-To Guide,* ed. Kathleen Fellows et al. Chicago: American Library Association, 1995, pp. 51–62.

———. "For All the Wrong Reasons? Implementing Volunteer Programs in Public Organizations." *Public Productivity and Management Review* 16(3) (Spring 1993): 271–282.

————. "Research You Can Use: Marketing to Children." *Journal of Youth Services* 7(3) (Spring 1994): 283–288.

————. "Volunteers and Bureaucrats: Clarifying Roles and Creating Meaning." *Journal of Voluntary Action Research* 16(3) (July-September 1987): 22–32.

————. "The Information Needs of Children." *Advances in Librarianship* 18 (1994): 111–129.

Walter, Virginia A., Christine L. Borgman, and Sandra G. Hirsh. "The Science Library Catalog: A Springboard for Information Literacy." *School Library Media Quarterly*, in press.

Ward, Maribeth. "Expanding Access to Information with Z39.50." *American Libraries* (July/August 1994): 639–641.

Weigand, Shirley A. *Library Records: A Retention and Confidentiality Guide.* Westport, Conn.: Greenwood Press, 1994.

Weingand, Darlene E. *Administration of the Small Public Library.* 3d ed. Chicago: American Library Association, 1992.

————. *Marketing/Planning Library and Information Services.* Littleton, Colo.: Libraries Unlimited, 1989.

Westin, Alan F., and Anne L. Finger. *Using the Public Library in the Computer Age: Present Patterns, Future Possibilities.* Chicago: American Library Association, 1991.

White, Anthony G. *Matrix Management/Public Administration: A Selected Bibliography.* Monticello, Ill.: Vance Bibliographies, 1982.

Wildhorn, Jane, Maryann McGuire, and Betsy Ryan, eds. *Return on Vision: Collaborative Ventures in Training and Education.* Los Angeles: Institute of Industrial Relations, Publications Center, 1993.

Willard, Patricia. "Microcomputer Availability to Public Library Clients." *LASIE* 17(2) (September/October 1986): 39–46.

————. "Public Access Personal Computers in Australian Public Libraries." *International Journal of Information and Library Research* 1(3) (1989): 157–174.

————. "The Browser and the Library." *Public Library Quarterly* 4(1) (Spring 1983): 55–63.

Willett, Holly G. *Public Library Youth Services: A Public Policy Approach.* Norwood, N.J.: Ablex, 1995.

Williams, Gordon et al. *Library Cost Models: Owning versus Borrowing Serial Publications.* Washington, D.C.: Office of Science Information Service, National Science Foundation, 1968.

Wilson, David L. "A Journal's Big Break" (electronic journal on Medline database). *Chronicle of Higher Education*, 40(21) (26 January 1994): A23.

Woo, Junda. "Publisher Sues CompuServe Over a Song." *Wall Street Journal*, 16 December 1993.

Wood, Elizabeth J. *Strategic Marketing for Libraries: A Handbook.* Westport, Conn.: Greenwood, 1989.

Wood, M. Sandra, ed. *CD-ROM Implementation and Networking in Health Sciences Libraries.* New York: Haworth Press, 1993.

Woodhead, Nigel. *Hypertext and Hypermedia: Theory and Applications.* Reading, Mass.: Addison-Wesley, 1991.

Young, Dennis. *If Not for Profit, for What? A Behavioral Theory of the Nonprofit Sector.* New York: Lexington Books, 1983.

"Z39.50: Lousy Sports Car, Great Library Standard." *American Libraries* (October 1990): 903.

Zaleznik, Abraham. *The Managerial Mystique.* New York: Harper & Row, 1989.

Index

About the Authors

ROBERT M. HAYES is the former Dean of the Graduate School of Library and Information Science at UCLA. He holds a doctorate in mathematics and has published several books on libraries and automated information systems. He is the author of *Strategic Management for Academic Libraries: A Handbook* (Greenwood, 1993).

VIRGINIA A. WALTER is Assistant Professor of Library and Information Science at the Graduate School of Education and Information Studies at UCLA, where she teaches courses in management and library services and programs for children. She has worked as a children's services coordinator, principal librarian, senior librarian, and young adult librarian at the Los Angeles Public Library. She has published numerous articles, and her books include three professional works for librarians and a children's book.